Narrative
Methods
for the
Human
Sciences

For Nicholas and Sage

Narrative Methods
for the Human Sciences

Catherine Kohler Riessman
Boston College

SAGE Publications
Los Angeles • London • New Delhi • Singapore

For information:

Sage Publications, Inc.
2455 Teller Road
Thousand Oaks,
   California 91320
E-mail: order@sagepub.com

Sage Publications Ltd.
1 Oliver's Yard
55 City Road
London EC1Y 1SP
United Kingdom

Sage Publications India Pvt. Ltd.
B 1/I 1 Mohan Cooperative
   Industrial Area
Mathura Road, New Delhi 110 044
India

Sage Publications
   Asia-Pacific Pte. Ltd.
33 Pekin Street #02–01
Far East Square
Singapore 048763

Printed in the United States of America.

Library of Congress Cataloging-in-Publication Data

Riessman, Catherine Kohler
Narrative methods for the human sciences / Catherine Kohler Riessman.
     p. cm.
Includes bibliographical references and index.
ISBN 978-0-7619-2997-0 (cloth: alk. paper)
ISBN 978-0-7619-2998-7 (pbk.: alk. paper)
   1. Narrative inquiry (Research method) I. Title.

H61.295.R54 2008
001.4'2—dc22   2007037953

This book is printed on acid-free paper.

13   10   9   8   7   6   5

Acquisitions Editor:	Lisa Cuevas Shaw/Vicki Knight
Associate Editor:	Sean Connelly
Editorial Assistant:	Karen Greene/Lauren Habib
Production Editor:	Karen Wiley
Copy Editor:	Gretchen Treadwell
Typesetter:	C&M Digitals (P) Ltd.
Proofreader:	Kristen Bergstad
Indexer:	Michael Ferreira
Cover Designer:	Michelle Kenny
Marketing Manager:	Stephanie Adams

Contents

Preface/Acknowledgments

Every book is positioned in a context and this one is no exception. Although narrative theory has been around for centuries, when I published *Narrative Analysis* nearly fifteen years ago, its methodological focus seemed to meet a still unmet need. The "little blue book" was brief—eighty-three pages long—summarizing a literature and proposing several ways to systematically analyze "personal stories" generated during research interviews with examples from studies of health and illness. The idea of narrative was hardly new, with well-developed traditions in literary studies, narratology, social linguistics, and other academic disciplines, but my pragmatic, methods-focused book apparently appealed to a broad group of human science investigators.

In the years since the little blue book was published, narrative study has come into its own in qualitative research; diverse viewpoints can be found in narrative journals, book series, handbooks and encyclopedias, and international conferences. I was gratified by the mushrooming of the field in the human sciences but also daunted when I was approached by Sage in 2002 about writing a second edition. It soon became clear that a bigger book was needed, a more extensive treatment of methodological aspects that distinguishes the wide range of social research that now comes under the broad narrative umbrella. During the next four years it took to produce what I thought was a "good enough" manuscript, Lisa Cuevas Shaw was a patient and supportive editor, while Karen Greene handled many details with skill, and Sean Connelly took charge of the final process. Karen Wiley sensitively oversaw the production process.

Like the earlier book, the perspective of this one was shaped in major ways by a network of relationships that has guided my thinking over many years about what narrative is (and isn't), what a story accomplishes in human interaction, what human scientists can learn from studying stories, and how narrative research can be evaluated. For twenty-one years, I have been part of a narrative study group led by Elliot Mishler that includes a cross-disciplinary group of scholars from several universities in the Boston area and neighboring states. More than anyone, Elliot's teachings infuse this book, in dialogue with the lively discussions of the narrative study group that occur in his living room every month. My deepest thanks to him, to my narrative friends in the group, and to graduate students in my methods classes over many years at Boston University and Boston College. Dialogues with graduate students from different disciplinary backgrounds have also played a pivotal role in my intellectual development. A few deserve special mention (Makiko Deguchi, Dana Cervenakova, Laura Lorenz, and John Rich), but many others will see ideas throughout the book that germinated during our classroom conversations. Another area to recognize is the administrative support that came from Dean Wilma Peebles-Wilkins at Boston University School of Social Work, and Stephen Pfohl and Julie Schor as successive department chairs in the Sociology Department at Boston College.

The manuscript was completed while I was on the move in more ways than one. Aware that contemporary narrative research was incorporating visual data, I ventured into the terrain (with more than a little help from colleagues) to learn about visual methods. Sensing that narrative research was becoming international in scope, I connected with narrative networks across the globe. In the United Kingdom—the location of the Centre for Narrative Research, at the University of East London—I spent enjoyable hours lecturing and meeting with teachers and students at the Centre (coled by Molly Andrews, Corinne Squire, and Maria Tamboukou) and with other British colleagues, and I spent many hours in the British Library. Funds from the British Academy enabled a lengthy period at the Centre, and a Leverhulme fellowship provided an extended time at University of Bristol. Briefer teaching assignments in Sweden introduced me to narrative traditions in social work, nursing, and communications research.

Exemplary work from all these places is folded into the manuscript. The last months of writing and revising were spent in Australia (funded by the Division of Humanities at Curtin University, and several other Australian universities), where I learned a great deal from colleagues in social work, Aboriginal studies, critical psychology, ethics, narrative history, creative studies, and other fields. The interdisciplinary perspective of the book is due in large measure to conversations with colleagues and students in these various settings. I thank my British and European, Australian and New Zealand, and Boston area colleagues for spirited conversations, computer assistance, wonderful meals, and a bed in their welcoming homes—friends too numerous to list (but you know who you are).

A prior group got me through a difficult personal time, making it possible to begin to think about doing another book: Caroline and Charlie Persell,

Linda and Michael Brimm, Cynthia Shilkret, Genevieve and Joe Coyle, Elliot Mishler and Vicky Steinitz, Mary-Beth Fafard, Pam Frank, Gail Hornstein, Eileen Julien, Lyndy Pye, Aylette Jenness, Jane Liebshutz, Natalie Schwartzberg, Cynthia Poindexter, Connie Nathanson, Judy Smith, Sarah Rosenfield, and many Cape Cod friends. Soothers of stress and providers of shelter, I thank you all.

As all books do, mine went through many drafts, diligently read and reread by colleagues. Maria Tamboukou commented on early versions of chapters, teaching me in the process a great deal about working with letters and paintings. I owe a particular debt to my writing group, extraordinary feminist sociologists (Marj DeVault, Lisa Dodson, and Wendy Luttrell) who improved early draft chapters with incisive comments and came through with enthusiasm when I lost mine. Detailed critical comments on what I had hoped would be the final draft were provided by Susan Bell, Bowdoin College; Elliott Mishler, Harvard Medical School; and Stefinee Pinnegar, Bringham Young University. Because I was traveling in Australia and New Zealand during the final revision, I could not locate every suggested reading or newly published work, but the three reviewers' comments saved me from some serious blunders and certainly strengthened the book. Susan Bell has always been one of the best critics while remaining a close friend; she was the person who in the 1980s initially sparked my interest in narrative at a women's studies conference. My debt to her and all the busy people for the time and thought they generously gave at various points goes beyond words. Of course, they are not responsible for errors and omissions that remain.

A final note of thanks to my family. Always honoring my need for alone time, they understood that "Camp Grandma" in summers had to fit around a writing and production schedule. During many fun times together, we crafted some good stories.

—Catherine Kohler Riessman
Truro, MA 2007

If the word "text" is understood in the broadest sense—as any coherent complex of signs—then even the study of art . . . deals with texts. Thoughts about thoughts, experiences of experiences, words about words, texts about texts.

—M. Bakhtin, *Speech Genres and Other Late Essays*, 1986

1

Looking Back, Looking Forward

One day, I was visiting my granddaughter Sage's classroom in Washington, DC, and saw the teacher's plan for the day on the blackboard, including the following directions:

Writing a Personal Narrative

   make sure the events are in the right order

   use the pronouns "I" and "me" to tell the story

   check to see that
         —the beginning is interesting
         —the narrative sticks to the topic
         —there are details that tell what, who, why, when, where
         —the last part tells how you felt

   check for
         —neatness
         —spelling
         —grammar

At first I thought it was a joke; the teacher knew I was coming and had selected a lesson to fit with my book project. Dismissing this self-centered thought, I settled into my role as volunteer for the morning in the public school. The diverse class included many children whose first language wasn't English, as well as African American, Asian American, and white children.

Alas, the teacher never got to the lesson on writing personal narrative, and I never saw the children's productions.

* * * * * *

Why begin the book with a story about a moment in a second grade class-room? Including this example underscores how early in schooling narrative emerges (it arises even earlier in human development[1]) and how highly regulated the practice is. Although the storytelling impulse may be natural and universal across the globe,[2] the teacher's instructions highlight normative criteria in one kind of classroom for one kind of story—the first person ("personal") narrative. Sage and her diverse classmates were being schooled in dominant Western narrative conventions for writing about personal experience: use the pronoun "I" (not "we," privileging the individual over family and community); place events "in the right order" (an ambiguous instruction, asking for "truth," perhaps, or the temporal ordering of events); the beginning must be "interesting" (to whom, I wondered—the writer, teacher, other children, family members?); the narrator must "stick to the topic" (privileging topically centered over episodically or spatially organized narrative); and there must be specificity—what, when, where events happened (disallowing personal narratives that report habitual or general states). A final instruction is the most revealing: the last part of the narrative must tell how the child felt (demanding the display of emotions to secure the "point" or meaning of the story in the emotional life of the child).

These instructions ring of contemporary North American individualism. To be fair, the second graders of diverse ethnic and racial backgrounds were being taught writing skills and a way to construct stories to help them succeed in U.S. public schools. Perhaps they were also being taught a way to construct a "self" in a particular historical and cultural context and prepare for the "interview society"[3] of late modernity. Even so, I couldn't help but imagine how the instructions would confuse South Indian children, Aboriginal children in Australia, and those in other contexts where I have lived—regions of the world where a singular feeling self is not necessarily the primary axis of signification. I also wondered about definitions of a "good story" that children in the classroom might have brought with them to school. Would the lesson honor the varied storytelling practices of children from the many ethnic communities in Washington, D.C.? I feared narratives could be evaluated as deficient when children developed them differently than the teacher outlined—an outcome others have found in urban settings in the United States that has disadvantaged African American children (research reviewed in Chapter 3). Was I witnessing the reproduction of inequality in schooling in this brief instance?

By using the incident, I do not mean to fault Sage's teacher or her wonderful school. The teacher was positioned in her world of experience and training, as I am positioned in mine. She built her lesson on dominant standards in education, and she used excellent pedagogical strategies (listing on the board the tasks for the day, and providing simple descriptions for concepts). I introduce the story to anticipate key issues I take up in the book: the central place of narrative when personal lives and social institutions intersect in the "ruling regimes"[4] of schools, social welfare departments, workplaces, hospitals, and governments. The classroom exercise illustrates how transforming a lived experience[5] into language and constructing a story about it is not straightforward, but invariably mediated and regulated by controlling vocabularies. Narratives are composed for particular audiences at moments in history, and they draw on taken-for-granted discourses and values circulating in a particular culture. Consequently, narratives don't speak for themselves, offering a window into an "essential self." When used for research purposes, they require close interpretation—narrative analysis—which can be accomplished in a number of ways depending on the objectives of the investigation.

Four broad approaches to analyzing narrative texts are presented in core chapters to follow. But first some orientation is given about what narrative is, and what it does in human communication. I introduce readers to the broad field of narrative inquiry, asking when the "narrative turn" began in the human sciences[6] and suggest some reasons why so many scholars in such diverse disciplines are now drawn to working narratively with data. The chapter closes with the organizing plan for the book.

What Is Narrative?

The term "narrative" carries many meanings and is used in a variety of ways by different disciplines, often synonymously with "story."[7] I caution readers not to expect a simple, clear definition of narrative here that can cover all applications, but I will review some definitions in use and outline what I think are the essential ingredients. Briefly, in everyday oral storytelling, a speaker connects events into a sequence that is consequential for later action and for the meanings that the speaker wants listeners to take away from the story. Events perceived by the speaker as important are selected, organized, connected, and evaluated as meaningful for a particular audience.[8] Later chapters will expand and complicate the simple definition with research based on spoken, written, and visual materials.

Viewed historically, articulating what the narrative form is, and what it does, began with Aristotle's examination of the Greek tragedy. Action is imitated *(mimesis)*: the dramatist creates a representation of events, experiences, and emotions. The tragic narrative is "complete and whole and of a certain amplitude" (size). There is a classic structure with "a beginning, middle, and an end" (sequence rather than haphazard organization). There is plot, "the ordering of the incidents," which constitutes the life blood of a narrative, and plot is enacted by characters, who take a second place. It is the plot that awakens emotions, such as fear and dread, when "things happen unexpectedly." Something goes awry: there is a breach in the expected state of things *(peripeteia)* that awakens response in the audience.[9] Aristotle understood that narratives are often moral tales, depicting a rupture from the expected—interpretive because they mirror the world, rather than copying it exactly. Later, narrative theory shifted with French structuralism, Russian formalism, poststructuralism, cultural analysis, and postmodernism.[10] Contemporary narrative researchers carry different traditions forward, as later chapters illustrate.

Although narrative theory developed initially from examining literary works, the Bakhtin epigraph to the book suggests that many kinds of texts can be viewed narratively, including spoken, written, and visual materials. Compositions made after lengthy periods of observation (ethnography) can be narratively organized ("texts about texts"). Just as interview participants tell stories, investigators construct stories from their data. Barthes notes the universality of the form and lists many sites where it can be found:

> Narrative is present in myth, legend, fable, tale, novella, epic, history, tragedy, drama, comedy, mime, painting . . . , stained glass windows, cinema, comics, news item, conversation. Moreover, under this almost infinite diversity of forms, narrative is present in every age, in every place, in every society; it begins with the very history of mankind (sic) and there nowhere is nor has been a people without narrative . . . it is simply there, like life itself.[11]

To add to the diverse sources Barthes lists, I would include memoir, biography, autobiography, diaries, archival documents, social service and health records, other organizational documents, scientific theories, folk ballads, photographs, and other art work. As later chapters reveal, most investigators tend to work with one kind of text (but there are exceptions[12]). In a word, narrative is everywhere, but not everything is narrative.

While everywhere, in my view, there still must be some boundaries around the concept. In contemporary usage, narrative has come to mean anything beyond a few bullet points; when someone speaks or writes more than a few lines, the outcome is now called narrative by news anchors and even some qualitative researchers. Reduced to little more than metaphor, everyone has a "story" that, in turn, feeds media culture, whether it entails telling one's story on television, or at a self-help group meeting in our interview society.[13] Here, a person's "story" seems to speak for itself, not requiring interpretation, a kind of "narrative seduction" that all storytellers strive for, and great ones achieve: "their telling preempts momentarily the possibility of any but a single interpretation."[14] Politicians even speak of the need for "new narratives" to steer them through election periods.

The concept of narrative has achieved a degree of popularity that few would have predicted when some of us, several decades ago, began working with stories that developed in research interviews and medical consultations. More than ten yeas ago, I began to be uneasy about what I called the tyranny of narrative,[15] and the concern has only increased. It is not appropriate to police language, but specificity has been lost with popularization. All talk and text is not narrative. Developing a sequenced storyline, specific characters, and the particulars of a setting are not needed in many verbal and written exchanges, nor are they present in many visual images. Storytelling is only one form of oral communication; other discourse forms include chronicles, reports, arguments, and question and answer exchanges.[16]

Among serious scholars working in the social sciences with personal (first person) accounts for research purposes, there is a range of definitions of narrative, often linked to discipline. Readers will find major differences, but all work with contingent sequences. Phil Salmon put it wisely: "A fundamental criterion of narrative is surely contingency. Whatever the content, stories demand the consequential linking of events or ideas. Narrative shaping entails imposing a meaningful pattern on what would otherwise be random and disconnected."[17] Beyond this commonality, the narrative concept is operationalized differently.

On one end of the continuum of applications lies the very restrictive definition of social linguistics. Here narrative refers to a discrete unit of discourse, an extended answer by a research participant to a single question, topically centered and temporally organized. The instructions that Sage's teacher wrote on the board were designed to elicit this kind of narrative in written form. William Labov provides classic examples in oral discourse: he analyzed tape-recorded answers to a question about a violent incident (presented in Chapter 4).[18]

On the other end of the continuum, there are applications in social history and anthropology, where narrative can refer to an entire life story, woven from threads of interviews, observations, and documents. A creative example is Barbara Myerhoff's ethnography of Aliyah Senior Citizens' Center in Venice, California. From taped conversations of Living History classes, combined with observations of the life of the center and poems and stories written by members (refracted through her biography), she composed compelling narratives of elderly Jews living out their days, crafted from the stories they had performed for her.

Resting in the middle of this continuum of working definitions is research in psychology and sociology. Here, personal narrative encompasses long sections of talk—extended accounts of lives in context that develop over the course of single or multiple research interviews or therapeutic conversations. The discrete story that is the unit of analysis in Labov's definition gives way to an evolving series of stories that are framed in and through interaction. An example here is Elliot Mishler's study of the trajectories of identity development among a group of artists/craft persons constructed through extended interviews with them.[19]

The diversity of working definitions in these brief examples from research anticipates complexities to come in later chapters and underscores the absence of a single meaning. The term narrative in the human sciences can refer to texts at several levels that overlap: stories told by research participants (which are themselves interpretive), interpretive accounts developed by an investigator based on interviews and fieldwork observation (a story about stories), and even the narrative a reader constructs after engaging with the participant's and investigator's narratives. Analytic work with visual materials pushes boundaries of narrative definition further, as Chapter 6 shows.

Distinctions are important for three nested uses of the term I employ throughout the book: the practice of storytelling (the narrative impulse—a universal way of knowing and communicating that Barthes articulated above); narrative data (the empirical materials, or objects for scrutiny); and narrative analysis (the systematic study of narrative data). Oral narratives can emerge in naturally occurring conversation—stories told around a dinner table, for example—which are usually treated differently than elicited stories, such as those told in research interviews or professional settings. Finally, there is the distinction between story and narrative. In my earlier book on narrative analysis, I made a great deal of the difference: a story is one kind of narrative, while there are other kinds (e.g., habitual and hypothetical narrative) that have distinctive styles and structures.[20] Sociolinguists reserve the term narrative for a general class, and story for a specific prototypic form:

> Stories can be described not only as narratives that have a sequential and temporal ordering, but also as texts that include some kind of rupture or disturbance in the normal course of events, some kind of unexpected action that provokes a reaction and/or adjustment.[21]

Although this definition of story (reminiscent of Aristotle) remains relevant for projects located in social linguistics (see Chapter 4), I have come over time to adopt contemporary conventions, often using the terms "story" and "narrative" interchangeably in writing.

It is also important to note that while personal stories are certainly prevalent in contemporary life, reflecting and producing the cult of "the self" as a project in modernity,[22] narrative has a robust life beyond the individual. As persons construct stories of experience, so too do identity groups, communities, nations, governments, and organizations construct preferred narratives about themselves (although this book concentrates on individual and group narrative). Perhaps the push toward narrative comes from contemporary preoccupations with identity. No longer viewed as given and "natural," individuals must now construct who they are and how they want to be known, just as groups, organizations, and governments do. In postmodern times, identities can be assembled and disassembled, accepted and contested,[23] and indeed performed for audiences.[24]

Oral storytelling is an everyday practice, yet it can disrupt research protocols when brief answers to discrete questions are expected, as I illustrate in Chapter 2. Speakers take long turns to create plots from disordered experience, giving reality "a unity that neither nature nor the past possesses so clearly."[25] Scholars debate whether there is such a thing as prenarrative experience or whether, on the other hand, experience is organized from the beginning.[26] Is "raw" experience formless, without plot, a series of isolated actions, images, and sensations that are then "cooked?" That is, is raw experience placed in memory in meaningful temporal sequences? While differing in important ways, both philosophical positions agree on the time ordering function of narrative. Typically, narrators structure their tales temporally and spatially, "they look back on and recount lives that are located in particular times and places."[27] Temporal ordering of a plot is most familiar (and responds to a Western listener's preoccupation with forward marching time—"and then what happened?"), but narratives can also be organized episodically, as Chapter 4 shows. (The teacher's instructions for writing a personal narrative did not allow for this form of organization.) In conversation, storytelling typically involves a longer turn at talk than is customary.

What Does Narrative Do?

When research participants engage in the practice of storytelling, they do so because narrating has effects in social interaction that other modes of communication do not; what the narrative accomplishes can become a become point of entry for the narrative analyst. Most obviously, individuals and groups construct identities through storytelling. Yuval-Davis develops the point: "Identities are narratives, stories people tell themselves and others about who are (and who they are not)." But the identity is fluid, "always producing itself through the combined processes of being and becoming, belonging and longing to belong. This duality is often reflected in narratives of identity."[28] Personal narratives can also encourage others to act; speaking out invites political mobilization and change as evidenced by the ways stories invariably circulate in sites where social movements are forming. Stories of abortion experiences, for example, promote "empathy across social locations," essential to organizing and activism.[29] In a word, narratives are strategic, functional, and purposeful. Storytelling is selected over non-narrative forms of communication to accomplish certain ends. Mark Freeman qualifies this observation:

> This is not to claim that the intentionality of narratives is always conscious and deliberate; the ends that are being achieved may be utterly obscure to those whose narratives they are. Rather, the claim is simply that narratives, as sense-making tools, inevitably do things—for people, for social institutions, for culture, and more.[30]

Narratives often serve different purposes for individuals than they do for groups, although there is some overlap. Individuals use the narrative form to remember, argue, justify, persuade, engage, entertain, and even mislead an audience.[31] Groups use stories to mobilize others, and to foster a sense of belonging. Narratives do political work. The social role of stories—how they are connected to the flow of power in the wider world—is an important facet of narrative theory.[32]

Turning briefly to each function, remembering the past is the most familiar. In therapeutic settings and in life writing, individuals turn to narrative to excavate and reassess memories that may have been fragmented, chaotic, unbearable, and/or scarcely visible before narrating them.[33] There is, of course, a complicated relationship between narrative, time, and memory for we revise and edit the remembered past to square with our identities in the present.[34] In a dynamic way then, narrative constitutes past experience at the same time as it provides ways for individuals to make sense of the past. And stories must always be considered in context, for storytelling occurs at a historical moment with its circulating discourses and power relations. At a local level, a story is designed for particular recipients—an audience who receives the story, and may interpret it differently.

Second, narrators argue with stories. This function is well illustrated in courtroom dramas, where lawyers organize facts to make claims to provide an advantage for their clients.[35] Third and related, all storytelling—whether in courtroom settings, halls of parliament, local bars, or therapy offices—involves persuading an audience that may be skeptical. Rhetorical skills are summoned by the storyteller—this is how it "really" happened. Positioning can, in turn, become a topic for inquiry, in therapeutic conversations ("it's interesting how you cast yourself as powerless in these family arguments . . .") or in critical studies of media ("note how the story of the war does not include reference to the origin of the weapons . . ."). Narratives work to convince audiences of veracity, but the "truth claims," in turn, can be questioned.

Fourth, storytelling engages an audience in the experience of the narrator. Narratives invite us as listeners, readers, and viewers to enter the perspective of the narrator. Interrogating how a skilled storyteller pulls the reader/ listener into the story world—and moves us emotionally through imaginative identification—is what narrative analysis can do. Narratives also engage audiences through modes of artistic expression, well illustrated in writing, painting, and the performing arts.

Fifth, the entertaining function of narrative deserves brief mention. We can all think of times around the dinner table when a speaker held forth and had everyone laughing uncontrollably by the end as bizarre events unfolded in a story. Professional entertainers do this for a living, using storytelling with great skill.

Sixth (and an often neglected function), stories can function to mislead an audience. A "con job" is accomplished by a storyteller to dissuade listeners from thinking that the speaker is responsible for misdeeds. Precisely because of their persuasive power, narratives are constructed by politicians to purposefully mislead the populace. Witness justification for the invasion of Iraq in 2003, for instance: as many have now observed, the Bush and Blair governments cobbled together a storyline from problematic "facts" that persuaded a fearful population—for a time.

Finally, on a positive note, stories can mobilize others into action for progressive social change. Major resistance movements of the twentieth century (including civil rights, feminist, and gay and lesbian movements) were born as individuals sat together and told stories about small moments of discrimination. Commonalities in the stories created group belonging and set the stage for collective action. For instance, oral *testimonios* got facts out in Latin American contexts regarding state-sponsored violence, helping to form revolutionary movements. These stories documented realities erased by governments in "official" documents. More recently, in the United States, the personal story continues to be a tool for organizing and mobilizing identity groups, with one example being the use of personal stories by gay and lesbian activists, fueling a movement to challenge discrimination in sexual citizenship (e.g., marriage and cohabitation policies).[36]

The functions of narrative are obviously overlapping: a teller must engage an audience in order to argue, persuade, mobilize others to action, and the like. Some individuals and groups narrate their experiences in ways that engage, convince, and move an audience, while other tellings can leave listeners or readers skeptical. In professional settings (a case conference, for example, or a courtroom), one speaker can persuade others of a particular formulation, while another fails to convince—a process that can be studied by close analysis of the rhetorical devices each employs to "story" the case.[37] Lawyers construct narratives in courtrooms to persuade judges and juries,[38] social workers use documents and interviews to construct stories about clients in written reports to persuade colleagues and governmental bodies,[39] and some programs in medicine ask students to think narratively about their cases, and their lives as physicians-in-training.[40] These brief examples illustrate what narrative can accomplish and potential points for analytic investigation.

Many investigators are now turning to narrative because the stories reveal truths about human experience. Those who work with oral narratives of trauma survivors can see Isak Dinesen's wisdom at work: "All sorrows can be borne if you can put them in a story . . . tell a story about them."[41] Joan Didion extends the point: "We tell ourselves stories in order to live."[42] Telling stories about difficult times in our lives creates order and contains emotions, allowing a search for meaning and enabling connection with others. My own research, which has examined lives interrupted by chronic illness, divorce, and infertility, is built around the meaning-making function of narrative. When biographical disruptions occur that rupture expectations for continuity, individuals make sense of events through storytelling. Interrogating the stories uncovers how we "imbue life events with a temporal and logical order to demystify them and establish coherence across past, present, and as yet unrealized experience."[43] Jerome Bruner goes further: narratives actually structure perceptual experience, organize memory, and "segment and purpose-build the very events of a life."[44] Individuals, he argues, *become* the autobiographical narratives by which they tell about their lives. To be understood, these private constructions of identity must mesh with a community of life stories, or "deep structures" about the nature of life itself in a particular culture. Connecting biography and society becomes possible through the close analysis of stories.

What Is Narrative Analysis?

Narrative analysis refers to a family of methods for interpreting texts that have in common a storied form. As in all families, there is conflict and disagreement among those holding different perspectives. Analysis of data is only one component of the broader field of narrative inquiry, which is a way of conducting case-centered research.[45] Analytic methods are appropriate for interpreting many kinds of texts—oral, written, and visual. The "cases" that form the basis for analysis can be individuals, identity groups, communities, organizations, or even nations (in political narrative), although the focus of this book is primarily on analysis of individual and group narrative. Particular histories of individuals are preserved, resulting in an accumulation of detail that is assembled into a "fuller" picture of the individual or group.

Attention to sequences of action distinguishes narrative analysis—the investigator focuses on "particular actors, in particular social places, at particular social times."[46] As a general field, narrative inquiry "is grounded in the study of the particular";[47] the analyst is interested in how a speaker or writer assembles and sequences events and uses language and/or visual images to communicate meaning, that is, make particular points to an audience.[48] Narrative analysts interrogate intention and language—*how* and *why* incidents are storied, not simply the content to which language refers. For whom was *this* story constructed, and for what purpose? Why is the succession of events configured that way? What cultural resources does the story draw on, or take for granted? What storehouse of plots does it call up? What does the story accomplish? Are there gaps and inconsistencies that might suggest preferred, alternative, or counter-narratives?

There are many ways to narrate experience; how a speaker, writer, or visual artist chooses to do it is significant, suggesting lines of inquiry that would be missed without focused attention. Rita Charon, writing from her dual position as physician/literary scholar, emphasizes the need for "close reading":

> the kind of reading taught in graduate programs in literature in which the reader . . . pays attention not only to the words and the plot but to all aspects of the literary apparatus of a text . . . [including] ambiguity, irony, paradox, and "tone" contained within the words themselves. . . . [Recent literary criticism interrogates] those texts historically, politically, semiotically, economically, in terms of gender or sexuality or colonial status . . . [grounding] their critique in their own close readings of texts. What texts "do," we all ultimately realize, they do in the resonance achieved between the words themselves and the worlds that surround them, elicit them, and are reflected and transformed by them.[49]

Narrative texts that social scientists collect require a similar level of close reading. But as later chapters display, some investigators attend to language, form, social context, and audience more than others do.

Elliot Mishler contrasts variable-centered approaches in social research, which strip individuals of agency and consciousness, with case-based approaches that can restore agency in research and theory. He argues that case-based methods are no less scientific a form of inquiry than population-based, variable-centered approaches. These case-based methods grant individuals "unity and coherence through time, respecting them as subjects with both histories and intentions."[50] Such approaches to generating knowledge are part of a long tradition, supported in moral philosophy by casuistry[51] and used throughout history to form theoretical propositions. Mishler wisely notes that in psychology, theories of great significance were developed through the study of individual cases: Freud, Piaget, Lewin, Erikson, and Skinner. In the physical sciences, too, major challenges to beliefs about the natural world came from detailed study and comparison of particular instances (e.g., theories of Galileo and Darwin, among others), generating knowledge that is unquestioned in science today.[52] When the investigator's objective is to understand and compare experiences of individuals in historical contexts, narrative analysis has aspects in common with other case-centered approaches such as auto/biographical study, life story/history, and oral history.[53] In most of these, however, particular sequences of action, choice of language and narrative style, and audience/reader response are not of analytic interest, although scholars of auto/biography do draw attention to the discursive limitations of time and place, and shifts in audience response through time.

Narrative study relies on (and sometimes has to excavate) extended accounts that are preserved and treated analytically as units, rather than fragmented into thematic categories as is customary in other forms of qualitative analysis, such as grounded theory. This difference (discussed further in Chapter 3) is perhaps the most fundamental distinction: in many category-centered methods of analysis, long accounts are distilled into coding units by taking bits and pieces—snippets of an account often edited out of context. While useful for making general statements across many subjects, category-centered approaches eliminate the sequential and structural features that are hallmarks of narrative. Honoring individual agency and intention is difficult when cases are pooled to make general statements. I believe, however, that category-centered models of research (such as inductive thematic coding, grounded theory, ethnography, and other qualitative strategies) can be combined with close analysis of individual cases.[54] Each approach provides a different way of knowing a phenomenon, and each leads to unique insights. In narrative study, however, attention shifts to the details—how and why a particular event is storied, perhaps, or what a narrator accomplishes by developing the story *that* way, and effects on the reader or listener. Who elicits the story, for what purpose, how does the audience affect what is told, and what cannot be spoken? In narrative study, particularities and context come to the fore. Human agency and the imagination of storytellers (and listeners and readers) can be interrogated, allowing research to include many voices and subjectivities.

Other forms of textual analysis (e.g., hermeneutics, semiotics, discourse, and conversation analysis) have contributed important ideas to narrative inquiry, although the particular theoretical perspective that guides each of these approaches may not be shared by the narrative scholar. Ricoeur's phenomenology, for example, is embraced by some doing narrative work, but for others the very idea of lived experience or a world behind the narrator (that is knowable) is rejected. Narrative scholars are a diverse bunch; we draw insights from many traditions and have disagreements. Research exemplars in later chapters illustrate the diversity.

Although narrative analysis is case-centered, it can generate "categories" or, to put it differently, general concepts, as other case-based methods do. The history of medicine, for example, is filled with stories of instances—cases where pathologies were noted and studied closely, leading to new disease categories. Similarly, in social research, knowledge about general aspects of social organization have sprung from close study of behavior in a particular instance.

A good narrative analysis prompts the reader to think beyond the surface of a text, and there is a move toward a broader commentary. Just because narrative approaches interrogate cases (rather than population-based samples) does not mean results cannot be generalized. But inference is of a different kind. Generalizing from a sample to the entire population is the statistical approach; case study involves "generalisation to *theoretical propositions*,"[55] which are, to some degree, tranferable. Making conceptual inferences about a social process (the construction of an identity group, for example, from close observation of one community) is an equally "valid" kind of inquiry with a long history in anthropology and sociology. As noted above, major theories in the medical, natural, and psychological sciences were developed from close analysis of instances. Case-centered models of research can generate knowledge that, over time, becomes the basis for others' work— the ultimate test. (In Chapter 7, I take up issues of validation.)

In sum, the field of narrative studies is cross-disciplinary, a many layered expression of human thought and imagination. Narrative inquiry in the human sciences is a twentieth century development; the field has realist, postmodern, and constructionist strands, and scholars and practitioners disagree on origins and ways to conduct analysis. The general approach has a great deal to offer disciplines and professions that want to see how knowledge is constructed in the everyday world through an ordinary communicative act—storytelling.

The "Narrative Turn"

At what point did the practice of treating a narrative as an object for careful study (centuries old in literature) migrate into the human sciences? Just as there are different ways of defining narrative, and contrasting approaches to interpretation, so too are there several histories that I now sketch. Scholars begin the process in different times, places, theoretical shifts, and political movements. In my reading of the debate about beginnings, differences also turn on epistemological position. Narrative study buds early, but flowers in the mid-1980s with challenges to realism and positivism. Today, the field is a veritable garden of cross-disciplinary hybrids.

Susan Chase locates beginnings in Chicago School sociology: in the early twentieth century, investigators collected life histories and documents to examine experiences of a variety of groups—Polish peasants, urban boys and men, and the situations of tenant farm women. Anthropologists began about the same time to adapt life history methods to study communities during cultural change, a tradition that persisted into the 1960s.[56] The historical sociology of Daniel Bertaux in France continues this realist tradition.[57] The language a particular informant may select, the narrative style, and audience (who elicits the story, for what purpose, and how meanings shift with different audiences) warrant attention only rarely. In the realist tradition, narrative accounts represent a means—one source of data—for the investigator's analytic description of cultures and lives.

Stories continue to be used for historical documentation, with little attention to particulars of the narratives themselves. Slave narratives collected after emancipation in the United States have provided a rich resource for documenting history that was invisible previously. Some contemporary scholars go beyond merely documenting and analyze the political work slave narratives did at contrasting moments in U.S. history.[58] Important social movements of the twentieth century were built from practices of storytelling, and the stories themselves can become objects for close reading and analysis.

Kristin Langellier locates the beginning of the "narrative turn" in the 1960s and the gradual shift away from realism. Four movements shaped the turn: (1) critiques in social science of positivist modes of inquiry, and their realist epistemology; (2) the "memoir boom" in literature and popular culture; (3) the new "identity movements"—emancipation efforts of people of color, women, gays and lesbians, and other marginalized groups; and (4) the burgeoning therapeutic culture—exploration of personal life in therapies of various kinds.[59] In the last several decades, institutions in North America and Western Europe began to provide numerous "autobiographical occasions" (Robert Zussman's felicitous phrase), which are "special occasions when we are called on to reflect in systematic and extended ways on who we are and what we are."[60] Although such occasions certainly existed before, in the autobiographical age of contemporary Western preoccupation,[61] there are opportunities galore: job and school applications, reunions, self-help groups, and, of course, therapy sessions. Given such opportunities, scholars began to examine how "selves" were constructed in these contexts. Corinne Squire, going further, locates the narrative turn in larger currents of late twentieth century Western thought: interest in language, the biographical, the unconscious, the visual, power in the research relationship, reflexivity, intersubjectivity, and the trend in scholarly work toward interdisciplinarity.[62] Clearly, the narrative turn is part of larger moves in the social sciences away from discipline-specific and investigator-controlled practices.

Going beyond epistemological, theoretical, and political shifts of the 1960s, were there other developments that fed an interest in narrative inquiry and close reading of texts? Although rarely mentioned, developments in technology were important in making narrative research a subfield in qualitative inquiry. Miniature recording technologies made detailed studies of everyday speech possible. Recording technologies offered alternatives to previous ways of gathering data that Chicago School and other "realist" ethnographies had relied on. New forms of analysis of first person accounts became possible with verbatim transcripts, opening up questions about language use, and the relationship between participants' utterances and investigators' interpretations of them. Classic work on narrative structure developed by Labov and Waletzky in 1967 (a touchstone for narrative analysis featured in Chapter 4) would not have been possible without miniature recording technologies, nor would the many other studies of naturally occurring conversation.[63]

Inexpensive cameras, television, and, more recently, video cameras made visual texts available, setting technological conditions in place for study of visual narrative (see Chapter 6). Cinematic images now play in living rooms around the world and expose large numbers of people to sequences of events they would not know otherwise, including images of survivors of state-sponsored violence. Analyzing stories recorded on camera provides new ways of interpreting historical events, cultural processes, and resistance movements.

Although the 1960s saw the budding of a field, the 1980s saw it flowering with landmark work, some guided by the feminist dictum: the personal is political. A fertile space developed in women's studies—interdisciplinary, with major participation from scholars in literary and auto/biographical inquiry. Attention shifted over time to the diversity of women's experiences, eventually clearing space for writings of women of color.[64] The classic volume *Interpreting Women's Lives* appeared in 1989, including work of anthropologists, historians, literary scholars, and others; the editors chose to be identified by their collective name, the Personal Narratives Group, indicating the solidarity of a cross-disciplinary intellectual movement.[65] Narrative inquiry turned a significant corner with these scholarly and political shifts, decentering realist representations of the (female) subject told from a distant standpoint and focusing, instead, on narrator-interpreter relations, context, and narrative form—topics others also explored. Women arguably led the narrative turn in anthropology along with the foundational work of Clifford, Geertz, and others.[66]

The narrative path widened when Labov and Waletzky's article was "rediscovered" by scholars in the 1980s. The classic paper and work in conversational analysis provided the basis for Elliot Mishler's radical revisioning of the research interview as a narrative event (discussed in Chapter 2). His book was published in the watershed year of 1986, the same year as Ted Sarbin and Jerome Bruner's classic contributions to narrative theory in psychology, with Donald Polkinghorne contributing a few years later.[67] These works assume fluid boundaries between the humanities, arts, and social sciences—a stance that differs sharply from earlier "realist" traditions. Bruner[68] dates the "paradigm shift" to the appearance in 1981 of a collection of essays of a cross-disciplinary group from literary theory, historiography, anthropology, and psychoanalysis that were asking comparable questions about textuality.

A final influence I would add to my brief sketch of the "narrative turn" in the human sciences is the general turn away from Marxian class analysis in the post-Soviet era—a trend Stephen Seidman includes in the broader shift toward postmodernism.[69] Social theories that privilege human agency and consciousness gained importance (particularly in the United States), in contrast to macro structural views of social relations. Theoretical shifts worked hand in hand with developments in methods designed to preserve agency and subjectivity. Detailed case analysis of narrative texts could occur under new conditions. As Norman Denzin says, theoretical and methodological shifts happen reciprocally, as narrative "forces the social sciences to develop new theories, new methods and new ways of talking about self and society."[70] As one of my students recently put it, "Narrative is the proverbial ferry between the abstract and the concrete, between cognition and behavior, and between the symbolic and the material."[71]

My preliminary listing of facilitating conditions—far from complete—suggests how diverse shifts in Western thought, epistemology, technology, and social practices that began in the 1960s fed the narrative turn. Langellier summarizes key elements:

Diverse sources converge on stories of experience, indicated by the term narrative, and the performance of identity, as indicated by the term personal. Embedded in the lives of the ordinary, the marginalized, and the muted, personal narrative responds to the disintegration of master narratives as people make sense of experience, claim identities, and "get a life" by telling and writing their stories.[72]

Analyzing those stories, rather than merely presenting them, was the logical next move.

In sum, the precise beginnings of narrative study in the human sciences are contested; there are taproots in a variety of fields that converged and informed narrative inquiry. Susan Chase argues that it remains "a field in the making."[73] In any event, the realist tales[74] of early twentieth century sociology and anthropology are now making room for ethnographies that include subjectivities of investigator and participant alike, an extension of a larger "interpretive turn" in the social sciences away from the realist assumptions of positivism. The mechanical metaphor adopted from the natural sciences—investigators provide an objective description of the world and position themselves outside the field of study to do so—has given way to narrative studies that position the investigator as part of the field, simultaneously mediating and interpreting the "other" in dialogue with the "self." Readers can expect narrative analysis to take diverse forms precisely because investigators rely on diverse theories and epistemologies.

Whatever its beginnings, analytic study of narrative can now be found in virtually every field and social science discipline. The movement is international and cross-disciplinary, not fitting within the boundaries of any single scholarly field or nation. The narrative turn has entered history, anthropology and folklore, psychology, sociolinguistics, communications, and sociology. The idea of narrative has energized the study of an array of topics—social movements, organizations, politics and other macro-level processes. The professions, too, have embraced the idea of narrative, along with investigators who study particular professions—law, medicine, nursing, education, occupational therapy, and social work. It is impossible to keep up with the wealth of work going on, as any list of citations quickly becomes obsolete.[75] Methods of narrative analysis are ripe for a detailed methodological inquiry.

Organization of the Book

The book is organized into seven chapters, purposefully crafted for beginning investigators. The four middle chapters take up particular methods of narrative analysis in a typology I originally developed for teaching graduate students. Others have developed different typologies, and I do not claim final authority with mine.[76] It is descriptive and provisional—a heuristic that I have evolved over years of teaching research methods to map a family of methodological approaches suited to the analysis of narratives of individuals and groups. The typology is not intended to be hierarchical or evaluative, although I do interrogate how investigators (whose work serves as the exemplars of each approach) deal with issues I think important: definition of narrative, the task of transforming talk into text, attention to language and narrative form, focus of an inquiry and associated unit of analysis; and attention to context (local and societal).

The four approaches to narrative inquiry are not mutually exclusive; in practice, they can be adapted and combined. As with all typologies, boundaries are fuzzy. In these postmodern times of boundary crossing, I encourage students to innovate and transgress the borders created by my separate chapters. Please, do not see the methods as a set of disciplining practices. Interrogate your projects in light of the exemplars presented in each chapter, rather than "applying" a particular analytic approach.

As I wrestled with how to construct a book about narrative methods, I decided to organize it around candidate exemplars of various analytic approaches, rather than a set of instruction points. This strategy is how many of us actually teach qualitative methods—detailed study of paradigmatic cases, rather than a listing of principles. The form seemed uniquely appropriate to presenting the case-based methods of narrative analysis. Thomas Kuhn argued that in the history of the social sciences, skills and practices are organized into exemplars: they serve as reference points, "practical prototypes of good scientific work" against which other scholarly activities can be acknowledged or rejected as "good science."[77] I chose selected exemplars for each of the four analytic approaches in the typology precisely because they are strong, and can function as focal points for different schools of thought in narrative inquiry. Conflict and controversy are as much a part of our "family" as they are in "normal science."[78] Because narrative analysis is grounded in close study of the particular, it seemed best to present exemplars where investigators detail their particular ways of working with narrative data.

The analytic approaches I outline are useful for studying certain research questions and not others. The methods are not appropriate for studying large numbers of nameless, faceless subjects. Analysis is slow and painstaking, requiring attention to subtlety: nuances of language, audience, organization of a text, local contexts of production, and the circulating discourses that influence what can be narrated, and how.

Before presenting the typology of analytic methods and candidate exemplars, I turn in Chapter 2 to an issue many narrative investigators confront even before they even begin formal analysis—how to construct their data for inquiry. I focus primarily on interviews and less on documents and visual data. The chapter explores the complexities of narrative interviewing, transcription, translation, and interpretation. Designed as an aid to investigators who are new to narrative research, I work through problematics by using instances from an interview study I conducted on infertility in South India. Detailed transcripts of interview conversations constitute the heart of the chapter, and I hope they will help students in research classes to think critically about their data.

Subsequent chapters present the typology—four broad approaches to narrative analysis. Candidate exemplars from published research (mostly the work of others) illustrate and explore key methodological questions that students should consider in relation to their own work. Chapter 3 examines thematic narrative analysis, the most widely used analytic strategy, which interrogates "what" is spoken (or written), rather than "how." Chapter 4 provides an introduction to structural forms of narrative analysis, with the focus on "how" a story is told. The next two chapters incorporate aspects of the previous ones (I see thematic and structural approaches as the basic building blocks) and add unique elements. Chapter 5 examines a broad tradition of research I call dialogic/performative analysis, which examines how talk among speakers is interactively produced and performed as narrative. Here the investigator becomes an active and visible presence in data gathering, analysis, and in the written report. Chapter 6 describes an emerging area of interpretive narrative inquiry, visual analysis. Here images are the data to be interpreted alongside the words of the image-makers. Chapter 7 concludes with some practical guidelines: ways of thinking about facets of validity relevant for narrative inquiry.

This is a large vision for a small book. I cannot discuss in any depth many issues in the complex field of narrative studies, which now crosses the borders of many academic fields. To further understanding of ideas I can only touch on here, I hope students will seek out the many sources provided in endnotes.

2

Constructing
Narratives for Inquiry

How can we know the dancer from the dance?

—W. B. Yeats, "Among School Children"

Before turning to methods of analysis in subsequent chapters, I devote some space here to the production of texts for inquiry, a task all investigators face even before formal analysis begins. It is generally acknowledged in the human sciences that "the researcher does not *find* narratives but instead participates in their creation."[1] This process occurs in particularly complex ways when data are written and visual, but the complexity is graphically apparent with research interviews. If, as Chapter 1 argued, the narrative impulse is universal, how can we facilitate storytelling in interviews? If audio recordings are made, how do we transform the spoken word into narrative text—a written representation—that conveys the dynamic process of storytelling? What about working with translated materials, particularly interviews that are mediated by a translator and varied in meanings across languages? This chapter focuses primarily on interviewing and transcription and the interplay between them (transcription and interpretation are often mistakenly viewed as two distinct stages of a project[2]). Following a general introduction relevant to all kinds of data (oral, written, and visual), I turn to interviewing and transcription by showing how I constructed two different transcripts based on the same interview segment. I look finally at interpreting a translated interview. Although the research examples in the chapter come from my research experience in India, similar issues arise in narrative projects that examine spoken discourse.

Investigators don't have access to the "real thing," only the speaker's (or writer's or artist's) imitation (*mimesis*). Cheryl Mattingly notes that the mimetic position involves both action and experience. Narratives are event-centered—depicting human action—and they are experience-centered at several levels:

> They do not merely describe what someone does in the world but what the world does to that someone. They allow us to infer something about what it feels like to be in that story world. Narratives also recount those events that happen unwilled, unpredicted, and often unwished for by the actors, even if those very actors set the events in motion in the first place. . . . Narratives do not merely refer to past experience but create experiences for their audiences.[3]

A few examples illustrate the persistence of the mimetic position across various kinds of data. In historical research, an investigator may begin with witness accounts and/or archival documents that recount a sequence of incidents. In clinical settings, investigators may begin with notes entered into a medical chart and/or audio or video recordings of office visits. In projects that include art, investigators may begin with a series of photographs. Most commonly, investigators conduct interviews (single or, ideally, multiple interviews with the same person) to learn about a process—identity construction among a group of artists, for example. Although substantively different, in all of these examples the investigator's access to knowledge about the prior—"real"—events and experience is mediated, at least one step removed.[4] We need, consequently, to think consciously and critically about how we as interpreters constitute the narrative texts that we then analyze.

Documents, of course, are already organized and "packaged," that is, cast in recognizable written forms (e.g., government reports, letters, or diaries in archives). They have a material existence before an investigator encounters them, unlike memories recollected in interview conversations—spoken first, and then transformed into text by an investigator. Interpretive issues arise, nevertheless, for those working with historical documents and autobiographies, as several exemplars in later chapters reveal, including imagined audience and other contexts implicated in production. Documents do not speak for themselves; decisions by the author and/or archivist have already shaped the texts an investigator encounters. Decisions, too, have shaped organizational documents, such as the narratives of causality constructed by social workers and physicians in case notes and team conferences about, for example, a case of suspected child neglect.[5] Artists' decisions have shaped photographs and other images that we work with. In sum, all investigators, no matter the kind of data—oral, written, and/or visual—lack access to another's unmediated experience; we have instead materials that were constructed by socially situated individuals from a perspective and for an audience, issues made vivid in interview situations. Unlike written documents and visual data, however, oral data require transformation into a textual form. And, if narratives of experience are desired, storytelling must be allowed.

Interviews as Narrative Occasions

Most narrative projects in the human sciences today are based on interviews of some kind. Generating oral narrative requires substantial change in customary practices. While survey and some qualitative researchers implicitly apply a stimulus/response model during interviews, Mishler suggests the alternative:

> Looking at how interviewees connect their responses into a sustained account, that is, a story, brings out problems and possibilities of interviewing that are not visible when attention is restricted to question-answer exchanges.[6]

In his (now classic) book, Mishler reconceptualizes research interviewing as a discursive accomplishment: the standardized protocol (where question order is invariant) gives way to conversation where interviewees can develop narrative accounts; speaker and listener/questioner render events and experiences meaningful—collaboratively. The model of a "facilitating" interviewer who asks questions, and a vessel-like "respondent" who gives answers, is replaced by two active *participants* who jointly construct narrative and meaning.[7] Narrative interviewing has more in common with ethnographic practice than with mainstream social science interviewing practice, which typically relies on discrete open questions and/or closed (fixed response) questions. The goal in narrative interviewing is to generate detailed accounts rather than brief answers or general statements. As argued in Chapter 1, narratives come in many forms and sizes, ranging from brief, tightly bounded stories told in answer to a single question, to long narratives that build over the course of several interviews and traverse temporal and geographical space—biographical accounts that refer to entire lives or careers. Establishing a climate that allows for storytelling in all its forms requires substantial changes in practice.

When the research interview is viewed as a conversation—a discourse between speakers—rules of everyday conversation will apply: turn-taking, relevance, and entrance and exit talk (where a speaker transitions into, and returns from, the past time story world). Generating narrative requires longer turns at talk than are customary in ordinary conversations, and certainly in research interviews of the survey variety. One story can lead to another, as narrator and questioner/listener negotiate openings for extended turns and associative shifts in topic. When shifts occur, it is useful to explore, with the participant, associations and meanings that might connect several stories. If we want to learn about an experience in all its complexity, details count. These details include specific incidents and turning points, not simply general evaluations. Susan Chase, for instance, relates how her sociologically worded questions in the early phase of a study of women school superintendents generated terse "reports" of work histories. Changing the wording of initial questions to simple, more open and straightforward ones elicited long narratives that recounted women's daily experiences in a white male-dominated profession—specific incidents and particular moments in careers.[8]

Creating possibilities in research interviews for extended narration requires investigators to give up control, which can generate anxiety. Although we have particular paths we want to cover related to the substantive and theoretical foci of our studies, narrative interviewing necessitates following participants down their trails. Giving up the control of a fixed interview format—"methods" designed for "efficiency"[9]—encourages greater equality (and uncertainty) in the conversation. Encouraging participants to speak in their own ways can, at times, shift power in interviews; although relations of power are never equal, the disparity can be diminished. Genuine discoveries about a phenomenon can come from power-sharing (vividly illustrated in photovoice, and other collaborative projects discussed in Chapters 6 and 7).

Storytelling in interviews can occur at the most unexpected times, even in answer to fixed-response questions (I present an example below), demonstrating the ubiquity of the narrative impulse. Especially when there has been major disruption in a life—in the normative social biography—I have learned through many interview studies that individuals often want to develop long accounts, and will do so at unexpected times.

Traditional survey interviewing practices offer little guidance for such moments (they are defined as "digressions"), but feminist researchers who attend to the research relationship provide insight.[10] The specific wording of a question is less important than the interviewer's emotional attentiveness and engagement and the degree of reciprocity in the conversation. But it is also true that certain kinds of open-ended questions are more likely than others to provide narrative opportunities. It is preferable, in general, to ask questions that open up topics, and allow respondents to construct answers in ways they find meaningful. For example, in my infertility study, I asked, "How did you first become aware that you were having difficulties with childbearing?" The question encouraged women to begin at the beginning (in South India it was often during the first year of marriage), to relate in a chronological sequence how they came to suspect fertility problems, and how understandings changed over time with new events, such as medical examinations and miscarriages. But, not all women began at the beginning, and some moved back and forth in time. There are many ways to organize a narrative account; investigators and interviewers can suppress the narrative impulse, or encourage diverse forms of storytelling. Confusion and misunderstanding can occur when participants in a conversation do not share the convention of temporal ordering of a plot ("and then what happened?")—a process I analyzed long ago in a conversation between an Anglo interviewer and a Latina.[11] (Chapter 3 takes up nontemporal forms of storytelling.)

Compare "When did X happen?" that requests a discrete piece of information, with "Tell me what happened?" that invites an extended account. However, some participants may not want to develop lengthy accounts of experiences with a stranger; the assumption that there is a story wanting to be told can put pressure on participants. Some investigators, after an introduction, have asked a participant to "tell me your story." In some of these cases, experience may exceed possibilities for narrativization; events may be fleetingly summarized, given little significance. With time and further questioning participants may recall details, turning points, and shifts in cognition, emotion, and action—that is, narrate—but others may chose not to, and summarize. To meet these challenges, investigators studying the life course have developed life history grids together with participants during the initial interview that are filled in over the course of subsequent conversations. Jane Elliott underscores the conversational utility of grids, stating, "Respondents are likely to find it easier to talk about specific times and places rather than being asked about a very wide time frame."[12]

In my interviewing practice, I sometimes followed up a participant's general description with a question: "Can you remember a particular time when . . . ?" I might have then probed further: "Tell me why that particular moment stands out?" While this is often effective, Cortazzi and colleagues, studying the education of health professionals, asked a direct question that could have been answered with a yes/no response: "Have you had a breakthrough in your learning recently?" "Oh yes" typically followed and (because participants weren't interrupted) the narrator proceeded with an outpouring of emotion and metaphor about a particular moment—"a clap of thunder," one student said.[13] Narration, in other words, depends on expectations.

If extended accounts are welcomed, some participants and interviewers collaboratively develop them, but if brief answers to discrete questions are expected, participants learn to keep their answers brief (or, if they don't, their long accounts are typically disregarded by transcriber or analyst, and seen as "digressions").

Sometimes it is next to impossible for participants to narrate experience in spoken language alone. Wendy Luttrell, working as an ethnographer in a classroom for pregnant teens (mostly African American), expected "stories" from each girl about key events such as learning of pregnancy, telling mothers and boyfriends, making the decision to keep the baby, and other moments. Luttrell confronted silence instead, only to discover a world of narrative as she encouraged the girls' artistic productions and role plays. When invited to make art, the girls performed the key moments for each other, creating group storytelling situations (see Chapter 6).[14] Investigators studying severely traumatic experiences in the lives of participants confront even greater interviewing challenges. Words do not come easily for victims, as Veena Das remarks: "Even the most articulate among us face difficulties when we try to put ambiguous and jumbled thoughts and images into words. This is even truer of someone who has suffered traumatic loss."[15] Attentive listening in these situations is difficult as our vulnerabilities become exposed.

In sum, although I emphasize the importance of careful transcription in the examples from my research below, it is limiting to rely only on the texts we have constructed from single interviews, and we must not reify our "holy transcripts" of these conversations. In later chapters, I discuss how scholars combine observation, ongoing relationships, and conversations over time with participants; some projects also incorporate their images. Interviews, though important and the most widely used method of data collection in the human sciences, represent only one source of knowledge about a phenomenon or group. Narrative interviewing is not a set of "techniques," nor is it necessarily "natural." If sensitively practiced, it can offer a way, in many research situations, for investigators to forge dialogic relationships and greater communicative equality. Toward these ends, it is preferable to have repeated conversations rather than the typical one-shot interview, especially when studying biographical experience.[16] Working ethnographically with participants in their settings over time offers the best conditions for storytelling. I also recommend that, whenever possible, the investigator also serve as interviewer, because the interpretive process begins during conversation (evidenced in the subtle give and take between speaker and listener in transcripts below). We must also learn to listen attentively. Despite the significance of listening, Molly Andrews notes that the complex process is rarely included in social scientists' professional training. Yet when we learn to listen in an emotionally attentive and engaged way, we expose ourselves and enter the unknown with "new possibilities and frame-works of meaning." It is "hard work, demanding as it does an abandonment of the self in a quest to enter the world of another; and it takes time."[17] The listener's identities and preconceptions come into play, particularly when interviewing across the divides of geographical, religious, class/race, and age difference—a process illustrated below.

Transcription as Interpretation: Research Examples

I referred earlier to my research in South India, where I interviewed (usually with a research assistant, Liza) childless women in towns and villages, and where I observed an infertility clinic in operation at a government hospital.[18] Briefly as context, I was drawn to the topic and setting because of the institutional importance of motherhood in India. Although family life is undergoing rapid change, the normative social biography for an Indian woman mandates childbearing after marriage; culturally, it is a master narrative. Motherhood is a woman's sacred duty—a value enshrined in religious laws for Hindus, Muslims, Sikhs, and Christians alike. Bearing and rearing children is central to a woman's power and well-being, and reproduction brings in its stead concrete benefits over the life course. A child solidifies a wife's often fragile bond with a spouse in an arranged marriage, and improves her status in the joint family and larger community; with a child, she can eventually become a mother-in-law, and this is a position of considerable power and influence in Indian families. Additionally, in old age, women depend on children (particularly sons) for economic security in a country with few governmental social welfare programs and, upon death, a son makes possible essential rituals for Hindus. Even further, for families with significant property or wealth, sexual reproduction allows for social reproduction, or the orderly transfer of privilege through inheritance to the next generation of kin. Motherhood, in sum, serves critical cultural functions in India's hierarchical society (stratified by gender, caste, and class) that are masked by psychological or sentimental discourses (e.g., it is "natural" for a woman to want to bear a child). Indian women are keenly aware that their reproductive capacities are an important source of power, especially when they lack it from other sources.[19]

Given this context (rapidly changing as I write), I wondered what happens when the normative biography is ruptured and a woman does not conceive. How is the situation defined and managed? How do differently situated women account for being childless, and what explanatory interpretations are possible? How does the local culture influence the actions women can take in their families and communities?

I struggled with how to represent what I heard in conversations with childless women. Remembering *mimesis,* I could never "know" their experiences. All I had were imitations, memories of past events recalled in the present and folded into "messy talk" that I had to transform into text suitable for narrative analysis. Because there is no universal form of transcription suitable for all research situations, investigators make decisions, Mishler argues, based on theoretical concerns and practical constraints, including an investigator's perspective about relations between meaning and speech, the specific aims of a project and relevant aspects of speech, and available resources.[20] In constructing a transcript, we do not stand outside in a neutral objective position, merely presenting "what was said." Rather, investigators are implicated at every step along the way in constituting the narratives we then analyze. Perhaps an example will help.

The study of infertility in South India was designed to explore the relationship between meaning and action: the sense women made of their situations and the actions they took in families and communities. Given my research on other biographical disruptions, I fully expected narrative accounts to emerge in the infertility project. But they appeared sometimes when I least expected them. For example, I had questions at the beginning of interviews that elicited factual and demographic information. But some participants answered at length. Sunita (a pseudonym) represents a case in point. I asked her early in an interview what I thought was a yes/no question, but she shifted the terms of conversation and responded with a long account of her relationship with her mother-in-law and a miscarriage almost twenty years earlier.

A Conversation in English: Two Contrasting Transcriptions

Sunita was a forty-two-year-old Hindu woman from an advantaged caste who had been married for twenty years. Having an advanced degree, she is economically advantaged (her husband runs a successful business), and she works professionally, mostly in English. I interviewed her in English in her home, audiotaping a conversation that lasted more than two hours. By consenting to be a participant in a study of infertility, Sunita had implicitly agreed to look back on her life, particularly when she was younger and trying to conceive. From the totality of her lived experience—a demanding career, a long marriage, as well as other important relationships and accomplishments—the research required that she attend to one specific component of her biography. My research interest constrained to a large degree which of her many identities would be relevant.

About ten minutes into the conversation, I asked Sunita a factual question about her reproductive history. On my interview schedule, there were two possible responses (yes/no). Sunita, however, thought otherwise and seized the question ("have you ever been pregnant?") as an opening for a long account that ends with a miscarriage. I learned later that she never became pregnant again. Some readers might wonder why Sunita engaged in storytelling at that point. I can only speculate that she knew the topic of my research, understood I was a sociologist with an interest in Indian families, and she was accustomed in the workplace to exercising authority in conversations. Perhaps the miscarriage long ago continued to hold meanings she wanted to express. Whatever the reasons, Sunita took control of the interview to insert a long story that recounted painful days and weeks—a sequence of events that had occurred eighteen years previously. Like all stories, it is selective and perspectival, reflecting the power of memory to remember, forget, neglect, and amplify moments in the stream of experience.

From the taped conversation, I constructed a written record that, like all transcripts, straddles a border between speech and writing. I transformed a complex verbal exchange into an object that would serve as a representation— my imitation on a two-dimensional page of what had been said between us. An audio recording is more selective than a video would have been, of course, but in neither case can the fluid and dynamic movement of words and gestures be captured. Much is lost, and key features slip away. Sunita's clipped Indo/British speech and the linguistic markers of her social position disappear in the transcript. Some of the qualities she expresses visually become invisible, and the particular cadence of her speech is flattened. Translating dynamic talk into linear written language, then, is never easy or straightforward (it is also time consuming, requiring three to four hours for every hour of interview). Some mistakenly think the task is technical, and delegate it. However, transcription is deeply interpretive as the process is inseparable from language theory.[21] The "same" stretch of talk can be transcribed very differently, depending on the investigator's theoretical perspective, methodological orientation, and substantive interest.

There are several ways my conversation with Sunita could be represented. I present two here, based on contrasting perspectives about language and communication. Incidentally, each also assumes a different theory about "the self." Simply stated: (1) the act of storytelling in dialogue *constitutes* the autobiographical self, that is, how the speaker wants to be known in the interaction; vs. (2) autobiographical narrative *reflects* a preexisting self; there is constancy across speaking situations because the self exists independently of social interaction.[22] The first requires a transcription that includes the interactional context, while the second privileges the narrator's speech—the way to "know" the person. Later, I will complicate this simple binary, but now it serves to contrast two transcriptions. The first is based on the theory of a co-constructed "self" produced dialogically, and the second transcription is based on the idea of a reflected "self."

Transcript 2.1

01 C: And have you ever been pregnant?

02 S: Yes (p) I think it was second or third year of marriage. (I—Aha)
03 that I was pregnant and then in the third month I started spotting
04 (I—Mmm). I think I was overworking (I—Mmm). Since it was a
05 choice marriage, I had a lot of—(p) We were trying to get my in
06 laws to be more amenable to the whole situation (I—Mmm). In
07 laws were against the marriage (I—Mmm) and so I used to work
08 the whole day, then go to their place to cook in the evening for a
09 family of seven (I—Mmm). Then pack the food for two of us and
10 bring it home (I—Mmm).

11 C: So you were living separately from them?

12 S: We were living here, my in-laws were staying in [city], some
13 distance away.

14 C: But you went there to cook everyday—

15 S: We—I went there to cook everyday and not everyday could he
16 come (I—Yes) you know, to pick me up or to come, so that we
17 could come together. (I—Mmm). And whenever my father-in-law
18 was at home, he used to see to it that the driver came to drop me
19 home. (I—Mmm) But when he wasn't at home, I had to, you
20 know, come on my own (I—Mmm). I think that was overdoing it,
21 (I—Mmm) and then I carried some of the food stuff you know, the
22 grains and things (p) the monthly stuff, groceries (p) from that
23 place, because my mother-in-law insisted that I carry it back
24 that day and the next day I started spotting and I was so frightened
25 (I—Mmm) because, you know, I didn't know really what to do.
26 So I rang up my doctor and told her and she said, "You just lie
27 down, you are okay but only thing is you need to rest." You know,
28 "don't move around and things like that." So then I went over to
29 my mother's (p) and stayed there for a month and doctor said,
30 "You are okay." But in the next (p) examination she said, "No, I
31 don't think the foetus is growing so (p) we should take a second
32 opinion." So we went to see another gynacologist and she—he said
33 that "definitely, you know, there's a problem, and foetus is stopped
34 growing, we'll wait for another 15 days (I—Mmm).

35 If there is (p) if you abort naturally, fine otherwise we'll have to
36 have a abortion," you know "it'll have to be with—, you'll have to
37 remove it." So that was very traumatic. Because (p) though (p) we
38 weren't totally prepared for it at that point, you know we weren't
39 using any contraceptives, but (p) I don't know, we weren't totally
40 prepared for the baby (I—Mmm) but when we realised that I was
41 pregnant, we were quite (p) ready for it, quite excited about it. So
42 (p) it was quite traumatic at that point. But the doctor, in fact I was
43 very thin. I weighed under 100 pounds (I—Mmm). So the doctor
44 said, "Look you have to put on weight before you— (p) decide to
45 get pregnant again" and (p) everybody agreed and after that I
46 stopped going everyday to my in-laws because my husband said
47 "this is ridiculous," I mean, you know . . .

Transcript 2.1 is detailed, for Sunita's and my utterances appear on the page as the primary speaker and listener/questioner. Sunita constructs herself in the context of a miscarriage and family expectations. Readers can see my initial question, later ones that ask for clarification, my "back-channel" nonlexical expressions (Mmm, uh huh), the break-offs (marked "—", when one of us begins to articulate an idea and stops midstream), and even long pauses (marked "p" on the transcript). This transcript reveals how a "personal" narrative is social at many levels. At the local level, it is composed jointly, crafted in a collaborative conversational interaction. Psychologist Phil Salmon reminds us of the widespread acceptance now of this feature of communication:

All narratives are, in a fundamental sense, co-constructed. The audience, whether physically present or not, exerts a crucial influence on what can and cannot be said, how things should be expressed, what can be taken for granted, what needs explaining, and so on. We now recognize that the personal account, in research interviews, which has traditionally been seen as the expression of a single subjectivity, is in fact always a co-construction.[23]

Investigators who take co-construction seriously struggle with decisions about how to represent physically present and absent ("ghostly"[24]) audiences. There is no simple rule for how to display a speaker and listener/questioner constructing narrative and meaning together.

My representation in Transcript 2.1, one attempt, is not nearly as detailed as some analysts work with,[25] but it was informed by decades of research on micro features of language use. It displays the co-construction process, or as some might put it, a story that is recipient-designed; Sunita developed her account (and her "self") for a particular listener, me, a white Western woman who needed to be educated about the Indian family context, and expectations mothers-in-law have for new daughters-in-law. If she had been talking with friends around a dinner table, or with an Indian interviewer, she would have assumed some knowledge was shared, and developed the account (and the "self" constructed in it) differently. Instead, Sunita cast her experience in terms a Western woman could understand. It was a "choice" (love) marriage, not arranged, and her in-laws "were against the marriage."

Looking briefly at Transcript 2.1 with co-construction in mind, my puzzlement is clear. I interrupt to ask about the couple's living arrangements (line 11). They were living separately from his parents, Sunita says, not in the joint family as would have been the custom. She went nevertheless to their home to cook every day. Interpreting Sunita's narrative as we constructed it together, I sensed a young woman going to great lengths to please a demanding mother-in-law, supported by a husband who seemed to want a degree of separation from his parents. Note here that my listening is already saturated with concepts, such as gender and generational hierarchies in India. Prior concepts, in other words, shaped my listening and questioning, allowing me to selectively see what I then described—a component of all observation ("the priority of the signifier over the signified"[26]). Prior texts constituted what I saw in the transcript even as I was composing it. There was an inevitable gap between Sunita's experience and her talk about it. Telling another about something that happened depends on language that, as Nietzsche wrote, is a "prison house"[27] because there is no way to break through to the ideas and events to which words refer. Language is "uncommunicative of anything other than itself."[28]

Much could be said about the narrative represented in Transcript 2.1, yet I draw attention to a few significant points. It displays tension between an "I" narrative and one about family and community expectations. Readers can also see two subjectivities at work as Sunita and I attuned our responses to the other (note my encouraging signs of involvement in the back-channel utterances, as well as my interruptions as I try to understand obligations in her Indian family). There are medicalized discourses taken for granted in the language community we shared (e.g., a miscarriage is "traumatic"). Sunita was an active research participant, not responding in scripted ways to discrete questions. She reworked questions so as to be able to tell me what she thought was important. Infertility, though the centerpiece of my research, was only a small part of her "self"—a difference she made clear to me in a letter written after the interview (discussed below).

The topic of pleasing a mother-in-law hovered over our two-hour conversation, which I can only summarize due to space considerations. When Sunita spoke moments later about the first year of her marriage (dialogue not included in Transcript 2.1), I returned to my puzzlement: "So you went there everyday as a—as a way of getting them to agree, and to like you? Is that—?" However awkwardly expressed, I was trying to understand the nature of Sunita's relationship with the woman who (I knew from reading) was immensely powerful in Indian families. Sunita responded by educating me about her culture ("I was very clear that I had somehow to get her to like me. My husband is very fond of his mother."). She continued by appealing to cultural knowledge we shared about regional foods in India ("My mother-in-law wanted me to learn uh their ways of cooking, you know . . .). She briefly introduced emotions and blame ("I think my mother-in-law also was uh fairly uh shocked when uh I had this mis—abortion. . . . And she's never blamed me, otherwise, you know, for not having children"). For whatever reason, I interrupted Sunita as she introduced the topic of blame and returned to the question that initiated our conversation ("So, did you ever get pregnant again after that?"). Perhaps I wanted to take back control of the interview and finish getting basic demographic information so we could move on. My interruption here does not illustrate good narrative interviewing, because I did not follow Sunita down *her* trails, but instead returned to my agenda. The theme of blame was left hanging, only to return again as we ended our conversation (presented below).

Transcript 2.2 displays a second transcription of the miscarriage narrative, which excludes my participation in the conversation (for heuristic purposes here[29]). It subtly implies that the "self" Sunita presents is independent of interaction. The mode of transcription is informed by the work of James Gee, a social linguist whose theory of narrative discourse is discussed at greater length in Chapter 4. His structural method requires that the transcriber/investigator listen to oral features—how a narrative is actually spoken with pauses and "pitch glides" (subtle falls in the pitch of voice). Listening carefully to intonation results in parsing a narrative into units consisting of lines (a single sequence of words comprising an "idea unit") that form stanzas (groups of lines with similar content that are separated by pauses and shifts in pitch) and, in very long narratives, parts and strophes. As Chapter 4 demonstrates with several interview texts, investigators have fruitfully adapted Gee's method of transcription to different research situations.

Transcript 2.2

Timing of pregnancy and spotting	Stanza 1

01   I think it was the second or third year of marriage
02   that I was pregnant
03   then in the third month
04   I started spotting

Overwork	Coda

05   I think I was overworking

In-laws response to marriage	Stanza 2

06   Since it was a choice marriage
07   we were trying to get my in-laws
08   to be more amenable to the whole situation
09   in-laws were against the marriage

Overwork	Stanza 3

10   And so I used to work the whole day
11   then go to their place to cook in the evening
12   for a family of seven
13   then pack the food for two of us and bring it home

Help from husband	Stanza 4

14   I went there to cook everyday
15   and not everyday could he come
16   to pick me up
17   so that we could come together

Help from father-in-law	Stanza 5

18   And whenever my father-in-law was at home
19   he used to see to it that the driver came to drop me home
20   but when he wasn't at home
21   I had to come on my own

Overwork	Coda

22   I think that was overdoing it

Mother-in-law's demand one day	Stanza 6

23   And then I carried some of the food stuff
24   the grains and things
25   from that place
26   because my mother-in-law insisted that I carry it back that day

	Fear of miscarriage	Stanza 7
27	And the next day	
28	I started spotting	
29	and I was so frightened	
30	because I didn't know really what to do	

	Getting medical advice	Stanza 8
31	So I rang up my doctor and told her	
32	and she said, "You just lie down	
33	you are okay but only thing I think you need to rest	
34	don't move around and things like that."	

	Going to her mother's and doctor's evaluation	Stanza 9
35	So then I went over to my mother's and stayed there for a month	
36	and the doctor said "you're O.K."	
37	but in the next examination she said	
38	"No, I don't think the fetus is growing so we should take a	
39	second opinion"	
40	[text about visiting another gynecologist, his advice,	
41	waiting, and a miscarriage that was "very traumatic"]	

	End of overwork	Coda
42	And after that I stopped going everyday to my in-laws	
43	because my husband said "this is ridiculous"	

Source: Riessman, C. K. (2000a). "Even if we don't have children [we] can live": Stigma and infertility in South India. In C. C. Mattingly & L. C. Garro (Eds.), Narrative and cultural construction of illness and healing (pp. 128–152). Berkeley: University of California Press. Reprinted with permission.

Note how in this version, Sunita's speech is organized into a series of thematic stanzas, or meaning units. Following Gee, I have given titles to each stanza (the thematic point), "cleaned" speech of disfluencies, and deleted my presence in the conversation. Some readers may find this written representation more accessible than the earlier version, while others will find it sorely incomplete because it excludes audience participation. The representation is compact and compelling, but it is also highly interpretive, carrying serious implications for how a reader will understand the narrative. Most obviously, it erases the entire process of co-construction and presents the narrative as if it arose, full blown, from within "the self" of the speaker.

The theme of overwork, however, does come sharply into focus. "Overworking" and "overdoing it" become codas that interrupt and comment on the unfolding sequences of action. The meaning of the final stanza—where Sunita gives a speaking role to her husband ("this is ridiculous")—is contingent on overworking, which Sunita did because of his mother, she said earlier. Readers usually make causal links when one event follows another, and Transcript 2.2. suggests overwork (and, implicitly the mother-in-law) caused the miscarriage. The precise sequence that points to this outcome is more difficult to discern from Transcript 2.1, which generates other knowledge.

With this brief exercise, I have shown how two transcriptions of the "same" segment of an interview are deeply interpretive; each points readers (and narrative analysts) in a different direction. The first one (2.1) leads readers into the conversational context; it is an exchange between two women from different cultures about a major event in the life of one. Jointly, they produce a narrative about a miscarriage that might, for example, initiate inquiry into how women speak across difference about difficult reproductive experiences. The second representation (2.2) leads the reader/analyst into the experience of one woman—Sunita—caught in a web of a job, a new marriage, and the demands of a mother-in-law; she connects themes into a causal narrative about a miscarriage. I have used the second representation (together with other narrative accounts) to study thematically Indian women's explanatory accounts of infertility—precisely how older women story themselves and their situations in ways that deflect blame and minimize stigma.[30] Each line of inquiry is productive; one does not necessarily lead to "better" analysis. Each can answer a research question and provide valid insights supported by textual evidence. In the first, we see how a complex narrative gets jointly produced in a storytelling context and, in the second, how a narrator structures her tale to shift responsibility for a reproductive failure. My simple point is that different theoretical assumptions about language, communication, and "the self" are embedded in each transcript.

Before moving to a later section of the interview with Sunita, some historical context is needed for the simple binary I set up earlier about "the self"—as constructed or reflected. The belief that a person could be known by examining her speech (excluding the interactional context that produced it) has a long history in the social sciences, exemplified in survey research, early Chicago School ethnography, and even some contemporary qualitative research. Case studies in the psychoanalytic literature, for the most part, also observe the custom of excluding the interviewer. Focus is on the patient/respondent/subject and underlying concepts contained in the talk. The practice continues in some grounded theory research and in the thematic narrative tradition displayed in Chapter 4. But with the "turn to language" in mid-twentieth century theory, a major shift began to take place in the research practice of some narrative researchers. The local context had to be taken into consideration, including *who* is asking the questions, *how,* and *why?* Dialogic and visual analytic approaches extend this line of inquiry further, as Chapters 5 and 6 show).

Mishler argues that methodological shifts in transcription practices led to the theoretical discovery of the "dialogic" or narrativized self.[31] If constructing the self is an ongoing project of daily living that happens through storytelling, attention moves away from "*who* I am" to questions of "*when, where, and how* I am."[32] In Mishler's view, methodological innovation led to this theoretical revision. To be sure, the change happened alongside other shifts in theory: for example, how gender intersects with race, class, ethnicity, and sexuality to produce (and maintain) discursively constituted identities. All these developments challenge ideas about a unitary and stable self that is simply *reflected* in language. This is the implication when we present a narrative account and erase the interviewer's role in producing it.

The two transcriptions open up issues that are often glossed in qualitative analysis. Investigators need to interrogate the decisions they make as they construct written representations of oral narrative. Transcripts contain invisible taken-for-granted theories of language and the "self."

I turn now to an issue that Chapter 7 takes up in earnest—the "truths" of our interpretations of oral narrative, drawing again on my interview with Sunita. I noted earlier that the topic of blame for the miscarriage returned in full force as she and I were ending the interview. We had been talking for almost two hours about a range of topics (some initiated by her, others by me). I then asked a question on my interview schedule about the reaction of others to her childlessness. The conversation that unfolded is presented in Transcript 2.3—my attempt to constitute in written form a moving conversation among women about a miscarriage.

Transcript 2.3

01 C: And your husband's family? (reaction to childlessness)

02 S: No, in fact I think uhh my mother-in-law (p) has felt (p) has
03 always felt guilty. (p) Because she was always felt that she has
04 been the cause of that miscarriage, you know. And because of
05 it she— it's its its something—

06 C: Because of the travelling and the bringing all the food and
07 so on?

(Continued)

(Continued)

08 S: Yeah, yeah. She insisted that day. And she said it to the extent,
09   uhh, "I've had 5 children and I've done all this work and I've
10   carried all these things" and things like that. And uhh I was
11   told by my doctor that "you don't—you are very anaemic, no,
12   you are not—you don't do such stupid things." And then
13   because she went on and on, and for that whole hour and a
14   half that I was at their place. (p) So finally I just dragged it
15   [food stuffs] towards the lift, to the elevator, just brought it
16   down towards the gate, you know.

17   [talks about security man who helped load a cab, elevator at
18   her flat not working]

19   So I just dragged it and—(p).
20   Now it may or may not be the reason
21   but (p) I think she feels- And that is why she has never ever
22   questioned me (p). Only (p) you know, 2 years—a year
23   ago when (p) her brother expired, youngest brother expired.

24   [talks about going to distant city on train with her mother-in-
25   law for ceremony, who stayed for 13 days, then returning to
26   pick her up because she is not in good health and brother's
27   death was hard]

28   So I went to pick her up and that time uhh, after so many years,
29   she actually asked me that—you know, "I have never had the
30   courage to ask you," but uhh, you know (p) "what has been
31   happening? I'm sure you've taken treatment and all
32   that, knowing you."

33   [talks about how she has worked outside home with her
34   husband's support, despite his family's objections, and about their
35   early struggles to be financially independent from his family]

36 C: So your mother-in-law asked after all these years? How many
37   years was that?

38 S: Almost 20 years.

39 C: Twenty years later she asked!

40 S: She asked me uhh—18 years that means after the miscarriage—
41   she asked me—

42   C: She knew about your miscarriage?

43   S: Yeah, yeah, she came at that time and all that. Uhh but uhh and
44   she said it also like that, "I've never had the courage to ask you
45   uhh but 'What?' you know 'Why?'" So then I (p) told her that
46   "No, well since you've never asked me, that's why I never said
47   anything." But uhh I explained to her, you know, what we have
48   done and uhh, the treatment we have taken and everything and
49   it hasn't worked so we've left it at that. (p) And uh well, she also
50   left it at that (p) and she didn't say anything more.

51   C: And you said before you think she feels quilty. How do you—?

52   S: Because she said that, you know uhh (p) "How did it happen
53   that—" you know, "you had conceived so why couldn't you
54   conceive again" (p) and uhh, "it shouldn't have happened that
55   way" (p) and uh you know uhh, "I suppose this generation is
56   different from my generation" and things like that, you know.
57   It's round round thing [gestures]. And I tried to tell her "I
58   don't blame you," (p) you know. Since she went round and
59   round I also had to go round and round. But I tried to tell her
60   that "I don't blame you." Because I don't think you know—

61   C: But you think that you were both talking about that moment?

62   S: Yeah, we were both talking about that moment. Uhm and I'm
63   glad that we could talk about it, we were talking in the train
64   as we were coming back from [distant city]. [voice lowers] Just
65   the 2 of us.

66   C: (p) Those conversations are very important when they happen.

67   S: Yeah, they are very important, yeah. [Long pause and sigh]

A great deal could be said about the long segment, yet again I emphasize only a few elements, leaving it to readers to grapple with the many meanings suggested in the text (readings, of course, will vary with one's interpretive framework). First and thematically, the topic of blame become explicit—responsibility for the miscarriage. A changed (and enduring) relationship between mother-in-law and daughter-in-law permits the topic to surface after eighteen years, albeit obliquely, on a long train ride after the death of a family member. Sunita indicates, through her choice of language, the conversational rules that both parties observed: they went "round and round" (lines 57–59), circling questions about the cause of the miscarriage. Still the dutiful daughter, Sunita followed her mother-in-law's lead about how to conduct herself ("since she went round and round I also had to go round and round"), just as twenty years earlier she had followed her mother-in-law's directive to drag foodstuffs "that day." Generational tensions about a woman's place in modern India cannot be addressed directly in the conversation on the train. Instead, political and institutional issues remain private—cast as an interpersonal conflict between women.

Second, notice the interviewer/questioner's *very* active presence in the conversation; any transcript that excluded her would be false. I repeatedly encouraged Sunita to expand on her relationship with a central character in the earlier miscarriage story ("So your mother-in-law asked after *all* these years? . . . Twenty years later she asked! . . . She knew about your miscarriage? . . . And you said before she feels guilty . . . "). Without my curiosity about the place of the mother-in-law, Sunita probably would not have expanded the miscarriage story (lines 8–20) or developed a new story about a conversation on a train many years later with her mother-in-law about the miscarriage (lines 22–65). The transcript shows co-construction vividly at work; topics and meanings are negotiated in dialogue between teller and listener (and new meanings, in turn, can be produced in the dialogue between text and reader—a topic I take up in Chapter 5).

Third, the transcript opens up issues of emotion in interviews, and how to present them.[33] Although many years have passed, I vividly remember the moment in the conversation with Sunita. Looking at the written representation, I still sense the muted unspeakable emotions in the depiction of the conversation on the train between two women from different generations that went "round and round" (the narrated event). Emotions also hang in the interview conversation between two women from different cultures about the past conversation (the narrative event). I am reminded of Aristotle's wisdom and Cheryl Mattingly's comment: "Narratives do not merely refer to past experience but create experiences for their audiences."[34] Sunita's description of a conversation between two women on a train created an experience for me, the audience. Thinking back, I remember feeling some discomfort when, after a long sigh (mine, not hers, on line 67), I returned to the next question on my interview schedule. I had attempted after a long pause to provide a kind of "resolution" for the narrative in the comment ("those conversations are very important when they happen"). Perhaps I was recalling difficult conversations in my own family. But there was no resolution for the strong emotions that the narrative tries to contain.

About five minutes later, after I had gone on to ask about the reaction of Sunita's natal family to her childlessness (a topic she did not find too meaningful), she broke into tears. We simply sat together for many minutes.

No words were needed. All I could do was bear witness and be with her. All a transcript could do is note her sobbing (although narrative analysts, of course, could inquire about the power of the feelings and possible sources of her tears).

Finally, the transcript opens up questions about determining the boundaries of a narrative—an issue all investigators face. This is one of the many ways that we participate in the creation of narratives, rather than "finding" them in interviews. Looking at the transcripts as a group that I presented from the interview with Sunita, an investigator could compose boundaries in several ways. The texts could be treated as discrete stories; the first segment (2.2) about the miscarriage, for example, could be analyzed alongside miscarriage stories from other women. Or, the texts could be combined to form a case study composed of linked stories that explored a theoretical issue of general interest to narrative scholars. Or even further, the texts could form the basis for an exploration of a single life story or biographical study. Some narratives that develop in research interviews are clearly bounded, with clear beginnings and endings, almost like the boundaries of folktales ("once upon a time . . . " and "they lived happily ever after"). Most personal narratives, however, like most lives, are more complex. In these cases, there are no clear rules for determining boundaries, but the analytic decision is important, for it shapes interpretation and illustrates once again how we participate in the construction of the narrative that we analyze.

If I had presented only the first transcript (2.1), inference would be different than when all the segments are included. Is it the story of a miscarriage, or a broad tale of family conflict, especially mother/daughter-in-law relations in a changing India? Is it a story about "getting her to like me"? Is it ultimately a moral tale about blame and forgiveness?

As our long meeting was ending, Sunita and I agreed to stay in contact. I wrote her when I had a draft of a paper completed and asked for reactions.[35] (I was seeking two kinds of reaction: her agreement to let me use the long segments from the interview in a disguised version, or a second chance at informed consent, and her reactions to my interpretations of the stories.) I did not hear from Sunita for over a year, when she wrote (on her company's letterhead) to apologize, explaining that she and her husband had moved to a larger flat, and my letter and draft had gotten buried in a box. She liked the paper, she wrote, and had no problems with my using her words. But, she wondered about my interpretation, because it was not how she thought about her life. I had developed the paper around my interest in infertility and its management in families. For Sunita, infertility was but a small part of her biography. She wrote about a recent job promotion and the many children in her life (neighbors' and servants' children whom she had mentioned repeatedly during our conversation), her husband's work, and their worries about aging parents. She was a "complete woman," not a childless woman as I had described her in the paper.[36] In Chapter 7, I return to Sunita's letter to interrogate different "truths" contained in our varying interpretations.

A Translated Conversation

Constructing a transcript from a translated interview involves difficult interpretive decisions. The conversation with Sunita occurred in English—a marker of her class advantage—but most women in the infertility study were interviewed in Malayalam, the local South Indian language. Interviews were translated later by Liza (my Malayalee assistant) who spoke both languages fluently, and who conducted most interviews; she introduced me alongside her as "Dr. Catherine." How to represent narratives from these conversations? How to present the English spoken word and not lose the Indian conversational context?

Many investigators present transcripts of translated interviews, but the politics of translation are rarely acknowledged. Given hierarchies of language power, scholars from non-English speaking countries are pressured to publish in U.S. or U.K. journals. Even aside from cultural imperialism when English is considered the language of science, there are other issues. Authors, for example, typically erase translation problems, assuming questions about equivalence of meaning are irrelevant. Like transcription, translation is often treated as a technical task, assigned to assistants, although anthropologists have long known the folly of such decisions. They are expected to speak the language of the group they are studying and, if they hire translators, they work closely with them.[37]

Bogusia Temple has brought the translator from behind the shadows for qualitative investigators not accustomed to thinking critically about the issues; she builds on work in feminist theory and literary studies about difference.[38] If meaning is constructed rather than expressed by language, "the relationships between languages and researchers, translators and the people they seek to represent are as crucial as issues of which word is best in a sentence in a language."[39]

To illustrate these complexities, I return to the infertility study, presenting narrative segments from an interview with Celine (a pseudonym), a Christian woman educated through the tenth grade, who was married to a Hindu fisherman. Twenty-six-years-old and married eight years, she had expected to conceive right after marriage but had not, and she was deeply sad. A visit to her village from "Dr. Catherine" may have carried hopes of a cure, despite the introduction that made explicit I was a sociologist studying childless women, not a gynecologist. Liza conducted the interview in Malayalam, translating periodically for me. It was difficult to find privacy in the small house (neighbors and family members watched and listened), and when we found a separate room her sisters brought a tray of tea and sweets. Elsewhere, I explore ethical issues in the interview[40]; here I focus primarily on relations between translation and interpretation.

Liza's initial transcript of the taped interview was literal—a "word for word" translation that was difficult for me to interpret. (She had, of course, already engaged in interpretation to find equivalent words in English for referential content—never easy in any translation.) We discussed her sense as a culture member of Celine's language, the equivalence in English of particular phrases, and the missing pronouns I noted in speech (characteristic of Malayalam).[41] Our conversations led to a revised transcript; sections were revised again to achieve greater clarity in English after discussion about syntax with South India specialists in the United States. I won't belabor the point: the interview excerpts presented below have been transformed several times over.

In contrast to Sunita's experience, a conversation about infertility was extremely relevant to Celine's life situation. At twenty-six, childbearing was still expected of her; in her small village she could not selectively disclose her situation or "pass as normal"—strategies available to women (such as Sunita) living in some more Westernized contexts.[42] It was common knowledge in her village, for example, that she cannot conceive, and (even though the fault may be her husband's) she was constantly reminded of her spoiled identity:[43] "Neighbors, they ridicule me. When I go out and all they call me 'fool without a child,' like that." As I worked interpretively with the translated interview and several others where managing a stigmatized identity was a central theme, I developed a new research question: what do women's stories reveal about how they contest stigma in words and action?

Transcript 2.4

Story 1

01 Liza: Has being childless affected your married life?

02 Celine: (lowers voice almost to whisper)

03 Initially very much.

04 because of not having children

05 he has beaten me.

(Continued)

(Continued)

06 Liza: During the initial years, I see.

07 Celine: Since 5 years
08 when we started going to hospitals
09 and even then didn't have children.

10 Initially, for 6 months after marriage,
11 I stayed with my husband's family.
12 Then for them—
13 what they are saying is because I don't have children
14 I should be sent away.

15 My husband's father, mother and siblings
16 they won't talk to me and all that.
17 Since I don't have children, they asked him to leave me.
18 His father and mother said that he should again marry.

19 (lowers voice). After that I quarreled with them
20 am living in this house [her family's home].

21 Liza: How long have you been here?

22 Celine: After marriage I stayed there for only six months.

Story 2

01 CR: [in English] But now her husband is with her. Is that right?

02 Lisa: I'll ask her.
03 [in Malayalam] Is your husband here always?

04 Celine: Yes

05 Lisa: For the past 8 years?

06 Celine: When they scolded him
07 told him he should marry another girl
08 their son used to hurt me a lot at first
09 [unclear] now he won't abuse me

10 Lisa: So your husband is staying here always?

11 Celine: Yes, yes, he is staying here.

12 Lisa: He doesn't go to his house?

13 Celine: No.

14 Lisa: What is your husband's reaction about remarrying?
15 Celine: I told him
16 since we don't have children
17 "remarry"
18 then when he remarries he will get children.

19 Lisa: You said to your husband?
20 Celine: So that it won't be so hard for him,
21 he will get children when he remarries, Right?

22 So he asked me, "Will you stay like this?"
23 I told him, "Yes, it's no problem for me.
24 I'll stay here,
25 you marry again and I'll stay."

26 But then he doesn't leave.
27 Even if we don't have children, can live.

28 Lisa: [in English] She tells her husband that he should marry again.
        So that he may have children, but he doesn't want to do that.

Source: Riessman, C. K. (2002). Positioning gender identity in narratives of infertility: South Indian women's lives in context. In M. C. Inhorn & F. van Balen (Eds.), *Infertility around the globe: New thinking on childlessness, gender, and reproductive technologies* (pp. 152–170). Berkeley: University of California Press. Reprinted with permission.

Buried in pages of translated interview transcript was a brief story (Story 1) where Celine relates that she was beaten by her husband and shunned by his parents when she didn't conceive after six months of marriage, and also included was an elaboration almost an hour later (Story 2). The stigma Celine faced because of infertility was the harshest and most punishing tale that Liza and I had encountered during the fieldwork. We were disturbed by the stories for different reasons (described below). I knew I had to present them, but was not sure how to do it—translations of two stories, separated by many pages of transcript, that involved a conversation among three speakers (Celine, Liza, and me [CR]) communicating in different languages.

Transcript 2.4 displays the text I ultimately constructed, which is two linked stories[44]—sparse (like the spoken version) and full of ambiguity. Because the materials were translated, readers and analysts can't interrogate particular words and other lexical choices (the meaning of a word is not always equivalent across languages). It is, however, possible to examine sequence, contexts in which topics appear, and participants' contributions to the evolving narrative. I have created structures to convey the sense I've made of the two stories by grouping lines into units on the page. As a kind of textual experimentation, I constructed poetic stanzas (groups of lines about a single topic) that make my reading of the organization of the brief stories clear for the reader.[45] The translated materials (which initially seemed daunting) opened up the text to shifting meanings.

Liza and I participated differently in the two stories, complicating the idea of co-construction: three speakers participating across two languages and several cultural divides. Looking first at Story 1, Liza begins with a question about whether childlessness had affected "married life," and Celine positions the infertility in the context of her arranged marriage and the joint family. Although lines 4 and 5 could have become an abstract for a story to follow—about beatings because of infertility—the story does not get developed that way.

The topic of physical abuse does not surface again until Story 2 (an hour later). There are several ways to make sense of the shift. Perhaps because the topic was so unexpected, Liza backs away from the beatings and comments on their timing ("during the initial years"), which, in turn, prompts Celine to give a chronology of the initial years of the marriage and to end with her decisive action to leave the joint family. Embedded in the tight temporal sequence are several stanzas that recount the family's response to her. Liza does not respond specifically to the family drama that the stanzas describe, but instead responds after a coda to ask again about time ("How long have you been here?"). The construction of a story gets shaped in this small instance by audience. Liza mediates how the story begins and ends, how it gets located in time and place, and what themes get developed. In this co-constructed narrative, the audience permits certain facts to come to the fore and get included in the drama, while others remain outside—momentary visitors who leave the stage when they are not given a part. Celine's husband, for example, has no role after the beginning because Liza does not respond to him as a major character in the drama. Like all narrative interviewers, Liza tries to make sense of what she is hearing, and locating the events in time and space aids her meaning-making process.

Perhaps a story of wife abuse is more than Liza can hear. She is a twenty-six-year-old woman (the same age as Celine, but with a master's degree) whose own marriage is about to be arranged. Liza asks about the marriage and, in this context, Celine and Liza collaborate to develop a theme salient to both of them—the evolution of an arranged marriage from inauspicious beginnings.[46] The ensuing story they craft presupposes shared cultural knowledge about gender and generational hierarchies in South India.

Returning to what researchers can and cannot do with translated texts, note that I have included in Transcript 2.4 certain performance features that intensify the narrative event (the present conversation about past events). Celine alters markedly the volume of her voice at two key places in Story 1: as she opens the story and as she moved to close it (lines 2 and 19). Lowering her voice almost to a whisper signals meaning and importance, as these are unspeakable events, unknown perhaps to her family in the next room. Given the privacy of the setting and the many topics that have been touched on in the hour interview, she decides to reveal the abuse and her actions against it—between women. Talk about family problems to strangers is not customary in India. Speaking out to Liza and me challenges social conventions, just as Celine's "quarrel" with her in-laws, and departure from their home, defied conventions in the Indian joint family.

Shortly after Story 1, our interview was interrupted by Celine's sister, who brought us tea and snacks, and then by Rajiv (Celine's husband). He came into the room to tell Celine he was going out and when he would be back. I watched their solicitous interaction. After he left, we ate food the family provided as people wandered into the room and asked more questions of Liza (Since she was twenty-six, why isn't she married?) and of me (Why did Madam come to India? Had she diagnosed Celine's problem yet?). We answered all questions, and I said again I was not a gynecologist.[47] While we had tea, Liza used the break from the formal interview to inquire about how the marriage was arranged, given religious differences between the families, which was a topic of obvious personal interest (she, like Celine, is Christian). She learned (and told me later) the marriage was held in Celine's village, "since they [his family] are Hindus." After she moved to their village, religious harassment began. They would not let her go to church and pressured her to attend their temple, which she refused to do. Meanwhile, her family had difficulty amassing the dowry promised, so they gave property instead of gold. Liza listened intently to Celine's descriptions and, as the tea things were collected, moved to complete the formal interview. She quickly summarized the preceding conversation for me ("She had a problem with not giving adequate dowry. After six months she's come back and stayed here.")

I was puzzled about the husband's place in the narrated events, specifically his reaction to his parents' directive to abandon Celine and marry again. Contradictions in Story 1 further puzzled me, for instance, he beat Celine but accompanied her after she quarreled with his family. His behavior to her during our visit was kind and attentive. (Earlier, I had asked Liza to clarify the structure of the household, and found that the couple was living permanently with her family, not his as is more common, and Celine refused to visit her in-laws.) I now sensed something further, and very unusual for a South Indian family; he is distant from his natal family and allied with his wife. My puzzlement stimulated a question-and-answer exchange, and then Story 2, linked to and expanding Story 1.

The narrated events in the second story raise questions about meanings in the first story—interpretive issues that arose with Sunita's narrative as well. Some uncertainties regarding Celine's situation are resolved in Story 2, but others remain. It is clear that Rajiv has distanced himself from his parents physically, and from their "scolding." Related to this, perhaps, he has stopped beating Celine.[48] But why does he resist her urging to remarry (lines 14–27)? I leave it to readers to work further with the stories, bearing in mind Temple's cautions: there are "constraints placed on the reading of a text by the need to make sense of it on its own terms, and thus while there may be many versions of the 'truth' of a text, each must be made possible by something within the text, by its logic, syntax and structuring resources."[49]

Returning to transcription practices, notice in Story 2 how I chose to represent the three participants in a "trialogue" consisting of a narrator (Celine), translator (Liza), and investigator/interpreter (CR), who, working together as narrator and audience, shape the performance of the story, including the events, plot, and characters allowed onstage. Rajiv, a shadow figure in the first story, returns as a central character in the second, prompted by audience puzzlement[50] and my explicit instruction to Liza to inquire about him. Similarly, Rajiv's response to his parents' directive to remarry (central to the plot of the first story, and introduced again in the second) is resolved because Liza explicitly asks about it (line 14). Whatever a reader might think about remarriage as a "solution" to infertility, Celine voices the recommendation here, not her in-law's to get rid of her. Is she taking back some power?

Yet, Rajiv does not leave. Many ambiguities remain, particularly in the last line made more so by translation: "Even if we don't have children, can live." I have presented the line exactly as translated, and a key pronoun is missing (not uncommon in Malayalam). Celine's wording in the final clause suggests two possibilities, "I can live" or "we can live"—statements that carry very different meanings. In relation to this, it is not clear who is speaking the last line of the story. Is remaining childless (the solution suggested) voiced by Celine or Rajiv? If it is her line, she is again challenging stigma and social convention, implying that life is possible even for a South Indian village woman who does not have children. If it is his line, the message carries other meanings, one being that perhaps he views their life together as important, even without progeny. He is willing to face stigma himself by permanently remaining with a wife who cannot conceive. Elsewhere, I bring observational data to bear—a tender interchange I witnessed between Rajiv and Celine—to suggest another provisional reading related to their their loving sexual relationship.[51] As in all stories, there are ambiguities and relative indeterminacies. The texts are sparse, there are gaps leaving considerable room for reader response. I eventually combined Celine's account with those of other women speaking about stigma to generate a theoretical framework about childless women's resistance practices in India to challenge stereotypes about women's victimization. Celine was certainly victimized, but she fought against it by leaving the joint family where she had become an object of scorn. Her marriage was surviving childlessness, an outcome I witnessed with others in the sample (including Sunita).

Liza was upset by the interview with Celine. As we were walking away from the house afterward, she said it was "the saddest case she had heard so far," and in her translation of the interview, and our discussion of it, she repeatedly returned to the "abuse"—her word. In our many discussions about this and other interviews (and related conversations about women's position in a changing India), she often recalled the "sad case." Her reading of the narrative differs from mine, a consequence no doubt of our contrasting positions, biographies, nationalities, and gender ideologies. Any text an investigator creates is "plurivocal, open to several readings and to several constructions."[52]

I have presented some of the difficulties of working with translated narratives, hoping to stimulate future investigators to bring the translator from behind the shadows. Investigators can include themselves and the translators as active participants in knowledge production. As Temple and Young write, the text any investigator constructs is "the researcher's view of what the translator has produced rather than any attempt to show that she knows their 'actual' meaning."[53] Multiple readings are potential in all narrative research, and the problem becomes highly visible when investigators work with narratives in another language and those that appear "strange" in other ways. Translation can open up ambiguities that get hidden in "same-language" texts. When we have a common language with our informants, we tend to easily assume that we know what they are saying, and alternative readings tend to get obscured, or even ignored, because of the methodological and theoretical assumptions we bring to our work. Temple summarizes key points:

> The use of translators and interpreters is not merely a technical matter that has
> little bearing on the outcome. It is of epistemological consequence as it influences

what is "found." Translators are active in the process of constructing accounts and an examination of their intellectual [and personal] autobiographies, that is, an analytic engagement with how they come to know what to do, is an important component in understanding the nature and status of the findings. When the translator and the researcher are different people the process of knowledge construction involves another layer.[54]

Conclusion

By our interviewing and transcription practices, we play a major part in constituting the narrative data that we then analyze. Through our presence, and by listening and questioning in particular ways, we critically shape the stories participants choose to tell. The process of infiltration continues with transcription, for language is not a "perfectly transparent medium of representation."[55] Mishler[56] makes the analogy between a transcript and a photograph, which seemingly "pictures reality." Yet the technology of lenses, films, printing papers, and darkroom practices (even before the digital age) has made possible an extraordinary diversity of possible images of the same object. An image reflects the artist's views and conceptions—values about what is important. Photographers, like interviewers, transcribers, and translators, fix the essence of a figure. I return to these issues in Chapter 6 and discuss how visual narrative analysts have dealt with them.

Transcribing discourse, like photography, is an interpretive practice. Representing "what happened" in an interview is a "fixation" of action[57] into written form. Transcriptions are by definition incomplete, partial, and selective—constructed by an investigator (who may or not also be the transcriber). Each transcript prepared is "a partial representation of speech . . . a transformation . . . each includes some and excludes other features of speech and rearranges the flow . . . into lines of text within the limits of a page."[58] Decisions about how to display speech reflect theoretical commitments (and practical constraints); they are not simply technical decisions. By displaying text in particular ways and by making decisions about the boundaries of narrative segments, we provide grounds for our arguments, just as a photographer guides the viewer's eye with lenses and cropping. Different transcription conventions lead to and support different interpretations and theoretical positions, and they ultimately create different narratives. Meaning is constituted in very different ways with alternative transcriptions of the same stretch of talk.[59]

I turn in the next four chapters to specific forms of analysis. Readers will see investigators constructing transcripts that represent speech in ways that suit their particular theoretical aims, including the interviewer/questioner to varying degrees. The four approaches to narrative analysis are broad group-ings with boundaries that are not always distinct, for they often overlap and blur. Within each chapter, I present candidate exemplars (sometimes it is my own work, more often it is the research of others) that serve as models of the approach, electing to write about method by focusing on how different investigators actually carried out analytic work. Exemplars illustrate the general pattern and the diversity within each approach. I hope the candidate exemplars inspire students to formulate their own projects, and determine the kind of analysis that suits their questions.

3

Thematic Analysis

What do we think a narrative means? What information is communicated that can aid exploration of our study issue? All narrative inquiry is, of course, concerned with content—"what" is said, written, or visually shown—but in thematic analysis, content is the exclusive focus. The general approach is probably the most common method of narrative analysis and, arguably, the most straightforward and appealing in applied settings. Many studies in nursing and other health occupations (including those influenced by interpretive phenomenology and hermeneutics) have implicitly adapted the approach to uncover and categorize thematically patients' experiences of illness.[1] Thematic narrative analysis is akin to what scholars in folklore and history use with archival data. It is often confused with grounded theory in the qualitative methods literature. There are key differences that I develop more fully at the end of the chapter but, to note an obvious one, narrative scholars keep a story "intact" by theorizing from the case rather than from component themes (categories) across cases.

The chapter articulates specific features of thematic narrative analysis by working through selected exemplars that use oral and written data. (A similar approach to visual data is discussed in Chapter 6.) I make explicit how particular scholars did their work, that is, how they thematically analyze narrative materials. Because the candidate exemplars are extremely different (in kinds of data, theoretical perspective, epistemological position, research questions, even in definition of narrative), students looking for a set of rules will be disappointed. Instead, my objective is to excavate concrete practices or ways of working with narrative data where primary attention is on "what" is said, rather than "how," "to whom," or "for what purposes." The exemplars are diverse in other respects. Several researchers come from university settings in the United Kingdom with ongoing programs in narrative inquiry, reflecting the international and multidisciplinary scope of the field. Two of the exemplars use research interviews as data, another draws on documents, and another combines ethnographic observation with analysis of interviews and published biographical accounts. The diversity illustrates how the thematic approach is suited to a wide range of narrative texts; thematic analysis can be applied to stories that develop in interview conversations and group meetings, and those found in written documents. Several exemplars illustrate how stories can have effects beyond their meanings for individual storytellers, creating possibilities for social identities, group belonging, and collective action.

Adapting Mishler's distinction, the research featured in this chapter focuses almost exclusively on the "told"—informants' reports of events and experiences, rather than aspects of "the telling."[2] Data are interpreted in light of thematics developed by the investigator (influenced by prior and emergent theory, the concrete purpose of an investigation, the data themselves, political commitments, and other factors). There is minimal focus on *how* a narrative is spoken (or written), on structures of speech a narrator selects, audience (real and imagined), the local context that generated the narrative, or complexities of transcription (issues discussed in Chapter 2). These are taken up in other approaches described in chapters to follow.

Turning to the four exemplars, I begin with the questions that frame each study, summarize briefly the general findings, and then focus intensely on methods—the pragmatic steps each researcher took to thematically interpret their data (not always fully described in the published work). Drawing on points I made in earlier chapters, I interrogate each exemplar in light of four issues: (1) how the concept of narrative is used; (2) how data are constructed into text for analysis with attention to language and form, if present; (3) the unit of analysis (or focus) in each investigation; and (4) the investigator's attention to contexts, local to societal (micro and macro). I address these foci as I move through each exemplar, summarizing in Table 3.1 at the end. The chapter concludes with some general observations and questions about thematic analysis.

Working With Interviews

The sociologists' work that is featured can be contrasted on the dimension of time, specifically when and where each article appeared in the history of the "narrative turn" in the human sciences. Gareth Williams (from the U.K.)

published his research in 1984 in a British medical sociology journal, antic-ipating (and shaping in key ways) the emerging area of narrative inquiry that was to flower several years later. Patricia Ewick and Susan Silbey (from the U.S.) published their narrative article in 2003 in a general top-tier sociology journal (*American Journal of Sociology*) that in recent decades has published little qualitative work, let alone narrative work; they could take full advan-tage of more than twenty years of narrative scholarship (and a supportive journal editor). I take up each exemplar in turn.

1. A Study of Illness Narrative

Gareth Williams uses thematic methods to analyze interviews about illness.[3] Building on prior theoretical work by British sociologist Michael Bury and others,[4] he develops the concept of narrative reconstruction, mean-ing the imaginative work individuals do when chronic illness disrupts the expected life course. Not unlike the issue I explored in my infertility research, Williams asks how individuals explain and account for the biographical dis-ruption of rheumatoid arthritis. He argues that beliefs about the causes of misfortune are human interpretive practices, and meet our need to narratively reconstruct discontinuities in an imagined biography (continuing the ancient tradition of reflecting on origin and purpose, or *telos*).

Williams conducted and tape-recorded thirty interviews with individuals who had been diagnosed with rheumatoid arthritis. Many interviewees told long stories in response to Williams's brief and simple question, "Why do you think you got arthritis?" They expanded on the stories as the research relationship developed. Williams then constructs three case studies to illus-trate the process of making sense of the genesis of disability. Cases were not selected to be representative statistically, but instead to develop a theoreti-cal argument: the arrival of chronic illness initiates a process of cognitive reorganization—meaning-making. Individuals revealed through their stories different attempts "to establish points of reference between body, self, and society and to reconstruct a sense of order from the fragmentation produced by chronic illness."[5] They "reaffirm the impression that life has a course and the self has a purpose or *telos*."[6] (Negative cases are not presented, that is, biographical accounts in which narrative reconstruction doesn't occur, are resisted or remain incomplete.

The three cases illustrate marked variation in individuals' interpretation of the genesis of the same disease. While the interpretations are different, each narrator rejects (in a different way) simple medical formulations of etiology. To help illustrate this, the interview material is quoted extensively. For instance, to account for why his biography has been disrupted, one narrator

("Bill") develops a story that connects his job as a factory worker and fore-man ("working gaffer") with the onset of symptoms:

> I was a working gaffer . . . but, you know, they were mostly long hours and the end result, in 1972, was every time I had a session like, my feet began to swell and my hands began to swell. I couldn't hold a pen, I had difficulty get-ting between machines and difficulty getting hold of things.

As Bill relates the subsequent events of his life—referrals to doctors, blood tests, hospitalization—he explicitly connects work and illness:

> I didn't associate it with anything to do with the works [factory] at the time, but I think it was chemically induced. I worked with a lot of chemicals, acetone and what have you. We washed our hands in it, we had cuts, and we absorbed it. Now, I'll tell you this because it seems to be related. The men that I worked with who are all much older than me—there was a crew of sixteen and two survived, myself and the gaffer that was then—and they all complained of the same thing, you know, their hands started to pull up. It seems very odd.

Doctors dismissed his hypothesis about workplace toxicity, pursuing instead a genetic hypothesis to explain his illness:

> I was assured by them [the doctors] that this is what it was, it was arthritis. Now, it just got worse, a steady deterioration, and I put it down that it was from the works. But with different people questioning me at the hospital, delv-ing into the background, my mother had arthritis and my little sister, she died long before the war, 1936/7, and she had not arthritis, just rheumatism and that naturally did for her.

Bill refuses the medical explanation of genetic transmission and, as he returns later in the interview to the topic of the workplace, he picks up the theme of toxic exposure:

> But thinking back to the way the other blokes were who are now gone, so we can't ask them, and what I remember of them, they more or less came to it in the same manner . . . I wasn't in there with them all the time, I was travelling between floors so I was coming out of it and getting fresh air and washing more frequently than they did. So this is something to do with it.

Bill's causal narrative also includes a graphic description of the physical decline of a fellow worker. He develops a political critique of exploitative social relations where workers were the victims of injustice and neglect. Williams notes that the company eventually accepted some degree of liabil-ity, and paid compensation to surviving dependents.

I reproduced Bill's full narrative account as Williams presents it to make an essential point about his analytic method. Williams does not fracture the biographical account into thematic categories as grounded theory coding would do, but interprets it as a whole. Given his focus on the imagined genesis of illness, he roots Bill's explanatory account in political criticism, for he "linked his own demise with that of others, transcended the particulars of his own illness, and redefined his personal trouble as a public issue."[7] The sociologist brings prior theory to bear to interpret the case (in this instance, C. Wright Mills[8]).

Williams uses a similar thematic approach with the biographical narratives of two others in his sample to uncover strikingly different explanations for the genesis of arthritis. One is rooted in everyday understandings from social psychology (stress and hardship associated with a woman's place in the modern world), and the other is rooted in religious beliefs (the mysterious working of God's will). Each of the three case studies serves to thicken Williams's theoretical argument: "narrative reconstruction is an attempt to reconstitute and repair ruptures between body, self, and world." Individuals confront the assault of a major chronic illness by "linking up and interpreting different aspects of biography in order to realign present and past and self and society."[9] Analysis interprets and compares biographies as they are constituted in the research interviews.

Williams's implicit definition of narrative (it is never explicitly defined) is the biography as a whole, and specifically the story of the illness that unfolds over the course of a single interview. The definition is inclusive, referring to all speech that relates to the illness and typical of one strand of work in the thematic narrative tradition. The investigator works with a single interview at a time, isolating and ordering relevant episodes into a chronological biographical account. After the process has been completed for all interviews, the researcher zooms in, identifying the underlying assumptions in each account and naming (coding) them. Particular cases are then selected to illustrate general patterns—range and variation—and the underlying assumptions of different cases are compared. Williams is not interested in distribution (e.g., how many individuals rely on "political" as compared with "religious" or "social/psychological" explanations), although other researchers have used thematic narrative analysis to do that. Instead, he seeks to map the contours of the interpretive process that happen with biographical disruption—*telos*.

Williams reproduces excerpts or segments (some fairly lengthy, from the long interview narratives) that are interspersed in the written report with his interpretation, theoretical formulation, and references to prior theory. Speech quoted from interviews is "cleaned up" to some degree, for his texts erase dysfluencies, break-offs, interviewer utterances, and other common features of interview conversations. In thematic narrative analysis, emphasis is on "the told"—the events and cognitions to which language refers (the content of speech). Consequently, "messy" spoken language is transformed to make it easily readable. Although ambiguity remains, the investigator does not explore it, assuming a reader will "fill in" and make sense of the main point.[10]

Investigators in the thematic narrative tradition typically pay little attention to how a story unfolds in a conversational exchange or the questioner's role in constituting it. In other words, readers usually learn little about the local context—conditions of production of a narrative. Consequently, in the written report, it appears that a biographical account emerges "full blown" from the "self" of the narrator, rather than in conversation between a teller and a particular listener/questioner. Issues of audience, and the subtle give and take between speakers as they make meaning together, slip away. The active participation of interviewer, transcriber, and analyst disappear from writing. Ironically, Williams's use of an open research interview is consistent with Mishler's general approach to narrative interviewing (presented in Chapter 2), but insights about the co-construction process are erased in the written report. Bill's account, for example, is presented as if it came out of a vessel, uncontaminated by human interaction.

Williams does attend to the research relationship briefly in one of the three case studies. He is conversing with a woman who has rheumatoid arthritis and he notes that her medical vocabulary ("virus") provides a "shared concept and a common understanding." He contrasts this with another comment, by the same woman, that he "couldn't understand." Her model for the genesis of her illness—the stress of womanhood—"was not something I could possibly have encompassed with my social experience."[11] With this fleeting acknowledgment, Williams locates himself in the interview and interpretative context, rather than pretending he wasn't there (customary in studies using thematic analysis).

Although attention to local contexts is minimal, Williams attends in a sustained way to broader contexts that shaped the "personal" accounts. Individuals' varying explanations for the genesis of illness draw on and, in turn, reinforce specific discourses—ordinary citizens' beliefs about the unjust workings of the world. A causal narrative about motherhood and stress leading to illness, and another about workplace toxicity, are firmly rooted in a particular history and industrial culture—the twentieth century Western world of late modernity. In his interpretive commentary about each case, Williams tacks back and forth between his respondents' theorizing about inequality and broader social structures that weigh heavily on their lives.

Lastly, how does Williams attend to narrative form and language choice? Because interest in thematic analysis lies in the content of speech, he interprets what is said in interviews by assuming meanings for an utterance that any competent user of the language would bring. In thematic narrative analysis (and in other thematic coding methods), language is viewed as a resource, rather than a topic of inquiry. In this respect, the approaches can mimic objectivist modes of analysis where themes appear to be unmediated by an investigator's theoretical perspective, interests, mode of questioning, and personal characteristics. Again, however, Williams fleetingly hints at complexities of language choice, drawing the reader's attention, for example, to metaphors that might be overlooked. For instance, in one case study, a participant "brings into play two metaphors, one religious and one mechanical, to suggest the inevitability of illness in society."[12] Williams "unpacks" the metaphors, exploring their functions in the narrative text—analogous meanings they may carry.

Although attending occasionally to particular word choices, thematic analysts generally do not attend to language, form, or interaction. In these ways, thematic narrative analysis is similar to grounded theory. The second exemplar illustrates the general pattern where the primary focus is on "what" is said, rather than "how" or "to whom" and for "what purpose."

2. Stories of Resistance to Legal Authority

Published in 2003, the study examines the problem of citizen resistance to authority. The authors, Patricia Ewick and Susan Silbey, are North American sociologists interested in the role of law in everyday life, for the law has an extended hegemonic reach in the contemporary United States While collecting data for a large survey on law in the lives of ordinary Americans, the authors were told "thousands of stories, some of which were stories of resistance to legal authority."[13] After their book was completed in 1998 (it relied on survey questions and a few open-ended items) the authors returned to the stories to inquire how persons in less powerful subordinate positions resist the law in "small acts of defiance." The investigators wondered, when greater power lies with others, how individuals in conflict situations at work and in the community develop "underlives" and engage in oppositional action. The research builds on and extends prior theory from social history, labor studies, sociology, and feminist studies, which articulates hidden, mundane everyday resistance practices that individuals employ to challenge oppressive social structures.[14]

The exemplar models a way of working carefully and systematically with stories about ordinary events to unmask how sociological concepts work in everyday life. Complex and fluid relations of power are made visible in Ewick and Silbey's analysis (topics essential to social movement theory), which help individuals and groups understand their situations, and engage in subversive actions to disturb social structures, or "impede the routine exercise of power." The authors posit that the narratives about resistance practices can have more power than the subversive act itself (i.e., actions reported in the narrative) by mobilizing others. The work emphasizes the social change potential of personal narrative noted in Chapter 1.

The paper begins by articulating a compelling relational theory of power that draws on Foucault and others but (in contrast to much macro sociology theorizing) seeks to include the thoughts and actions of actors, that is, individual agency. Individuals' acts of resistance invoke a reaction in the speaker, which can be considered "a consciousness of being less powerful in a relationship of power" and a "consciousness of opportunity" to challenge the powerful.[15] Acts of resistance make "claims about justice and fairness" and, because actions are typically "institutionally indecipherable," they are "officially unreadable," that is, they do not break the law in a narrow sense.[16] With this strong theoretical framework (which can be only cursorily summarized here), the investigators return to the interviews to look for acts of resistance (their unit of analysis) that took the form of stories. A subset of 141 interviews from the larger sample was then transcribed in full. As is typical in narrative analysis, sampling was purposeful, not random as Ewick and Silbey clarify, "Because . . . [the] principal analytical goal in this part of the project was not to generalize to the population but to interpret the meaning and function of stories embedded in interviews," the subsample was selected based on familiarity with the case and the "richness of the interview (in terms of length and degree of detail)."[17] The investigators used trained interviewers, and they conducted some interviews themselves.

Interview questions and probes inquired about problems and events that people might see as legal (vandalism, work-related accidents), and others less connected to traditional legal categories (division of household labor, obtaining needed medical care or schooling for a child)—instances where "a person might, if they chose, assert a legal right, entitlement, or status." Respondents, rather than answering "yes" or "no" in response to a list of possible problems in a survey item, told "dozens of stories" about small moments when they got the better of an oppressive system.

The investigators then identified a set of stories that met specific criteria: acts had to be intentional and purposeful, where a "reversal of power" was the goal of a participant's actions. "To identify stories of resistance, we examined whether the narrative described an opportunity to avoid the consequences of relative disadvantage,"[18] paying particular attention to the means through which resistance actions were achieved. After selecting stories that met their criteria they coded them, categorizing the different "means" actors used to get out from under a position of relative disadvantage. Working with well-defined criteria and a sizable sample of incidents, they then grouped the stories and constructed a typology of resistance practices. The typology includes the masquerade (where the actor is playing with roles in the story), rule literalness (playing with rules), disrupting hierarchy (playing with stratification), foot-dragging (playing with time), and colonizing space. Ewick and Silbey relate the typology to their prior theory of power and, as they present and interrogate the stories, the theory is complicated and qualified.

Below is a story told by a respondent ("Sophia Silva") about the tactic of colonizing space in a department store, which she subsequently taught to a young mother having difficulty getting service one day:

> I was in Sears one day, and this young girl was there with all these children around her. . . . She had bought a vacuum cleaner like a week before and it did not work, and they were telling her to mail it back [to the manufacturer]. . . . And she was distraught. I said to her, "Don't you move." I said, "You stay there, you'll have to stay two or three hours until they give you a new one." And I kept coming back to check, and they did give her a new one.[19]

Another woman used the same tacit—a kind of informal "sit in"—to advocate for her son's special needs in a high school when his requests were being ignored:

> My son wasn't getting any place [trying to obtain a copy of his transcript]. So one morning, I got up and I dressed nicely. Not jeans, but I got dressed nicely. And, I went to school with him at 7:30 in the morning and I went to the guidance waiting room and I sat in the chair and I said I'm going to sit here until I talk to him [the official]. And when he walked in and realized I was sitting with my son—because he recognized my son—he was very friendly. . . . So I got results. . . . But I feel that if I hadn't done that he'd probably, he may have missed out on the only school he wanted to go to, because they weren't sensitive to his needs. So I don't like to have to interfere like that but I learned back in elementary school when other mothers used to do it, and I used to be the type who didn't say much and sat back, that other parents were getting what their kids needed for them. . . . So I had to change my ways and I had to start speaking up.[20]

Note that Ewick and Silbey's conception of narrative contrasts sharply with the previous exemplar. The "story" here refers to a brief, bounded segment of interview text, rather than an extended biographical account. Their unit of analysis is the particular act of resistance. Like Williams, the authors "clean up" spoken language to construct an unambiguous plot line, using ellipses (. . .) to indicate deleted speech. Unlike Williams, the textual stories are short, with clear beginnings, middles, and ends. For example, Sophia Silva, in the incident about the defective vacuum, begins with a classic story introducer, "I was in Sears one day . . . "; she develops the middle of her story with a sequence of observations of a "distraught" young woman surrounded by her children, carrying a defective vacuum, who Sophia instructed to stay put; in the middle section she carries the plot forward over the next several hours ("I kept coming back to check"); she ends the story by resolving the plot ("and they did give her a new one"). Consistent with the investigators' theoretical interest, the stories Ewick and Silbey present resolve positively, that is, each act of resistance effects a desired change, however small, in the established order of things from the narrator's standpoint. As readers, we may wonder about negative instances (resistance actions are not always successful), just as in the Williams exemplar we might wonder about cases where biographical reconstruction did not take place.

Ewick and Silbey, like others who use thematic narrative analysis, are not generally interested in the form of the narrative, only its thematic meanings and "point." Interrogating the particular language a speaker selects is not relevant to their purpose; focus is on the act the narrative reports and the moral of the story. Exploration of the interpersonal conditions and "local" production of a story is irrelevant to the aims (although the authors acknowledge greater familiarity with some interviews, perhaps because they conducted them, and they acknowledge that narratives are "constructed interactively—with an audience and context"[21]). Readers learn little about the lives of individual narrators, except in relation to categories of power and subordination in the investigators' interpretive schema (e.g., the class, race, and gender positioning of the narrator). The authors frame a story of resistance in terms of the actor's one-down position (e.g., the mother of the youngster in the excerpt above was working class; she needed a school transcript from the guidance department of a "snooty" school). Like other researchers using thematic narrative analysis to interpret a large number of cases, local contexts tend to get eclipsed. Stories are presented as if they dropped from the sky, with interview excerpts contextualized only in relation to social structures of power. Readers, then, must assume that themes have similar meanings across narratives and narrators; they "transcend the subjective and the particular."[22] In these subtle ways, the analytic approach of Ewick and Silbey shares some features with the category-centered approach of grounded theory: primary interest is in generating thematic categories across individuals, even as individual stories are preserved and grouped, and the work is located in the narrative research tradition.

The exemplar illustrates a way of working with narrative data that will appeal to many sociologists who encounter stories in interviews. With a strong theory as a resource, an investigator can link everyday, seemingly insignificant acts that people engage in (e.g., refusing to leave a store until a defective item has been replaced) with social change processes (e.g., resisting power and authority). Telling a story "makes the moment live beyond the moment."[23] Stories function to alter the ways we view mundane everyday events. Stories can indeed accomplish change.

The final two exemplars in the chapter move away from sole reliance on interviews to show how thematic narrative analysis has been employed to interpret documents, and how it is also used in ethnographic work.

Working With Archival Documents

Thematic analysis is the usual approach to letters, diaries, auto/biographies[24]—documents historians and biographers draw on. When social scientists analyze archival materials in relation to a question, they tend to provide little information about how they work. Readers encounter compelling findings, but learn little about the circuitous route an investigator took to produce them. I selected the exemplar below because I was able to talk extensively with Maria Tamboukou, the author, about details that are only hinted at in her published work.

A sociologist, she examined life writings of women teachers in late nineteenth century England.[25] Given the occupational group's pivotal position in women's move beyond the domestic sphere, Tamboukou was interested in how women teachers thought about and imaged space. She asks how geographic and existential spaces are inscribed in women's subjectivities. How do they live and experience familiar spaces and reinvent themselves in new spaces? Like Ewick and Silbey in the previous exemplar, Tamboukou turned to personal stories because they can embody theoretical abstractions—sociological concepts are enacted as individuals talk and write. Building on Foucault's theorizing about space, power, and genealogy, she worked "with grey dusty documents, looking for insignificant details . . . discourses and practices that human beings [take up] . . . to make sense of themselves and the world."[26] Letters provided fertile primary data, and she interrogated the pages to understand the constitution of the female self—how women negotiate the "thematics of space" in self-writings.[27] The researcher discovered how the freedom of imagined spaces and the material reality of other spaces were important for women teachers working within the confines of gender during the late nineteenth century. These meanings were often encoded in brief narrative segments in women's long letters about their daily lives.

To examine the subjectivities of women teachers regarding space and place, Tamboukou began her research by reading available auto/biographies to gain general contextual knowledge about the times. Moving then to published letters and other archival materials, she made personal copies of relevant letters of women teachers, and read them at a surface level, drawing on Foucault's ideas: "instead of going deep, looking for origins and hidden meanings, the analyst is working on the surface, constructing [angles rather than many sides, noting] various minor processes that surround the emergence of an event."[28] During this nominal level of analysis, Tamboukou circles and highlights words and phrases that strike her. Regarding references to space in the letters, particular verbs appeared and reappeared, such as "go out," "get out," "be out," "spread my wings," "run away," and "leave."[29]

She then reads the documents again with spatial categories in mind, looking in the texts for additional statements that relate in a general way to the larger concept. As themes emerge during the process, the investigator interrogates them historically, using "discursive constructs of historical contingencies" that individual women might have questioned and reversed.[30] In the letters of teachers, for example, Tamboukou looked for statements about confinement and escape; these were received concepts for the sociologist (learned from prior feminist work), but related to her nominal analysis. The confinement in the home of white middle-class women in *fin de siecle* Europe and America is well established, as is the symbolism of travel—escape. How did women teachers experience confinement? Did they long to travel and, if so, how were these themes expressed in self-writings? Tamboukou finds ample evidence: "women's self-writings present selves on the move, always attempting to go beyond the boundaries of their families, their locality, their town or city and, in some cases, their country."[31] In these ways women constructed counter-narratives,[32] bending colonial practices and ideologies about women's proper place. Teachers during the period were positioned at a border between private and public worlds; because of school vacations, travel was possible for some, and could be only imagined by others.

The investigator confronted puzzles and paradoxes in the documents. Reading letters and autobiographical writings for spatial references, she came upon seemingly contradictory statements. Women wanted to "escape" enclosed spaces, and they wanted "a room." They wanted to get away from home, and they wanted a space of their own in it. The paradox sent the investigator to the library, where she discovered other scholarship that forced her to critically interrogate her thematic categories—who might they exclude? Black feminist scholars, for example, had written about home as a safer place for African American women during the same historical period. Thematic analysis then gained specificity. (What household space meant to white working-class women in England might also have been interrogated.)

Library reading sent the investigator to other documents in archives. Reading about the origins of the first women's college at Cambridge University (Girton, which opened in 1871), Tamboukou learned that each woman was given, in addition to a bedroom, another room, described as "a small sitting-room to herself, where she will be free to study undisturbed, and to enjoy at her discretion the companionship of friends of her own choice."[33] The writer of these words, Emily Davis, as she was preparing Girton College for its open-ing, realized that "the power of being alone" could be a distinctive feature of college life for women. Discovering Cambridge University documents about the allocation of space by gender (male students were not given two rooms) invigorated Taboukou's thematic analysis, reinforcing ideas she had begun to develop while working with the letters.

Knowledge about "the room" informed subsequent coding of narrative seg-ments in letters and other documents written by women teachers, most of whom would never experience the privilege of Cambridge University. For example, Molly Hughes came from a lower-middle-class family to attend a teacher training college, writing about the moment later in her autobiography:

> When my trunk was landed, I was shown my room. This was some twelve feet square on the ground-floor, with one small window flush with the pavement, a narrow bed, a scrap of carpet, a basket chair, one upright chair and a bureau. A fire crackled in the hearth. "Is this *mine?*" cried I in ecstasy (emphasis in original).[34]

"The room" became a central concept as the investigator interrogated the autobiographies and letters again. Tamboukou discovered that the documents were filled with spatial drawings that provided meticulous and enthusiastic detail about spaces where women found solitude and independence, and where they could invite others on their own terms. Theorizing from these materials, Tamboukou interprets "vocabularies of space" as ways that women could imagine themselves differently from their confined positions in the bour-geois family. Well before Virginia Woolf wrote her influential lecture about "a room of one's own," the theme was circulating among women. It was also an established housing policy in the women's colleges of Cambridge University.

Turning to my four questions, the definition of narrative that Tamboukou employs needs some explication. Individual letters took many forms, not all of them narrative. Some women simply reported news, without evaluation. Other letters were little more than lists of questions they hoped the recipient would answer by return mail. Some women, however, developed storied accounts in individual letters about important moments. Additionally, as other biographical researchers do, Tamboukou treats the entire epistolarium narratively, for lines of women's lives can be traced across letters.

Below is an extract from a letter written in 1902 by Winifred Mercier, a woman teacher who became a leader in the British reform movement of teacher training colleges, to her friend and fellow teacher, Jean Borland.[35]

[W]ouldn't you like to go to America, Canada or the great wide west? Where perhaps there might be more chance of finding out what manner of being you were?—where there is more room, more freedom, and one is not so hide-bound by conventions—where you could get nearer the soil, and as I said before not be stifled by artificialities and habits and conventions, your own and other people's. Oh wouldn't you like it, wouldn't you? Wouldn't you?

The poignant utopian narrative about longing for space is written in a hypothetical form.[36] It recounts a sequence of actions that *hasn't* occurred, but for which the writer fervently wishes. Because Tamboukou wants to make theoretical claims across her subjects about confinement and escape, she (like Ewick and Silbey) does not examine form and language choice. In the excerpt above, for example, one might theorize the meanings of North America (the "wide west," the "soil") for British women toiling in small classrooms in the polluted urban environments of early twentieth century England. Or, one might interrogate particular phrases, such as "artificialities and habits and conventions" from which the letter writer wants freedom, but which (she wisely sees) are both "your own and other people's", that is, self-imposed restrictions and cultural ones. As in previous exemplars in the chapter, there is little attention to local context. But future investigators could ask, where in the overall letter did a story appear? Who was the audience and what was the relationship between writer and recipient? Micro contexts need not slip away entirely when the goal is broad theoretical generalization.

Epistolary narrative (a corpus of letters) is a potentially rich resource for social scientists interested in biographical experience. Like those developed during research interviews, these stories have an embodied subject and recipient. Audience—the relationship between writer and recipient—can be brought to bear in interpretation.[37] Unlike spoken interview data however, a letter does not require textual transformation.

To summarize, Tamboukou's thematic analysis is careful and methodical. She begins by educating herself about contexts: her subjects' lives and times (biographical reading), and theoretical work that bears on the study issue (e.g., social theory about space and power). Examination of self-writings with thematic categories begins at a surface level. Classifying statements from let-ters into thematic groups is theory-saturated from the beginning. (Note the difference from grounded theory coding here, where a priori concepts are dis-couraged.) The investigator tacks back and forth between primary data and the scholarship of others, checking what she is seeing in the self-writings (e.g., themes of escape and traveling) against concepts others have elaborated (e.g., "narratives of elsewhere" in women's writing). A theme may emerge from reading a primary source, but it needs to be supported with other historical materials (e.g., "the room" at Girton College). Material from other sources enlivens an emerging theme and complicates it. The investigator is sensitive to seemingly unimportant issues in the materials, topics that the women themselves might take for granted (e.g., the geography of a room). Submerged aspects of women's subjectivities, thus, can come to life.

Discoveries about women's complex relations to space and place have opened up topics that continue to preoccupy Tamboukou, as readers will see in Chapter 6 where I feature her work in the visual narrative tradition; she examines the images, letters, and biography of the Welsh painter, Gwen John.[38] From letters, Tamboukou learned that Gwen John lived in Paris surrounded by cats. Tamboukou later told me, "I hate cats, I never thought I'd be writing about them." This is a small indicator of the detours, surprises, and disorderly trail implicated sometimes in thematic narrative analysis.

The final exemplar features a narrative study that integrates diverse kinds of data (documents, interviews, and observations).

Working Ethnographically

In the last twenty years, narrative concepts and methods have increasingly informed ethnographic research.[39] I selected an exemplar from a large corpus of possible work because of its relevance for students: Carole Cain was a doctoral candidate in anthropology when she published her study of "identity acquisition" among members of Alcoholics Anonymous (AA).[40] The exemplar provides a suitable bookend to a chapter that has featured diverse sorts of data. The author used thematic methods to interrogate documents, group meetings, and interview narratives.

Like Williams in the first exemplar, Cain studied individuals who had experienced great personal difficulty, but her interest was in the development of group identity. She asks, how does a person learn to be an alcoholic in Alcoholics Anonymous, that is, how does the cultural knowledge of the organization become self-knowledge for an initiate member? Put differently, how is a group identity created and sustained?

To explore the social construction of identity, Cain analyzed and related three kinds of data: (1) written documents published by the AA organization (diverse pamphlets and the *Big Book*); (2) field notes from her observations of open meetings at three AA groups; and (3) transcripts of taped interviews with individuals she met at AA meetings.[41] Narrative was everywhere as members reconstructed the past with "one device in particular . . . telling personal stories."[42] Stories also pervaded the organization's literature, dominated the AA meetings she observed, and her interviews with members. About the observational and interview data, she writes:

> I heard stories told in three settings: discussion meetings, speakers' meetings, and interviews. In some cases I had the chance to hear the same persons tell their personal stories, or parts of them, in more than one setting. . . . It became clear that there were regularities in the stories each person told, even as they were adapted to the different settings.[43]

Cain also sensed similarities between the spoken narratives and the written ones (in documents, such as the *Big Book* and shorter pamphlets). Detailed study of each data source followed. What precisely was similar and different?

Working first with the written texts from AA documents (which contained forty-six accounts of drinking), she did careful textual analysis, "for each paragraph noting main points, what episodes and events were included, and what propositions were made about alcohol, self, and AA. I sketched the overall structure of each story." [44] (By "overall structure," I interpret Cain to mean the broad storyline, including episodes and turning points in the plot.) Cain identified propositions that reappeared in the form of thematic assumptions taken for granted by the teller/writer. For example, alcoholism is seen as a progressive "disease," the alcoholic is "powerless" over alcohol, the alcoholic drinker is "out of control," AA is for "those who want it," and, "AA is a program for living, not just for not drinking." The propositions "enter into stories as guidelines for describing the progression of drinking, the desire and inability to stop, the necessity of 'hitting bottom' before the program can work, and the changes that take place in one's life after joining AA."[45] Certain episodes reappeared in predictable sequences: taking the first drink, the negative effects of drinking, progression of drinking, suggestion (by others) that drinking may be a problem, denial, attempts to control drinking, entering AA, giving AA an honest try, and becoming sober. In the language of thematic analysis, Cain found a common pattern of embedded assumptions, and also a common sequence of episodes—a kind of overarching master narrative, as some would call it.[46] She located many local instances of this storyline. There was variation, of course, depending on the audience for a given pamphlet (a drinker, a family member, or another audience).

Next, Cain examined her field notes, comparing the stories told in AA discussion group and speakers' meetings to the stories in the organization's literature. There were marked similarities in the form noted in the documents and that which was repeated by speakers. The episodes in the spoken stories at meetings were also thematically familiar, though the sequence of the plot was often telescoped, and the narrative shortened. Field notes revealed that the drinking history of individual members followed the biographical storyline in the AA literature, and contained its basic propositions about drinking.

Finally, Cain applied the thematic categories she was developing to narratives recorded in interviews with three AA members whom she had met at meetings. Like Williams's research, the narrative interviews began with a broad question asking each person to tell about their "drinking experiences." "Beyond this [opening question] I tried not to direct the narrative until it reached what seemed to be a natural ending."[47] Two of Cain's three informants "seemed to have a clear concept of a set of episodes that constituted a response to my request" and these two narratives closely paralleled the model AA story—the storyline and propositions of the master narrative she had found in AA literature. There was interesting variation however, in that one informant (who had been sober for fourteen years) very closely approximated the AA story structure, while the other informant (who had been sober for two years) told a drinking story that was not as fully reinterpretive, deviating from the AA storyline at key points. The third informant did not have a fully formed narrative at all, only bits and pieces of some thematic elements (e.g., the episode of the "first drink"), and he showed little integration of propositions (e.g., alcoholism is a "disease"). This man had been in and out of AA for over twenty years, but never stayed in the program for long at each interval. He left the program a few weeks after Cain interviewed him. Analysis of the three interviews was consistent with what Cain's emerging theory would predict. One learns to be an alcoholic in AA through a process of narrative surrender, and a group identity develops over time:

> I argue that as the AA member learns the AA story model, and learns to place the events and experiences of his own life into the model, he learns to tell and to understand his own life as an AA life, and himself as an AA alcoholic. The personal story is a cultural vehicle for identity acquisition.[48]

In coming to "perceive oneself and one's problems from an AA perspective," individuals "must learn to experience their problems as drinking problems, and themselves as alcoholics." [49] As Cain argues, the AA identity is neither natural nor simple to learn:

> People do not describe themselves as alcoholics and their lives as alcoholic lives because this is natural and obvious; rather, they learn to tell about themselves and their lives in this way, and the process of learning can take much effort and cooperation between the neophyte and other AA members. . . . Members must agree to become tellers, as well as listeners, of AA stories.[50]

A group identity is made and maintained, then, in the organization through highly regulated storytelling practices.

Turning to the questions I have asked of other exemplars, how does Cain conceptualize narrative in her research? Actually, she never does defines the term, but as other anthropologists do she views narrative as related to ritual, songs, and ceremonies—cultural mediating forms that groups use to initiate and integrate new members and maintain continuity. But Cain's citations suggest she has also been influenced by sociolinguistic definitions of narrative (she cites Labov, whose work is featured in Chapter 4). She says the "drinking-experience narrative" is a "bounded unit,"[51] meaning, I believe, that it is a response to a question—the (typically unstated) request made of new members at AA meetings, for example ("tell us your story"). The organization's literature also refers to the "personal story," suggesting it is a recognized discursive form in AA. As Williams was in the exemplar about illness, Cain is interested in the biography of the narrator and, in a similar way, she limits analytic attention to the "life story about drinking"—bounded, but a broad enough definition to include relevant career and family changes. Her focus (and unit of analysis) differs from Williams because Cain explores the biography of the narrator only to the degree that it reveals patterns, that is, episodes in the master narrative.

Regarding representational issues, Cain decides to present types of narrative in different ways. (Remember, she has three kinds of data: written accounts from documents, her field notes from AA meetings, and the interview transcripts.) Choices about the written narratives are straightforward; Cain reproduces a text verbatim from an AA pamphlet written for young people. For example, a man called Al begins a long personal story by saying, "My drinking resulted in trouble from the very first. I was a sophomore in high school when. . . ." The story continues with a detailed description of partying, having trouble in college, a psychiatric hospitalization, realizing "alcohol had the best of me," and going to his first AA meeting. He concludes:

> That was over two years ago. I have not had a drink since, one day at a time. . . . I am now back at the university, and will probably be on the dean's list this term . . . There is a balance in my life today between studies, AA, and doing other things I enjoy.[52]

The text is long and cannot be reproduced in full here, but Cain does present it.[53] It provides evidence for her claims; a reader can evaluate its goodness of fit with the prototypic storyline that, she argues, characterizes AA documents. Her decision about how to represent stories she heard at meetings is more complicated. Cain tells readers in a long footnote about fieldwork complexities and how she resolved them:

> Note-taking or tape recording during meetings would be inappropriate, so excerpts presented as quotations from meetings are reconstructions taken from notes I wrote up after each meeting. However, I believe the reconstructions to be fairly close to the original, and I have tried to both capture what was said and the contours of how it was said.[54]

The issue is unavoidable in sensitive research situations and Cain's strategy (to reconstruct the narratives she heard, creating summaries in field notes) is the typical solution, albeit problematic. Readers must trust the investigator's representation, blurring further the boundary between transcription and interpretation (an issue noted in Chapter 2). Cain writes that she tried to create a narrative that "capture[s] what was said and the contours of how it was said." It's impossible, of course, to "capture" the past; it is gone, and memory is always partial and selective. Below, for example, is Cain's representation of a moment constructed from her memory, encoded in field notes she made after a meeting:

> One night as some members shared anecdotes about things they had done while drinking, Gary told this tale:
>   One morning I woke up after a night of drinking, and I thought I'd had this bad dream about running into the side of a bridge at 55 miles an hour. Then I went outside. Three inches off the side of my car were gone. And I thought, "Man, I've *got* to stop *driving.*"

Was the brief narrative told in the precise way Cain represents it, with identical word choice and emphasis? Unlikely, and we will never know. All the reader has is Cain's reconstruction of what happened at the meeting. Does it really matter? Ethnographic work in the narrative tradition often rests on persuading the reader, a topic I take up in Chapter 7.

Representing the long interview narratives also presented problems for Cain; she ended up creating synopses of each interview (presenting them in an appendix). Each is several pages long and written in the third person, with an occasional direct quotation, as the following synopsis (further abbreviated by me) illustrates:

> Hank begins his narration with an orientation in which he says who he is: a person who wants to educate young people about alcoholism. . . . He describes the kind of person he was before he started drinking. . . . He began to have serious physical effects from drinking, and was taken to the hospital several times. . . . Eventually, when he was in the service, he was caught drinking on the job, and had to cut back on the amounts he drank. . . . One morning he found he could not get up even after several drinks. . . . When he did get up, he found AA, although he cannot remember how he knew where to go. . . . From the morning when he contacted AA, he did not drink again for over five years. . . . Life improved, he got himself in better shape and got back together with his wife. After several years, the marriage broke up again, and in anger with his wife, he went back to drinking for another five years. He again reached a point where he had to do something about his drinking, and started back at AA. This time he went for six years without a drink. Problems in his life, and the death of his two sons led to the beginning of his third period of drinking. He began

to drink really heavily when his second wife died. He states that this period of drinking almost killed him. He went into a deep depression for which he was hospitalized . . . he reached a point when he felt that nothing was going to save him. It was at that point that he reentered AA, 14 years before this interview. "AA has been my life ever since" . . . he decided that if he was going to live, he would have to "take the AA program, its directions, and *live* it."

"This time I decided, you know, I was gonna do it . . . that way. And part of it is, is realizing that, you know, from the beginning that I'm powerless over it."

In the rest of the interview Hank tells about different ways he has been involved in AA and about different people he has helped become sober, and how they have recovered. Cain relates at the end of her long synopsis that two years after the interview, she visited Hank again; he'd had a stroke. He remained "heavily involved with AA, and had extended his period of sobriety to over sixteen years since his last drink."[55]

The life story the investigator constructs is thematically compelling, despite its third person voice and distant clinical tone. Hank's biographical account could be interpreted a number of ways, depending on the theoretical orientation and interests of the analyst. For instance, a dynamically oriented psychologist might interpret connections between a series of tragic losses and his drinking, while Cain (from anthropology) interprets the text in light of group identity formation—how the speaker integrates and reproduces through narrative the cultural knowledge of the AA organization. Note that her decision to use a synopsis limits attention exclusively to thematic content. Readers have no access whatsoever to aspects of *the telling* (except sequence), only *the told*. In a similar way, use of field notes necessarily limits analytic attention to thematic content. For example, the way a new member might speak at an open AA meeting—pauses, break offs, and word-finding problems that are common in spoken discourse—cannot be included.

Regarding context, Cain's work strongly emphasizes the social forces at work in personal narrative. The author skillfully moves back and forth between individual biographies of drinkers and broader institutional frames. In AA, alcoholism is understood as a disease (not moral weakness, an expression of psychological distress, or inappropriate social conduct); individual members must groom their accounts over time, the ethnographer suggests, to conform to medicalized understandings that the organization values. She contextualizes further by showing that seeing human problems as diseases is a historically and culturally situated practice, "the general Western trend toward medicalizing deviance."[56] As Williams did, Cain connects biography and history, but adds organizational culture and group expectations to the mix. Regarding the local context, Cain generally leaves herself as observer/interpreter out of the report (she was a graduate student when she published the research in 1991; the times and expectations of the university may have shaped decisions).[57] We don't learn much about how she gained access, nor are readers invited into the construction of the ethnography—how an anthropologist negotiated relationships, in this case with AA members and groups, whose stories she then presents.

Lastly, how does the investigator attend to narrative form and language? Cain pays careful attention to sequence—the ordering of events into a personal narrative and inclusion of particular propositions—and she finds recurrent patterns. "AA members learn to tell personal stories, and learn to fit the events and experiences of their own lives into the AA story structure. . . . Members also learn appropriate episodes to serve as evidence for alcoholic drinking, and appropriate interpretations of these episodes."[58]

The work hints at the importance of narrative form and language use. Readers might wonder, for example, what happens when a story is told at an AA meeting that doesn't conform to the group narrative? Precisely how, over time, is it shaped in conversation to conform to the expected storyline? Is there resistance, and if so, how is it expressed, or does a reluctant storyteller simply drop out of the group? Focus, instead, is on the broad contours of narratives—the scaffolding. Like others working with ethnographic materials, words are taken at face value, and they call up referential meanings competent users of the language routinely accept.

Conclusion

By working through four very different research projects, researchers can see how thematic narrative analysis generates significant findings. In each instance, prior theory serves as a resource for interpretation of spoken and written narratives. The exemplars (all strong representatives of the thematic approach) were drawn from a large number of studies that examine primarily what content a narrative communicates, rather than precisely how a narrative is structured to make points to an audience, although several studies trouble the borders here. Several exemplars (Ewick and Silbey, and Cain) suggest how stories function socially to create possibilities for group belonging and action. Future work could extend this line of inquiry, by examining, for example, how individual's stories of resistance actually generate collective action in social movements.[59]

A thematic approach often appeals to novice researchers who are working with narrative data for the first time. It appears intuitive and straightforward, but the exemplars show how methodical and painstaking analysis can be. The approach is suited to many kinds of data; it can generate case studies of individuals and groups, and typologies.[60] Theorizing across a number of cases by identifying common thematic elements across research participants, the events they report, and the actions they take is an established tradition with a long history in qualitative inquiry.[61] Continuing this tradition, while also preserving narrative features, requires subtle shifts in method. Of the four approaches featured in the book, thematic narrative analysis is most similar to qualitative methods such as grounded theory and interpretive phenomenological analysis, and even approaches to data analysis not typically associated with qualitative traditions, such as oral history and folklore. But there are some differences, especially with methods of coding in grounded theory, with which narrative analysis is most often confused.[62]

First, the two methods differ on the place of prior concepts in the analytic process (generally eschewed in the early stages in a grounded theory study). Prior theory guided inquiry in all the narrative exemplars, at the same time as investigators also searched for novel theoretical insights from the data. Second and most important, analysts in the four exemplars preserve sequences, rather than thematically coding segments. In narrative analysis, we attempt to keep the "story" intact for interpretive purposes, although determining the boundaries of stories can be difficult and highly interpretive. In grounded theory according to Kathy Charmaz, "We take segments of data apart, name them in concise terms, and propose an analytic handle to develop abstract ideas for interpreting each segment of data."[63] There is debate among grounded theorists about the significance of "fracturing" data,[64] but narrative analysts do strive to preserve sequence and the wealth of detail contained in long sequences. Third, most narrative investigators attend to time and place of narration and, by historicizing a narrative account, reject the idea of generic explanations. Finally, although the size of the unit of text to be coded in grounded theory can vary considerably (Charmaz describes word-by-word, line-by-line, and incident-by-incident coding),[65] the objective is to generate inductively a set of stable concepts that can be used to theorize *across* cases. By contrast, narrative analysis is case centered (note that the "case" was the identity group in the Cain exemplar). At a fundamental level, the difference between narrative methods and grounded theory flows from this case-centered commitment.

The four exemplars I selected to include in the chapter display a wide range of methodologies within the thematic narrative tradition. The table attempts to summarize the positions of the authors on the set of key issues I posed at the beginning of the chapter and discussed throughout. There is considerable variation in how each investigator defines a narrative unit, ranging from the entire biography, or "life story," to a bounded (spoken or written) segment

Summary Table 3.1   Thematic Analysis

Author of Exemplar	Definition of Narrative	How Represented: Attention to Form and Language	Unit of Analysis; Focus	Attention to Contexts
Williams (1984)	Extended account of a speaker; story of the illness	Lengthy interview excerpts; cleaned up speech; some attention to metaphors	A narrator's understanding of genesis of his/her illness	Local: minimal Societal: considerable
Ewick & Silbey (2003)	Bounded segment of interview text about an incident	Brief interview excerpt; cleaned up speech	Acts of resistance reported in personal narratives	Local: minimal Societal: considerable
Tamboukou (2003)	Bounded segment of a document about space (implicit)	Segment of document as written	Subjectivities of women teachers as they reflect on meanings of space and place	Local: minimal Societal: considerable
Cain (1991)	Life story of speaker or writer about drinking	As written (documents); Reconstructed from memory (observations); Summaries of interviews (from tapes)	The narrative primarily (recurrent episodes across narratives); the narrator secondarily	Local: minimal Societal: considerable

about a single incident. Related to this, authors represent narratives differently, constructing some from edited transcripts of interviews, and others from memories of fieldwork observations. When written narratives served as data, they were reproduced as printed. Because each author's focus was distinct, the unit of analysis in the exemplars varied. It was on the narrator in some (e.g., Williams and Tamboukou), and on the narrative in others (in

Ewick and Silbey, and Cain). Lastly, contextual information varied. Although there was little "local" context—about audience, where a specific utterance or written narrative appears in a longer account, or the relational dimensions that produced it—there was considerable attention to macro contexts, as all the authors make connections between the life worlds depicted in personal narratives and larger social structures—power relations, hidden inequalities, and historical contingencies. Thematic narrative analysis has strengths that are lacking in the methods described in later chapters, but also limitations. Readers must assume, for example, that everyone in a thematic cluster means the same thing by what they say (or write), obscuring particularities of meaning-in-context.[66] The investigators' role in constructing the narratives they then analyze (the topic of Chapter 2) tends to remain obscure. Nor is thematic narrative analysis suited to all research questions. The next chapter displays what can be gained by close attention to speech.

4

Structural Analysis

How are narratives organized—put together—to achieve a narrator's strategic aims? How does a speaker attempt to persuade a listener that a sequence of events "really happened" with significant effects on the narrator? Are different narrative styles heard, or are some more familiar, easily recognized as stories? These questions shift attention from the "told" to the "telling" and from exclusive focus on a narrator's experience to the narrative itself. Like thematic analysis, structural approaches are concerned with content, but attention to narrative form adds insights beyond what can be learned from referential meanings alone. There are many ways, for example, that a witness could represent "what happened" at an accident (and we know that witness reports vary considerably). To be effective, persuasion must be accomplished rhetorically, through forms of symbolic expression, as Kenneth Burke[1] noted long ago. In a word, narrative structure matters in human communication.

Certain forms of storytelling are privileged in powerful institutions, such as schools, hospitals, and courts of law. When speakers do not conform linguistically, they can be misunderstood, or worse, defined as deficient in cognitive ability. The development of "narrative competence" remains a primary goal in preschools and elementary grades in the United States, although the narrow way that competence is defined can impede social justice. (I remind readers of the anecdote with which I began the book, showing a teacher's instructions to her second grade class on how to structure their personal narratives.) Because language inequalities are highly visible in classrooms, studies of narrative structure found an early home in education in the United States, and as I develop below, education continues to be an area for inquiry that includes teachers', children's and parents' narratives.[2]

Structural analysis is less familiar than thematic approaches, necessitating some clarification of terms and framing of its history and rationale as background. Before turning to exemplars of the methodological approach, I provide some background for those without training in linguistic disciplines. The term "structure" evokes meanings and particular theoretical positions in the social sciences (including Levi-Strauss) that differ from usage in the exemplars to follow. And across studies, the term means different things to narrative scholars. Structure can refer to genre, or to an overarching "storyline" (e.g., episodes included in the narrative of an AA member, as in the Cain exemplar in Chapter 3). Investigators can graph the contours of a career over time (as Cain did), marking the turning points, peaks, and valleys, thus creating a visual representation of the investigator's reading of patterns across a group of biographical narratives.[3] For other investigators, "structure" refers to brief embedded moments in a conversation that take a poetic form, well illustrated in John Rich and Courtney Gray's study of black men's reports of violence in the form of rap rhythms the young narrators construct from their recollections of recent traumatic incidents when they were shot or stabbed. Rich and Gray relied on thematic methods primarily to interpret their interview materials, but they embed bits of structural analysis into their compelling analysis of violence in lives of young black men.[4] In both of these examples, attention to narrative structure is folded into studies built primarily around other methods of analysis. Investigators can attend to narrative structure to varying degrees as readers will see, and structural analysis can be combined with other approaches, such as thematic narrative analysis.

Background

Structural analysis is tied to theorizing in narratology that initially interrogated literary texts. In linguistics, there was interest in identifying scientific rules of spoken language and, in social linguistics, practices of class reproduction— the deep and surface structures universal to speech (Noam Chomsky) and the relations between speech codes and class structure (Basil Bernstein). Attention turned to story grammar and genre because, as Todorov suggests, genres create "horizons of expectation" for readers and "models of writing" for authors (and, I would add, they operate in oral storytelling).[5] A story about an experience, for example, could be cast during a conversation in comic terms, or as tragedy, satire, romance, or another form. Gay men, for example, invoke different genres over time to tell their coming-out stories.[6] In another instance, Corinne Squire identifies how South Africans with HIV/AIDS invoke religious genres to make sense of their situations.[7] In chapters to follow, investigators use the concept of "genre" in various ways.

Classic work on narrative structure occurred in education and was part of a movement in the United States to address racial injustice by drawing attention to diverse forms of children's storytelling and the relationship to the legacy of slavery. Studying two groups in the South shortly after desegregation began, Shirley Brice Heath compared two contrasting rural working-class communities and classrooms (one white, the other black).[8] Close study of transcriptions of speech documented that the two groups of children spoke differently "because their communities had different social legacies and ways of behaving in face-to-face interactions."[9] Brice Heath's words are highly relevant for multicultural class rooms today, as children "hear different kinds of stories . . . develop competence in telling stories in contrasting ways"[10] and use stories to accomplish different aims.

Courtney Cazden taught teachers to adapt linguistic methods to interrogate their classroom practice, encouraging taping of classroom conversations to aid reflective teaching.[11] Teachers were encouraged to play excerpts back to children to foster discussion about classroom problems (e.g., marked gender or racial differences in participation). Cazden collaborated with Sarah Michaels to study children's participation in show-and-tell meetings (sometimes called "circle time") in the early grades in several U.S. schools.[12] They analyzed detailed transcripts to understand how teachers ask questions and make comments that help children clarify, sequence, and expand their stories; children learn through these brief exchanges how to be clear, precise, and put into words what a public audience needs to understand the story. Children's contributions to show-and-tell were invariably storied, but the investigators found teachers collaborated more successfully with some children (more often the white children), helping them to expand brief summaries; the success with these youngsters seemed tied to how they learned to create cohesive stories that were temporally ordered, organized around a single topic (recalling the classroom instruction with which I began the book).

Teachers collaborated less successfully with black children, whose narratives often consisted of several episodes that were linked thematically (not always explicitly stated); their stories were often associative, without a clear statement of the overall "point," and time and place could shift across episodes. Importantly, these latter productions were not heard as competent stories by the teachers. Interviews afterward revealed some black children felt derailed ("show-and-tell got on my nerves . . . she was always interrupting me"). There were exceptions, to be sure, in the overall racial pattern.[13] Nor were the black children's narratives "deficient." To illustrate, Michaels, in a later collaboration with James Gee, analyzed the complex narrative forms used by these students.[14] Taken together, the work shows how children are prepared in ordinary classroom moments for a pattern of literacy. They can learn a "discourse of power,"[15] provided teachers listen for and build on diverse forms of storytelling. (In Chapter 5, readers will see an example of such teaching practice.)

My brief and selective sketch of research on children's narrative styles, and teachers' responses to them, underscores how attention to diverse forms of storytelling can further racial justice—success in school for minority children, in this instance. With adults, too, certain ways of speaking can cause difficulty in institutions that privilege one form. Students from management programs in my narrative methods seminar cite examples of disruptions in transnational business conversations when speakers narrate differently; some executives, for example, use forms that circle around a subject, and they are misunderstood by U.S. executives. Communication in our global world must make room for different narrative styles. Narrative researchers should expect stories to be organized differently and, in their interviewing practice, they can collaborate with participants, as Rita Charon teaches physicians to do with patients.[16] Practitioners, she remarks, are the ones who need to develop "narrative competence" in the interviews they conduct and interpret. Fluency in hearing different narrative forms is one dimension of competence.

I turn now to five exemplars using structural narrative analysis, chosen to guide beginning investigators who might want to adapt the approach to their projects. The field is complex, with taproots in social linguistics and cognitive science; this kind of detailed analysis of forms of speech is less intuitive than thematic narrative analysis, and receives less attention in qualitative research generally. The research I have chosen is accessible to readers without strong backgrounds in relevant fields. I also chose candidate exemplars that deal with the kinds of problems human scientists typically investigate, such as violence, illness, other biographical disruptions (I use my own research here), and accounts of professional work in hospital settings. Some participants' accounts in these studies might not have been heard as narrative because they failed to conform linguistically, much like the children's oral narrative discussed above (and in the opening anecdote of the book, the ones I imagined second graders producing in response to the teacher's instructions). Structural narrative analysis allows topics and voices to be included in qualitative research that might be missing otherwise. As developed in the chapter, it is appropriate for interpreting spoken narratives that develop in interviews and naturally occurring conversations. (Literary methods and the field of narratology provide models for written texts, although adaptation for narrative research in the human sciences needs development.[17]) From a wealth of work that examines narrative structures, I concentrate on two approaches that have aided the work of students and colleagues, and my interpretive work with interview narrative. Each is appropriate for asking how an account is put together—made whole, coherent, and understandable—out of component parts we take for granted when telling (and hearing) personal stories. The rich resources referenced throughout can guide readers to specialized literature on syntactic and prosodic dimensions of narrative. At the end of the chapter, I discuss what structural narrative analysis can and cannot do and, building on the exemplars, show how the approach is particularly useful for constructing case studies.

An analogy to classical music may help readers who might be put off initially by the close attention to details of speech in several of the exemplars. To hear how a composition is structured and what each part contributes, musicians break the score down, see what each instrument or musical phrase adds, that is, its function in the overall composition. When we go to a concert, unless we are musicians, we typically just experience the work; the performers, on the other hand, have done considerable "unpacking" in rehearsal to construct the unity we hear. Structural analysis of oral narrative requires the same level of scrutiny; we slow down a narrative account (so to speak)—step back from it—to notice how a narrator uses form and language to achieve particular effects.

Attention to the Function of Clauses: The Approach of William Labov

Systematic study in social linguistics of narrative form began with the pioneering work of William Labov and Joshua Waletzky, who developed a model of narrative structure forty years ago. The work is paradigmatic in that most narrative scholars either cite it, apply it, or use it as a point of departure. In other words, the approach remains a touchstone for narrative inquiry.[18] Labov's subsequent work (his major book was published in 1972, the research completed by a multiracial team of investigators) examined the black English vernacular as spoken by youths in south-central Harlem and other inner-city areas; the research details the rules of discourse and ritual insults that structure conversation within street culture. Like work on young children's narratives (discussed above), an explicit purpose of the research was to challenge the "deficit theory of educational psychologists who see the language of black children as inadequate for learning and logical thinking."[19]

Labov's methods included long-term participant observation with adolescent peer groups (including the "Jets" and the "Cobras") and individual interviews with members, completed by black researchers who knew south-central Harlem as full participants. Labov and others were outsiders to the culture, but brought backgrounds in social linguistics. Together, the team of investigators produced a highly detailed description of vernacular language, including a chapter interrogating a corpus of personal narratives about violent incidents. The chapter specifies the narrative structures participants used to compose the stories, elaborating the structural coding system that Labov and Waletzky had developed earlier.

Below is a story told by John L., a young adult "gifted storyteller" (years later he joined Labov's research group as the fieldworker with the Jets and Cobras). The story begins with a lengthy buildup that contextualizes the violence, after which John L. recapitulates a fist fight he had with a girl in school. Note how in Transcript 4.1 he translates a personal experience into dramatic form.

Transcript 4.1

(What was the most important fight that you remember, one that sticks in your mind . . .)

a Well, one (I think) was with a girl.

b Like I was a kid, you know.

c And she was the baddest girl, *the baddest girl in the neighborhood.*

d If you didn't bring her candy to school,

    she would punch you in the mouth;

e And you had to kiss her

    when she'd tell you.

f This girl was only about 12 years old, man,

g but she was a killer.

h She didn't take no junk;

i She whupped all her brothers.

j And I came to school one day

k and I didn't have no money.

l   My ma wouldn't give me no money.

m   And I played hookies one day,

n   (She) put something on me.*

o   I played hookies, man,

p   so I said, you know, I'm not gonna play hookies no more 'cause I don't wanna get a whupping.

q   So I go to school

r   and this girl says, "Where's the candy?"

s   I said, "I don't have it."

t   She says, powww!

u   So I says to myself, "There's gonna be times my mother won't give me money because (we're) a poor family

v   And I can't take this all, you know, every time she don't give me any money."

w   So I say, "Well, I just gotta fight this girl.

x   She gonna hafta whup me.

y   I hope she don't whup me."

z   And I hit the girl: powwww!

aa and I put something on it.

bb I win the fight.

cc That was one of the most important.

Source: Labov, W., *Language in the Inner City: Studies in the Black English Venacular,* pp. 358–359. Copyright © 1972, University of Pennsylvania Press. Reprinted with permission.
*To put something on someone means to "hit him hard." See also *aa,* I put something on it means "I hit hard."

Labov wanted to identify sequences and structural parts of the narrative that recur across stories about experiences. Consequently, for analytic purposes, he keeps narrative segments of longer exchanges intact and closely analyzes their internal structure—component parts of the story and their relationship to one another. Looking at John L.'s story, note how the investigator parses the brief narrative into clauses and identifies lines for ease of reference (marked on right as *a–cc*). He then determines the function of each clause in the overall narrative, drawing on the approach he and Waletzky had developed earlier. Particular structures out of which a story is composed are a bit like the figures in a musical composition, for they hold an account together, enabling a listener to follow it and determine what's most important. John L.'s story is similar structurally to others collected during field-work, and it shares common parameters with the other stories.

A "fully formed" narrative includes six elements: an abstract (summary and/or "point" of the story); orientation (to time place, characters, situation); complicating action (the event sequence, or plot, usually with a crisis or turning point); evaluation (where the narrator steps back from the action to comment on meaning and communicate emotions—the "soul" of the narrative); resolution (the outcome of the plot); and a coda (ending the story and bringing action back to the present). Not all stories contain all elements, and they occur in varying sequences. As noted earlier, the approach remains a touchstone for narrative analysis despite limitations I discuss shortly.

Looking at John L.'s story in light of structural elements common to stories (see Transcript 4.1), Labov notes its structural similarity to others this narrator has told. The story begins with "an elaborate portrait of the main character: . . . clauses *a–i* are all devoted to the 'baddest girl in the neighborhood.'"[20] Verb tense in this orientation section indicates ongoing circumstances—"the kind of thing that was going on before the first event of the narrative occurred." Continuing the long orientation with lines about his not having money to give the girl candy, playing "hookies," and getting a "whupping" for skipping school, "the first narrative clause [complicating action, line *q*] brings John L. and the girl face to face in the schoolyard," and a quick punch from her (*powww!*) when he can't supply candy. A long embedded evaluation section follows (lines *u–y*)—"what he said to himself at the time." The evaluation here is dramatic fiction for Labov notes that "it is unlikely that all of this internal dialogue took place between the time the girl said *powww!* . . . and the time he hit her back."[21] But, because the sequence of action has been suspended, the resolution comes with "greater force" (lines *z–bb*). The coda (*cc*) signals the end of the narrative, putting off any possible "so what?" response from the listener. (This story was told in answer to a question about the "most important fight" John L. could remember.)

Labov went on from his fieldwork in south-central Harlem to examine first person accounts of adults from many backgrounds and ethnicities about violence—in bars, on the street, and other public settings. (Rarely does he include incidents in the home—the most frequent site of violence.) In answer to a single question ("What happened?"), narrators developed brief, topically centered and temporally ordered stories. To explain these seemingly senseless acts of violence, Labov goes beyond his earlier work and incorporates speech act theory, identifying relations in narrative between a speech exchange and a violent action.

Below is an excerpt from Labov's large corpus of accounts of violence; this one is told by a thirty-one-year-old man in Cleveland about an incident in Buenos Aires when he was in the Merchant Marines in his early twenties. With a sample of similar stories and prior work of Goffman, Labov builds a new theory about the "rule of requests." Violent actions, he argues, are the outcome of speech acts gone awry. Through detailed analysis of sequences of verbal acts, he develops a linguistically based explanation for violent eruptions in a variety of settings experienced by diverse groups.

Transcript 4.2

(What happened in South America?)

1 Oh I w's settin' at a table drinkin'.

2 And—uh—this Norwegian sailor come over

3 an' kep' givin' me a bunch o' junk about I was sittin' with his woman.

4 An' everybody sittin' at the table with me were my shipmates.

5 So I jus' turn arou'

6 an' shoved im,

7 an' told im, I said, "Go away,

8 I don't even wanna fool with ya."

9 An' next thing I know I'm layin' on the floor, blood all over me,

10 an' a guy told me, says, "Don't move your head.

11 Your throat's cut."

Source: Copyright ©1982 by Georgetown University Press. William Labov, "Speech Actions and Reactions in Personal Narrative," from *Georgetown University Round Table on Languages and Linguistics, 1981: Analyzing Discourse: Text and Talk,* Ed. Deborah Tannen, p. 229. Reprinted with permission. www.press.georgetown.edu.

The brief story in Transcript 4.2 reports a confrontation, told from the point of view of a victim of violence. This man had his throat cut by a "Norwegian sailor" in a bar, and lived to tell the tale. Although the storyteller uses structures common to stories and the story could be interpreted thematically (connecting alcohol and violence, for example), Labov is interested in identifying the *sequence of moves* in the interaction. An implicit request is made by the sailor (line 3), the speaker refuses to hear the sailor's request as valid (lines 6–8), which then reduces the latter's status and leads to violence (line 9). It is the *sequence of speech acts*—repeated over and over again in the stories Labov collected in a wide variety of settings (not only bars)—that culminates in a violent act. Labov explains, "The controlling dynamic of this situation is one of social status and challenge to social status."[22] Here, a form of structural narrative analysis generated knowledge about what can happen in social interaction when one party's relative social position is on the line. Rich and Gray, in their recent study of young black men who had been victims of violence, suggest the sequence can continue beyond an initial episode. As he recovers, the victim may want to defend himself from "being a sucker." The "code of the street" requires a move to regain respect, setting in motion the high reinjury rates of young black men.[23]

Analyzing Divorce Stories: An Application of Labov

As I noted in Chapter 1, my scholarly interests pivot around biographical disruption and the role of personal narrative. To interpret divorce stories, I used Labov's analytic model of structural elements. First, it will be helpful to provide a bit of theoretical background. In research interviews (as in all face-to-face interactions), storytellers have a task to accomplish; they must convince a listener, who wasn't there, that certain events *really* happened. One way a teller persuades is by making events reportable, that is, worthy of a long turn in conversation and fending off the "so what?" response of the listener. There is additional face work to accomplish with divorce stories, because a narrator must persuade a listener that particular actions were justified, especially if they go against the grain. It is the "teller's problem," as Dennie Wolf describes:

> The problem is, at least in one sense, to convince a listener who wasn't there that these were seriously troubled times and that the speaker hasn't just cooked up this account in order to entertain, lie, or get attention. It, like many other kinds of therapeutic discourse, faces a speaker with justifying her/himself as the main character—both in the sense that s/he was a central agent (not just furniture) and was deeply affected (not indifferent). A speaker also has to prove that the times really did have the qualities s/he says they did. To do this often means finding some way to provoke a similar state in the listener, at least enough so as to argue, "This is veridical. It did happen. I am justified in having felt as I did." [24]

Labov's analytic method helped me see how different storytellers solved the "teller's problem," at the same time as they used narrative forms to make sense of their marital experience and construct positive identities.

A thematic analysis of women's and men's lengthy accounts across a number of interviews suggested a common set of "reasons" for divorce action. But there were questions I couldn't answer with a thematic approach. What place did a "reason," or justification, have in the downward spiral of a marriage and the subsequent decision to end it, that is, what is the role of these "reasons" in the sequence? Reading through many transcripts, I sensed that the same event meant different things to different participants. I needed to look at how divorce stories were organized and sequenced to understand the range of meanings.

A case in point was a spouse's infidelity, a "reason" given by a group of participants. Using Labov's model, I compared how three participants combined story elements in contrasting ways because they had such different points to make about the relationship of their spouse's (long-term) affairs to their divorces. What, on the surface, appeared to be the same events turned out to be quite different ones, a finding I used to raise questions about life event scales in stress research.

Below is a bounded segment from a long narrative, told by Gloria (a pseudonym), a thirty-eight-year-old white woman with a professional education, who was married to a minister for fifteen years before she divorced him (see Transcript 4.3). Midway through a lengthy interview that took place in her home, I asked Gloria a standard question on our interview schedule, saying, "Would you state, in your own words, the main causes of your separation?" She responded tersely, "infidelity and alcoholism." I probed, "Tell me a little bit about that, what that was like for you." Gloria responded with a tearful narrative about her husband's affairs (she had talked about his drinking earlier in the interview). My adaptation of Labov's structural coding (from his 1972 work) appears to the right of the transcript below with a key at the bottom.

Transcript 4.3

01 (Crying) That's where the pain is	AB
02 (p) I guess that's where the dream ended	
04 We'd been married about eight—no ten years	OR
05 and we were in the parish	

(Continued)

(Continued)

06	(p) and Keith began having an affair with a parishioner	CA
07	twenty-five years his junior	OR
08	who claimed to be a counseling case for 6 months	
09	until I got wise	
10	(p) and I asked him	CA
11	and he said yes, he was having an affair but he was trying desperately to end it.	
12	Two years later he was still having it	
13	(p) and that nearly drove me literally nuts	EV
14	that drove me almost to suicide.	
15	And when we left the parish	OR
16	and he decided to go to Greenville	
17	I thought (p) "Oh good, maybe this will all end because he won't be near Miltown."	EV
18	And I remember when we bought our first house	OR
19	we'd lived in school houses and parsonages	
20	he was still seeing Bea	
21	And I said "Damn it, if you take that black mud pot of a relationship into our new home it will kill me."	CA
22	And he took it, for the first four or five months.	
23	And it was very difficult	EV
24	but I kept thinking maybe, maybe with Greenville	
25	and he gets into something he really likes	
26	maybe that will take care of it.	
27	Except he went to Greenville and he started up another one	RE
28	(p) and that is still going on.	Coda

AB = Abstract
OR = Orientation
CA = Complicating action
EV = Evaluation
RE = Resolution

Source: Riessman, C. K., Life events, meaning and narrative: The case of infidelity and divorce, in *Social Science & Medicine, 29*, pp. 743–751, Copyright © 1989. Used with permission of Elsevier.

The codes display my reading of the *function* of a particular *clause* in the overall structure of the narrative: does it carry the action forward (CA), comment on the meaning of an event for the narrator (EV), and provide information about setting and characters (OR), or resolve the narrative (RE)? I display my coding strictly for heuristic purposes here. Readers might debate coding of several clauses (I published the analysis in 1989 and would code differently now), and I would not recommend that contemporary researchers include coding of clauses in a published paper. The degree of attention to specifics of speech runs the danger of losing readers without social linguistic interests and is unnecessarily detailed for most publication purposes. But doing structural coding of clauses is extremely useful at the early stage of the analytic process. As an initial foray into any narrative segment, I often ask, how is this story put together? How are structural elements arranged by this storyteller? Examining strategic placement can be of enormous aid in interpreting the relation between meaning and action.

Gloria's account takes the classic form of a story identified by Labov and Waletzky, and later elaborated by Labov. It moves chronologically through time, reports specific past events, and it has a moral point that she helps us anticipate in the Abstract ("the pain . . . where the dream [of a happy marriage] ended"). The story, Gloria tells us, will be about her emotional pain. She draws listeners/readers into her experience and persuades us of veracity, not so much by the objective events she reports, but more through the context she supplies. She tells us how to read the plot—what it means to her—by contextualizing events, in orientation clauses (OR) that give background information about the particular women, when and where her husband became involved with them, and, most vividly, in evaluative statements (EV) that describe rationalizations and emotions—Gloria's despair. She could have organized the plot in many ways, but she chose to move back and forth among her various suspicions of infidelity (OR), confirmation (CA), and emotional response (EV). Alongside the manifested world of the marriage, a second world existed, created by his secret and the betrayal she experienced. The dialectic between these two worlds is embodied in the form of the narrative. It portrays the suffering of a real woman expressed in language that communicates real pain, realized in sequences of suspicion, discovery, and hurt.[25]

In a case comparison, I contrasted the structure of Gloria's account with two others in the divorce sample, who also lived with a spouse's long-term infidelity. For these participants (both men), the spouse's long-term infidelity did not seem to be a source of suffering; other events appeared to be more important. Case comparison here shows how close attention to story structure can yield different findings than a thematic analysis would. Although each of the three storytellers mentioned infidelity as a "reason," and used a similar set of narrative structures to develop their accounts (orientation, complicating action, evaluation, etc.), they combined the elements in such different ways because they had very different points to make. I analyzed linguistic choices—*how* the speakers composed their tales, not simply *what* they said about the relationship between infidelity and divorce. If I had relied only on thematic coding of the stories, and ignored sequence and narrative structure, I would have missed important differences in meaning of the "same" event for different participants. Thematic narrative analysis assumes that the accounts of individuals in a group resemble each other because the accounts are organized around the same theme. By combining thematic and structural analysis of divorce stories, I was able to describe broad patterns (thematic similarities across the sample) but also variation in meanings for individuals. Infidelity was not an objective event, but a phenomenologically different experience.

Analyzing Clauses Across a Group of Stories: An Example From Nursing

Catherine Robichaux, a nursing Ph.D. candidate collecting data for her dissertation, wanted to understand and describe the practices of expert critical care nurses when they face moments of ethical conflict. She adapted Labov's approach to identify structural commonalities across her cases, or similar elements nurses used to construct stories of ethical conflict. Her approach could help students who want to combine thematic and structural approaches in their research. Her analytic strategy, which involved comparisons across cases, illustrates how a thematic and a structural analysis can reinforce one another.

Robichaux's inquiry began with a puzzlement coming from her nursing experience with severely ill patients in hospitals, probing her to discover what specific actions critical care nurses took when they believed that continuing aggressive medical intervention was futile for a patient.[26] After selecting a sample of twenty-one critical care nurses (who worked in public and private units of several adult facilities in the southwestern United States and who were evaluated as "expert" nurses), the investigator began the research interviews with a statement:

> Sometimes critical care nurses find themselves in situations in which they believe the patient will not regain an acceptable quality of life despite the provision of all therapies and interventions. Caring for the patient at this time can become an ethical dilemma for the nurse if aggressive medical treatment is continued. I would like you to think about whether you have experienced this situation and tell me what you chose to do.[27]

Most nurses immediately recalled several instances, but Robichaux encouraged nurses "to recall and reflect on one or two patient situations," thus collaborating with participants to generate detailed narratives of specific instances. To clarify ambiguities that arose during analysis, she conducted second interviews or had phone contacts.

There were recurrent themes across the incidents nurses reported and, as thematic analysts often do, Robichaux constructed a typology of nurses' responses: protecting or speaking for the patient; presenting a realistic picture (often to the family); and experiencing resignation and frustration. The thematic analysis was strengthened by triangulation, specifically the use of a second analytic method. She examined the nurses' stories structurally and found particular sequences of action were repeated across diverse situations. Labov's model, then, helped her identify narrative components common across the accounts. For example, nurses typically began their stories with an abstract or summary of what was to follow, then provided a brief orientation to the situation, the patient, and the nurse's intervention. The nurse typically stepped back from the action—interrupting it—at various points to reflect on the situation and evaluate the meaning he or she wanted Robichaux to take away. In all the stories, the patient's situation was eventually resolved (not always ethically, from the nurse's point of view). By exercising agency in critical situations, nurses were able to challenge the technological imperative in some end-of-life situations, thus assisting a dignified death. In others situations, they remained active moral agents, "even when they could not change or guarantee the outcome."[28]

Looking at recurrent narrative structures in Table 4.1 (a composite that combines speech of several participants), nurses typically introduced their stories with phrases such as, "Well, we had this patient . . ." or "I remember this one patient . . ." The long accounts that followed were temporally sequenced, tracing complex situations to a resolution. Table 4.1 displays Robichaux's representation of a prototypic story that recurred across her sample. Labov's structural elements are identified in the left-hand column, their function is listed in the middle column, and illustrative examples of nurses' speech are in the right-hand column. Robichaux's research illustrates how a structural analysis of narrative can reinforce a thematic analysis, achieving triangulation. In this instance, content and form worked in tandem to accomplish nurses' communicative aims.

To summarize the chapter so far, the exemplars feature and/or adapt Labov's model of narrative structure. The particular definition of narrative (a bounded stretch of talk that answers a single question) is specific to this approach. The primary unit of analysis in each exemplar is the narrative, rather than the narrator. Each investigator examined how the narrative was organized, thus each needed to transform oral speech into a written form.

Table 4.1

Narrative Elements	Definitions	Examples From Interviews
Abstract (AB)	Summarizes point of the narrative	This is about a patient who did not want any more surgery. . .
Orientation (OR)	Provides time, place, situation, participants	When I came in that morning she had been in the unit over a week
Complicating action (CA)	Describes sequence of actions, turning point, crisis, problem	And this patient went into ARDS [acute respiratory distress syndrome]
Evaluation (EV)	Narrator's commentary on complicating action	. . . her face was so broken down . . . . . . it was pathetic.
(CA)		So I called the pulmonary fellow and told him my concern.
(EV)		And to me this was just like an abuse . . . totally futile.
(CA)		And so we ended up extubating her
Resolution (RE)	Resolves plot	and she passed away about forty-five minutes later
Coda	Ends narrative; returns listener to present	So now we tend not to go to the ethics committee because it has not proven useful for us.

Source: Robichaux, 2003. Reprinted with permission.

Authors represented idiosyncratic features of speech to a greater or lesser degree. Because analytic focus remained primarily on the narrative itself (rather than the content it may convey) attention to context was minimal, although others adapting Labov's approach could certainly interrogate where and how a story emerges in an interview conversation, and the larger social/historical discourses that shape it.

Attention to Units of Discourse:
The Approach of James Gee

Some narrators in research interviews develop stories that are extremely lengthy, with asides, flash forwards, and flashbacks in which time shifts; these narratives can be composed of episodes that build meaning through complex forms of telling. The misunderstood narratives of African American young-sters (described above) illustrate early versions of the form used by adults of all backgrounds to communicate complex experiences. These texts do not meet Labov's definition of a "story," and the component structures he iden-tified are not sufficient to analyze how they are put together, or organized. Ethnopoetic approaches, as linguists call the general mode, can be of aid.

James Gee extended this tradition when he developed a theory of narra-tive drawing on a combination of earlier work done by Cazden and Michaels with children's stories, his own reanalysis of the texts, and other sociolin-guistic work.[29] In later writing, Gee elaborated his theory using the spoken account of a woman in her twenties, hospitalized for schizophrenia.[30] Her narrative deviates markedly from the topic-centered, temporally ordered form that Labov posits as the prototypic story form.

Scholars in nursing, social work, sociology, psychology, communication studies, and other disciplines have found Gee's methods useful for analyzing extended narratives of experience.[31] Interpretation of meaning begins with close examination of how a narrative is spoken in *units* that we all use in planning speech, such as idea units, lines, stanzas, strophes, and parts. Stanzas are a series of lines that have a parallel structure and sound as if they go together; they tend to be said at the same rate and with little hesitation between the lines. Gee argues that stanzas are a universal unit in planning speech and that poetry, in fact, builds on what we each do all the time—poetry "fossilizes" and ritualizes what is in everyday speech.[32]

Unlike Labov's analytic approach (which attends to the *function* of a clause in a spoken narrative), Gee's method requires close attention to the audio recording to see how a sequence of utterances is actually *said*—"crucial to the structure we assign it."[33] Linguists understand that pitch signals the focus of a sentence—"the information that the speaker wants the hearer to take as new."[34] Simultaneously, listeners pay attention to prosodic features (including but not limited to intonation) because they offer cues as to what is important in a long stream of speech. Stanzas constitute particularly impor-tant prosodic units in Gee's model (signaled by subtle shifts in pitch and set off with other linguistic markers): each stanza in a narrative is typically four lines long (but length can vary) and about a single topic—a particular "take" on a character, action, or other feature of the narrative—a "vignette."[35] Larger units, composed of groups of stanzas, include strophes and parts in a long narrative. Importantly, Gee's theory is founded on a North American English prosodic system of stress and pitch, dictating how he parses a text. Applications to speech samples from other languages and other English prosodic systems must be attempted cautiously.[36]

When I teach Gee's theory of narrative structure, before the lecture I give students a traditional rough transcription of a stretch of speech that he studied, which was collected from a woman suffering from schizophrenia; I do not provide this information about the speaker (my re-transcription fills two typewritten pages). Before students have read Gee's argument and analysis, some find the speech sample "strange," even incoherent; one social work student said the woman had "a thought disorder." Given that the tape of the woman's speech was given to Gee "as an example of a text that made little overall coherent sense to those who had collected it,"[37] my students' responses were not unique, for mental health professionals had found the woman's speech senseless. How did Gee make it senseful?

Returning to my musical analogy, Gee slows down the woman's stream of talk to examine how each part fits into the whole, and what each topic shift contributes to the overall effect. The content of the narrative relates to the woman's childhood experiences (playing in storms, riding waves and horses, going to camp and caring for horses, and other "exciting" things); the narrative ends when the fear of others ("rich girls") toward her causes her to leave camp. Although many readers initially find the talk incoherent, Gee rescues meaning: "Her world of innocence—running to meet thunderstorms, riding bareback in the sea—is gone . . . the woman's narrative is 'perfectly and wonderfully senseful' . . . its structure quite clearly tells us the terms on which it requests to be interpreted."[38] The narrative is long, and cannot be reproduced here, but I urge students to read Gee's paper to see how he renders the speech understandable by closely examining how it is put together.

Analyzing Stories of Biographical Disruption: Applications of Gee's Approach

Chapter 2 discussed my research on the meaning and management of infertility, and included the long account of an Indo-English speaker, Sunita, who recapitulated events she thought had led to a miscarriage. Readers may remember that one version of her account was transcribed using Gee's method, which proved especially helpful for me in interpreting the causal narrative about the genesis of her infertility. To review, I parsed Sunita's narrative into stanzas by listening closely to the audiotape. Intonation guided decisions about line breaks. Pauses and nonlexical expressions helped determine stanza breaks. Discourse markers,[39] including connectives ("and," "so"), typically set off stanzas. The resulting transcript is tightly organized.[40] As Gee does, I give titles to the stanzas, and display another unit I heard in Sunita's speech: codas that were like a recurrent refrain, suggesting the problem of "over-working." (Remember, Sunita does not make an explicit connection between the demands of her mother-in-law, overworking, and the miscarriage; the listener/reader must infer a connection.) Adaptation of Gee's approach helped me identify thematic issues (in this instance, a veiled attribution of responsibility for infertility) that I would have missed otherwise. Although not its intent, Gee's form of structural analysis also accomplished data reduction; the lengthy and somewhat unwieldy text displayed in Transcript 2.1 was transformed in Transcript 2.2 to conform to length restrictions necessary for presentation. I also found Gee's approach extremely useful in making sense of the speech of participants in the divorce study.[41] In this instance, structural analysis of a single case opened up substantive questions about gender and mental health.

One speaker in the divorce sample, Rick (a pseudonym), was a thirty-three-year-old male academic, without children, who had been separated from his wife for two years at the time I interviewed him. His wife left him unexpectedly, in the middle of "a stupid argument," and he found out later that she had been involved with someone else (a neighbor) for some time. His initial reaction was "bleak depression," a term he didn't elaborate. During our long interview conversation, he talked about many topics—his new partner, a recent job change—but I remember wanting to know more about his emotional response and, specifically, what the "bleak depression" was like for him.

Transcript 4.4

01 CR: Go back a little bit in time—when [wife] left—you described
02   as bleak depression, very unhappy, tell me more about that.

03 Rick: I got a feeling that I'd never experienced before which is almost
04   a certain frant*icity*—a *frant*ic feeling, I don't know what I'm going
05   to do, it almost like I was running *right* on the edge and I don't
06   know on the edge of *what*—I was never able to put that into
07   *words* very well, but I had the feeling that almost—something'

(Continued)

(Continued)

08   got to give, now nothing ever gave, that I can see, things just sort
09   off backed off and eased out, but I was running sort of like wide
10   open, 90 miles an hour down a dead end street as the song goes
11   and I started drinking much more just because it was something
12   to do—I'd stop at the bar—between Greenboro and home there
13   was this little comfortable bar where everybody used to gather
14   about 5 o'clock and we were drinking pretty heavily, which
15   is—I used to *party* pretty well, but drinking that heavily it was
16   just something different, it was a total reaction and living just
17   much more wildly, like I said, just more—driving faster and just
18   *pushing* it—funny kind of feeling, kind of hard to put it into
19   words, I never really could when it was going on—I'd say to
20   people, "I feel like I'm on the *edge* of something," but I didn't
21   know what. I still can't describe it very well, that's not an ade
22   quate description but it's 'bout the best I can do right now. I
23   was monumentally unhappy. I did *not* want her to leave, which
24   I discovered after she left. But there's lots of songs about that
25   too, so, what can you do? Interestingly, I wrote a few songs—I
26   played guitar for years [continues on topic of playing guitar and
27   writing songs with "interesting melody lines."]

As our conversation was ending, I returned to the topic of "bleak depression" and asked Rick about the phrase. Transcript 4.4 displays exactly what Rick said (the raw version of his reply that the transcriber prepared from the audiotape). My participation is minimal and the transcript does not include back-channel contributions (uhm, and other brief utterances). The text was difficult to interpret, and it certainly does not meet many definitions of personal narrative in that it is not organized temporally and lacks a clear plot that resolves; it lacks characters, setting, and other features typical of stories. Yet during the interview conversation, it "felt" like narrative, since I did not interrupt as Rick spoke at breakneck speed about his emotions. As I was working with the interview transcript later, I wanted to find a way to present the segment as narrative, and to understand its organization, rather than fragment it into thematic categories.

I struggled with the boundaries of the segment: where should I begin and end my representation? The beginning seemed clear enough (Rick initiated his account of emotions after my question), but where to end it? He spoke about writing songs for several pages of transcript not included in Transcript 4.4, and after much wrestling, I constructed an ending with the rhyming coda, "lots of songs about that too/so what can you do," but other investigators might have included more (or less) text. Constructing boundaries in this case was highly interpretive. As I argued in Chapter 2, decisions about textual boundaries reveal one central way in which we actually compose our narrative data.

Transcript 4.5

Affect

01	I got a feeling that	**Stanza 1**
02	I'd never experienced before	
03	a certain fran*tic*ity	
04	*frantic* feeling	
05	like I was running *right* on the edge	**Stanza 2**
06	and I don't know on the edge of *what*	

Backing Off

07	I was never able to	
08	put that into *words* very well	

Affect

09	but I had the feeling that	**Stanza 2**
10	almost something's got to give	(Cont.)

Backing Off

11	Now nothing ever gave	**Stanza 3**
12	that I can see	
13	things just sort of backed off and eased out	

Affect

14	But I was running	**Stanza 4**
15	sort of like wide open	
16	ninety miles an hour	
17	down a dead-end street	
18	as the song goes	

Backing Off (habitual narrative)

19	I started drinking much more	**Stanza 5**
20	just because	

(Continued)

(Continued)

21	it was something to do	
22	I'd stop at the bar	
23	between Greenboro and home	
24	there was this little comfortable bar	Stanza 6
25	where everybody used to gather about five o'clock	
26	we were drinking pretty heavily	
27	I used to *party* pretty well	Stanza 7
28	but drinking that heavily	
29	it was just something different	

Summary

30   it was a total reaction

Affect

31	and living	Stanza 8
32	just much more wildly	
33	just driving much faster	
34	and just *push*ing it	

Backing Off

35	funny kind of feeling	Stanza 9
36	kind of hard to put into words	
37	I never really could	
38	when it was going on	
39	I'd say to people	Stanza 10
40	"I feel like I'm on the *edge* of something"	
41	but I didn't know what	
42	I still can't describe it very well	Stanza 11
43	that's not an accurate description	
44	it's 'bout the best I can do right now.	

Coda: Affect and Backing Off

45	I was monumentally unhappy	Stanza 12
46	I did *not* want her to leave	
47	which I discovered after she left	
48	But there's lots of songs about that too	Coda
49	so what can you do	

My interpretive decisions about boundaries and organization are displayed in Transcript 4.5, which takes considerable liberty with Gee's structural approach. Thematically, the narrative does not describe feelings of sadness and personal vulnerability that are typical of one type of depression, but suggests an entirely different idiom of distress—frantic activity and heavy drinking. Structurally, the narrative is saturated with patterns that reinforce thematic elements—talk about cars, bars, and guitars.

Rick recapitulates a time of "bleak depression" by adapting an approach/avoidance form, which allows him to speak about strong feelings, and to retreat from them. He states a feeling, backs off from it, restates it, and backs off again, in repeated cycles. He interrupts the flow of speech about his emotions to say he does not have a vocabulary, except through music. He repeatedly apologizes for not having a language for emotions, illustrating a further manifestation of distress. This is significant, since backing up to apologize for not having the words, particularly for an academic, is a way of saying, "I'm out of place in this field."

The form of the narrative here mimics the turbulent emotions it sets out to reveal as the feelings career around like a speeding car nearly out of control. Note how Rick breaks up stanza 2 with an aside ("I was never able to/ put that into *words* very well"), truncating what is otherwise a key stanza in a sequence of four stanzas that build toward the metaphor that Rick finally seizes upon, that "gets it"—a solo driver barreling down a "dead end street." The narrative pivots on danger and isolation, evoking "franticity."

Extending Gee's approach, I examined metaphors and figurative language. Rick relies on one several times to express his emotions—"running on the edge"—the antithesis of the abstract clinical language of depression. Pressure metaphors also recur throughout the text ("something's got to give," "running wide open," "driving faster," "just pushing it"). Regarding the metaphor of the speeding car, I did not realize at the time I was working with the text (nor when I published my analysis) that Rick's organizing metaphor came from a song Bob Dylan recorded, "Ninety Miles an Hour (Down a Dead End Street)."[42]

Rick returns to song lyrics as a language for emotion in the coda of the narrative ("But there's a lot of songs about that too"). A contradiction is apparent in that Rick is an academic in a business school, and yet the vocabulary he finds meaningful is musical.

There is a brief embedded episode about drinking at the "comfortable little bar," told in a familiar style—habitual narrative, recapping events that happened over and over. Habitual narratives are less dramatic than blow-by-blow reports of a single occasion; they tell of the general course of events over a period of time with verbs and adverbs marking repetition and routinization.[43] But, in general, Rick's speech does not conform to the temporally ordered sequential model of narrating personal experience. I might not have heard it as narrative, and divided up the long utterance into brief thematically coded segments, perhaps to illustrate recurring themes across the sample. Instead, I took the text on its own terms, respecting how it asked to be interpreted by the way it was spoken, paying close attention to its formal features. Meanings became clear only after repeatedly listening to the tape for relevant units of discourse and recurrent figurative language. When I finally constructed a textual representation that displayed my understandings from the raw material, it felt liberating.

For my broader theoretical aims, I used the case study of Rick to raise questions about past research in the sociology of mental health, where men's vocabularies of distress have been largely neglected. Rick's narrative about a time of "bleak depression" contains the seeds for inquiry into subtleties of men's modes of expressing distress—actions that enable some men to get through difficult times, not reflected in the lists of symptoms that appear on quantitative depression inventories. Although Rick's narrative of cars, bars, and guitars was one of a kind, other men in the divorce sample also adopted the approach/avoidance form to speak about feelings. They also spoke about risky activities they took up after marital separation. Emphasis was on doing, not feeling.

In sum, I have drawn on my research to illustrate how methods from social linguistics can be adapted for a research project in the human sciences. Gee's conception of narrative is broader and more encompassing than Labov's, and can include long stretches that are not linear and neatly sequenced, nor do they necessarily have a "point" that is clearly stated and a plot that resolves. In working with this model of narrative, investigators make interpretive decisions about units of speech by careful listening to the audiotape. The focus of analysis for interpretive purposes can vary depending on the purpose of a study; it could be the narrator (as in Rick's narrative of emotions) or the narrative itself (as in Gee's research). In all cases, however, interpretation is constrained by the structure of the overall narrative—how it is spoken in units of discourse. Attention to the local context of production is variable across the exemplars, more extensive in the case study of Rick, and nearly absent in Gee's study because, to work out his theory of narrative structure, he focused on the narrative alone. Scholars since have adapted Gee's approach to include the interaction between primary speaker and listener. [44]

Conclusion

Structural narrative analysis can generate insights that are missed when interpretation concentrates narrowly on "what" is said, ignoring how content is organized by a speaker. The model developed by Labov and Waletzky for clearly bounded narrative texts, and that used by Gee for more extended narrations, provide starting points for beginning investigators. The methods can illuminate the kinds of data human scientists work with in interviews and naturally occurring conversations. To return to my musical analogy, the analyst slows the composition down and notices relations (of parts to each other and to the whole), thus determining how the composition achieves its effects. Attention to structure can generate knowledge that reinforces an investigator's thematic analysis, but sometimes complicates it and takes inquiry in unexpected directions.

The exemplars showcase Labov's and Gee's very different but paradigmatic approaches. Each illustrates one way structural analysis can be done and what it yields. The models have aided graduate students in my courses who are not familiar with (or have backgrounds in) language and communication studies, and who have difficulty with detailed transcriptions of discourse. For those with more extensive backgrounds, and for beginning investigators who want to learn more, there is a wealth of research to explore.[45]

The summary table (Table 4.2) displays how each author dealt with issues I think are central to all forms of narrative analysis. Note the range of positions investigators take within the structural narrative tradition on the key issues, including how narrative is defined. It can refer to a brief and temporally ordered story that is in answer to an interviewer's question, or to an extended turn at talk that is organized in complex ways, with flashbacks, asides and, perhaps, an episodic rather than temporal organization. In both cases, however, the term "narrative" is reserved for a bounded unit of speech, rather than the entire biography (as in several exemplars in Chapter 3). The table underscores variation in each author's way of displaying speech, the unit of analysis (focus) in each study, and attention to relevant contexts. The table simplifies complexities to underscore diversity, emphasizing how investigators use structural approaches for distinctive purposes—to answer particular questions that, in turn, dictate the unit of analysis and focus of a study, the kind of texts they will include, how narrative texts will be presented, and level of contextual knowledge that is relevant to interpretation. Despite the danger of oversimplification, I present the table to aid the decision making of investigators who may want to interrogate formal features of their data.

Indicating how the authors incorporated context was particularly difficult to summarize in the table, and I urge readers to consult each author's writings. Regarding local context, placement of an utterance was always relevant—where a line (or clause) appears in the sequence, and how it is linked to previous ones. Other aspects of the local context, however, slip away in the exemplars. We do not typically learn, for example, when a narrative segment

Summary Table 4.2	Structural Analysis of Interview Texts			
Author of Exemplar	Definition of Narrative	How Represented: Structure	Unit of Analysis: Focus	Attention to Contexts
Labov (1972)	Brief; topic-centered, temporally ordered segment of speech	Clauses on lines	Common structural elements across stories	Local: placement of clause and function in a sequence Societal: minimal
Labov (1982)	Brief; topic-centered, temporally ordered segment of speech	Clauses on lines	Recurrent sequence of moves across stories	Local: placement of clause and function in a sequence Societal: minimal
Robichaux (2003)	Extended accounts, topic-centered segments from several speakers	Clauses from several interviews	Recurrent clauses across stories	Local: components common to narratives Societal: minimal
Gee (1991)	Extended, nonlinear segment of oral discourse with episodes; associative	Prosodic units in spoken narrative (lines, stanzas, parts, strophes)	Relationship of structure and interpretation	Local: relations among units of discourse Societal: none
Riessman ("Gloria") (1989)	Extended topic-centered, temporally ordered segment of speech	Clauses on lines	Meaning of event for narrator	Local: placement and function of clause Societal: minimal
Riessman ("Rick") (1990)	Extended stream of speech; nonlinear, nontemporal	Prosodic units (stanzas, codas); approach/ avoidance form; figurative language	The narrator's emotions refracted through structure and word choice	Local: research relationship Societal: media text appropriated by speaker

occurs in a conversation, and we see little about the evolving relationship between teller and listener that produced the emerging narrative. There is even less attention to "societal" contexts, a bad term referring to institutional constraints, power relations and cultural discourses that contextualize all narrative. Ironically, I began the chapter by noting that the early structural narrative researchers in education drew attention to these very issues. It is not inevitable, then, that the constraints of social structure be submerged when looking at how a personal narrative is told. It is not intrinsic to the method to decontextualize narrative segments, ignoring historical, interactional, and institutional factors.[46]

Investigators must decide, depending on the focus of a project, how much transcription detail is necessary. There is the danger that interview excerpts can become unreadable for those unfamiliar with social linguistic conventions, compromising communication across disciplinary boundaries. Structural narrative analysis is not suitable for large samples, but can be very useful for detailed case studies and comparisons across a few cases. Microanalysis of several narratives can build theories that relate language and meaning in ways that are missed when transparency is assumed, as in thematic narrative analysis. Because it takes language seriously, structural narrative analysis provides tools for investigators who want to interrogate how participants use speech to construct themselves and their histories.

5

Dialogic/Performance Analysis

T he approach in this chapter is a departure from the detailed methods of previous chapters. What I am calling dialogic/performance analysis is not equivalent to thematic and structural, but rather a broad and varied interpretive approach to oral narrative that makes selective use of elements of the other two methods and adds other dimensions. It interrogates how talk among speakers is interactively (dialogically) produced and performed as narrative. More than the previous two, this one requires close reading of contexts, including the influence of investigator, setting, and social circumstances on the production and interpretation of narrative. Simply put, if thematic and structural approaches interrogate "what" is spoken and "how," the dialogic/performative approach asks "who" an utterance may be directed to, "when," and "why," that is, for what purposes?

Stories don't fall from the sky (or emerge from the innermost "self"); they are composed and received in contexts—interactional, historical, institutional, and discursive—to name a few. Stories are social artifacts, telling us as much about society and culture as they do about a person or group. How do these contexts enter into storytelling? How is a story coproduced in a complex choreography—in spaces between teller and listener, speaker and setting, text and reader, and history and culture? Dialogic/performance analysis attempts to deal with these questions, applied here to ethnographic and interview data about identities. The investigator becomes an active presence in the text. As a kind of hybrid form, the approach pushes the boundaries of what is and is not included in narrative analysis. It draws on and extends theoretical traditions that emphasize the importance of interaction, including symbolic interaction theory and, to a lesser extent, aspects of conversational analysis.

Although different in important ways, both traditions share interest in how social reality is constructed through interaction—typically in mundane talk between speakers, although gaze, gesture, and other nonverbal aspects of communication are sometimes considered. What we as members of a culture take to be "true" (meanings that are taken for granted, for example, or social conventions such as taking turns in conversation) are actually produced in face-to-face exchanges every day, and the process of reality construction can be systematically studied. Microanalysis of narrative accounts can still occur, but both participant and listener/questioner must be included, and context becomes important. I hinted at this perspective in Chapter 2 and develop it further here, beginning with several theories that shape the analytic approach.

Using a dramaturgical metaphor, Erving Goffman[1] extended symbolic interaction theory toward the performative, thus transforming understandings of identity. We are forever composing impressions of ourselves, projecting a definition of who we are, and making claims about ourselves and the world that we test out and negotiate with others. In situations of difficulty, social actors stage performances of desirable selves to preserve "face." Language is the major resource we draw on (in literate societies), although bodily forms of communication also come into play. As Goffman elegantly put it, "What talkers undertake to do is not to provide information to a recipient but to present dramas to an audience. Indeed, it seems that we spend more of our time not engaged in giving information but in giving shows."[2] To emphasize the performative is not to suggest that identities are inauthentic (although this reading is suggested by the dramaturgical perspective), but only that identities are situated and accomplished with audience in mind. To put it simply, one can't be a "self" by oneself; rather, identities are constructed in "shows" that persuade. Performances are expressive, they are performances *for* others.[3] Hence the response of the listener (and ultimately the reader) is implicated in the art of storytelling. Including the audience as an active presence requires a shift in methods.

Since Goffman, ideas of performativity have reached a fever pitch in contemporary theory.[4] In the evolution of narrative inquiry, a key paper—invaluable theoretically and analytically—is Kristin Langellier's interview study of a performance of identity by a breast cancer survivor. The case study could well have served as an exemplar in this chapter. Langellier interrogates the woman's illness narrative as a performative struggle over meanings.[5] The concept of performance can also be used in a more limited way when a narrator appropriates certain conventions (e.g., setting up scenery and distributing roles) to dramatize an experience and engage an audience.[6]

Literary theory informs what I am calling dialogic/performance analysis. Bakhtin studied novels,[7] but his concepts have infused studies of interaction in everyday life, and all of the exemplars below draw on him. An antiformalist literary scholar who lived and worked in Soviet Russia until his death in 1975, Bakhtin situates all utterances in the "I-thou" relationship. Form and meaning emerge *between people* in social and historical particularity, in a dialogic environment.[8] Every text, he argues, includes many voices—hidden internal politics, historical discourses, and ambiguities—beyond the author's voice. Narratives (especially those that appropriate theatrical conventions) are polyphonic—multivoiced; the author (speaker) does not have the only word, that is, the authority over meaning is dispersed and embedded. These concepts are important to narrative research in the human sciences because they complicate the commonsense theory about language and meaning (e.g., language simply conveys information). A given word, Bakhtin argues, is saturated with ideology and meanings from previous usage; analysts never encounter a word from a "pure" position—it is not a neutral repository of an idea. An utterance carries the traces of other utterances, past and present, as words carry history on their backs.[9] No longer accepting the narrator as the "final" authority, the social scientist can interrogate particular words, listen to voices of minor characters, identify hidden discourses speakers take for granted, and locate gaps and indeterminate sections in personal narrative. Wolfgang Iser,[10] also a literary scholar, extends dialogue to include the reader. We bring current sensibilities and cultural tensions into reading, adding new voices to interpretation. Iser describes the process:

> [Innovating readings] would, of course, be impossible if the text itself was not, to some degree, indeterminate, leaving room for a change of vision. . . . Texts with . . . minimal indeterminacy tend to be tedious, for it is only when the reader is given the chance to participate actively that he [sic] will regard the text, whose intention he himself [sic] has helped to compose, as real.[11]

I introduced the general theoretical framework because it is embedded in each of the three exemplars. Performances of identity (a substantive commonality across the three) are treated as plurivocal, and the investigators all problematize meaning. Each interpreter has an active voice, yet never the only one, as readers are also invited to engage with the text. Turning now to the three studies, as in previous chapters I emphasize how each investigator did his or her analytic work. The research is broadly interpretive and purposefully varied: the first (my research, which continues the theme of biographical disruption) analyzes a conversation that develops during a single research interview, the other two (from education) work with group dialogues that were collected ethnographically in classrooms.

Performing the Last Day at Work: Disability and Masculine Identity

Burt was a white working-class man with advanced multiple sclerosis (MS) when I interviewed him in 1983. His name appeared in divorce court records and, when telephoned to ask about participating in a research project, he was enthusiastic. Going to his home, I was surprised when an aging man in a wheelchair answered the door, and wrote, "He looked much older than 43 years." We had a long and memorable conversation, which Burt redirected at every opportunity to talk about the progression of his illness over eight years, during which time his wife left him for another man. Burt's painful story is reminiscent of what Anatole Broyard, after his own battle with cancer, wrote: "Ill people bleed stories, and I've become a blood bank of them."[12] Taking charge of the interview early on, Burt bled stories from beginning to end.

Similar to that of other white working-class men, the job had provided a secure masculine identity. Burt had been the breadwinner in a traditional marriage that lasted twenty-one years. He had worked for a large well-known company for most of those years. When he got sick, he said with pride, "They got me an electric wheelchair"; they also gave him a desk job. He continued to work until he "couldn't sit for too long in a wheelchair." Since conducting the interview in 1983, I have returned to our conversation many times, reading it differently as Iser suggests.[13] I summarize earlier understandings here, and present yet another perspective on one story—a vivid moment in the interview when Burt performs his last day on the job. His identity as a worker permanently ended on that day.

My analysis is informed by Goffman's idea of performance, and the work of others who have extended his ideas. To review, Goffman theorizes that social actors stage performances of desirable selves to preserve "face" in situations of difficulty. In the interview, Burt not only provides information about his condition, he also performs—enacts—key moments in his life since chronic illness stopped him in his tracks. The moments he chooses to dramatize often turn on masculinity—particular moments when he was a motivated husband or factory worker. Constructing his identity—how he wanted to be known in our conversation—was accomplished in "shows" that were designed to persuade. To examine Burt's speech as performance, I must include myself as the immediate audience for it.

When a narrator "acts out a story," it has immediacy. Past actions appear as if happening in the present, for time collapses as the past and present fuse. The speaker's experiential involvement engages the listener emotionally, creating a "two way narrative contract between teller and audience."[14] When Burt performed moments in his life, I experienced the unfolding events *with* him, reliving the events and identifying with him. The pull of the narrative contract can obscure an important ontological distinction in that the performance is "both an 'act' and an enactment, a doing and a representation of a doing."[15]

Turning to the interview, the topic of employment functioned as bookends to our conversation. Within the first five minutes, Burt told me he was "planning on going back to work part time." Sitting across from him, it was hard to imagine. He said he had gone to see his boss several weeks earlier but had been told "things were kind of slow . . . there was nothing open right now . . . they would get in touch with [him]." I remember thinking (and wrote in field notes) that they were putting him off and learned later that the plant was downsizing; a year after we talked, another firm acquired the company, and the plant closed (a fact I expand upon below).

As our conversation was ending, Burt returned to the topic of work, creating an opening in a fixed response question (about sources of his income) to construct long a narrative (see Transcript 5.1). I asked a question about income, and Burt performed his last day at a factory job. In the story he positions himself as the central character in a heroic drama, with his boss and several doctors as supporting characters. He positions me, his audience, as witness to a moral tale depicting a man who wants to be a workingman. Multiple "selves" are performed as Burt casts about for threads of his prior identities, not tied neatly into the legitimately disabled man. The narrative is a poignant, quintessentially masculine tale that articulates failures of the male body. As if emasculated, Burt cannot stand up to urinate. The story entangles readers too in the bodily suffering of the man, and in his social suffering as he tries to return to work. A classic story in a formal sense, it bleeds the pain of disability in social space.

I wondered why Burt told the poignant story as our interview was ending and in response to a question about income. The dialogic approach explicitly invites such questions from listeners and, eventually, from readers, but there are risks when we open our work to different readings. For example, when I have included the transcript in public presentations, responses have been extremely varied. In the United Kingdom, a medical practitioner read it as a case of "claims-making"—a justification for continuing disability

Transcript 5.1

01 I had told my boss ahead of time that I was	**Scene 1**
02 goin' to see him [the doctor].	
03 And he said "well, let us know, you know, as soon	
04 as you find out so we can get your wheelchair all, you	
05 know, charged up and fixed up and everything."	
06 So I had seen him [doctor] on a Friday	
07 and I'd called soon as I got back Friday told him [boss]	
08 I'd be in that following Monday.	
09 And he said, "oh, it's goin' to be so good to have you back,	
10 you've been out of work so long."	

11 So I went in there [factory]	**Scene 2**
12 (p) and before I used to be able to stand up in the	
13 men's room, you know, and urinate that way	
14 but this one time I took the urinal with me	
15 just in case I couldn't do it.	
16 So I got up, I get in there at 7 o'clock that morning	
17 and at about 9 o'clock I felt like I had to urinate.	
18 And I went over to where I usually go to try to stand up	
19 I couldn't stand up the leg wouldn't hold me.	
20 They have a handicapped stall.	
21 So I went into the handicapped stall to try and use the urinal.	
22 Couldn't use it.	
23 I had the urge that I had to go but nothing was coming out.	
24 So back to my desk I went and I continued working.	
25 And about fifteen or twenty minutes later I get the urge again.	
26 So back to the men's room I go	
27 back to the handicapped stall.	
28 All day long this is happening.	
29 I couldn't move my urine, everything just blocked up.	

30 When I get home I figured well	**Scene 3**
31 maybe it's because I'm nervous	
32 coming back to work the first day on the job.	
33 So I get home (p) I still couldn't go.	
31 So I called my doctor, Dr George	
35 and he said "well, can you get up to [names hospital]?"	

36 I said, "well, I'm in my pajamas."
37 He said, "well, I'll send an ambulance."

38 So they sent an ambulance and brought me up there.   **Scene 4**
39 And he put a catheter on me
40   soon as he put that on I think I must have let out maybe
41   two pints.
42 Everything just went shhhhh.
43 You know, I felt so relieved.
44 And he said "well, I'm goin' to keep you in," he says
45 "I want, I want this uh (p) urinologist to take a look at you."
46 So it was Dr Lavini
47 I don't know if you know Dr Lavini he's one of the best around.
48 He looked at it and said, "we're going to have to operate."
49 Everything just blocked up.
50 They had to make the opening larger
51 so the urine would come out, you know, freely.
52 So I was in [name of hospital]—

53 I had gone to work for that *one* day   **Coda**

Source: Riessman, C. K., A thrice told tale: New readings of an old story. In Hurwitz, B., Greenhalgh, T. and Skultans, V. (Eds.). (2004). *Narrative Research in Health and Illness. British Medical Journal,* pp. 316–317. Massachusetts: BMJ books/Blackwell Publishing. Reprinted with permission.

payments. In the United States, several social researchers spoke of their "embarrassment"—details about the failure of the penis were too intimate for these strangers. Others have noted that a man's worth in a capitalist society is tied to what he earns; consequently Burt protects his masculinity by storying a day at the job when I asked about income. These different readings underscore a central point about the dialogic approach. Readers are inherently part of the interpretive process, bringing their positioned identities and cultural filters to interpretation. Investigators adapting dialogic/performative methods should be prepared, then, to acknowledge that audiences will read the narrative texts they produce in all sorts of ways. To counter the argument that all readings are equally plausible, I adopt the view of the structural approach—interpretation must be linked to features in the text, including how it is organized. Additionally, the analyst can bring information from the interview context to bear, which other readers may not have access to.

My reading develops a relational theme; the insertion of an intimate and detailed story about his masculine body sustains an intimacy Burt has been seeking all along in our conversation—connection with a woman. Many times during the research interview, Burt had tried to position me in a common world of meaning by connecting me to his life world. He asked my age, religion, whether I had children, and noted commonalities between us. He talked about sexual feelings for a nurse he met during a hospitalization. He said he wanted a woman companion, "someone to talk to, you know, someone to love."[16] Perhaps I represented some of that to him, a woman who listened and expressed interest in his life. He chose to disclose intimate details about his body in such a context.

The way the story is told supports this interpretation. Burt could have narrated the events in many ways, but he chose a dramatic presentation. Looking more closely at narrative form, he constructs what I call scenes—marked on Transcript 5.1—separated by time: Friday (Scene 1), Monday morning (2), that evening (3), and a final hospital scene (4). (The scene is an extension of Gee's concept of the stanza, described in Chapter 4). Burt creates characters, giving speaking roles to his boss, the two doctors, and himself. He positions himself in a moral drama about what it means to be a virtuous man.

In working with Burt's narrative over time, I have moved between two concepts of performance. Goffman alerted me to the preferred "self" Burt enacts. But performance is also a distinct genre of talk, Nessa Wolfson notes, used in certain speech situations and not others, an indicator of "received or proffered commonality between speakers"[17] and rarely used when conversationalists are remote from each other. By choosing to *dramatize* rather than simply report what happened in a more distant way, a narrator's plea for commonality cannot be easily ignored. Looked at more closely with the performance genre in mind, the excerpt displays nearly all its characteristic linguistic features. First, there is *direct speech*—Burt gives key lines to his boss in Scene 1:

> And he said, "oh, it's goin' to be so good to have you back, you've been out of work so long."

Using direct (often called reported or reconstructed[18]) speech builds credibility and pulls the listener into the narrated moment; as used here, it also allows Burt to communicate an important message about himself that it would be difficult to say in other ways. By appropriating the boss's voice, he can claim he was a valued worker at the factory.

Second, there are *asides*—points where he steps out of the action to engage directly with the audience:

They have a handicapped stall . . .

I don't know if you know Dr. Lavini he's one of the best around.

Third, he uses *repetition* to mark the key moment in the unfolding sequence of events, his body's recurring urge to urinate:

So I went into the handicapped stall to try and use the urinal . . .

So back to the men's room I go

back to the handicapped stall.

Fourth, he makes use of *expressive sounds* (alongside words) to signal the pivotal turning point in the action, and to resolve the crisis. With a catheter, he can finally urinate—made known with sound effects ("shhhhh").

Finally, Burt uses verb tense performatively. Stories are typically told in the past tense, but he alternates the past with the *historical present* at key junctures:[19]

So I got up, I get in there at 7 o'clock that morning . . .

So back to my desk I went and I continued working.

And about 15 or 20 minutes later I get the urge again.

So back to the men's room I go . . .

All day long this is happening.

Not only do these alternations make the story vivid and immediate, switching tenses underscores the agency of the narrator (Burt was not passive), and focuses attention on particular segments in the long narrative. He can emphasize his motivation to work (and how the body refused to go along), not what happened during the medical treatment (note, he does not alternate verb tense in Scene 4). The man's social suffering, not the biomedical plot, is the focal point of the story. An enactment or replay is "something that listeners can empathetically insert themselves into, vicariously reexperiencing what took place."[20] Burt's strategic decision to show, rather than to tell, accomplishes a vivid and involving portrait of the man. As our long conversation was ending, he performed his preferred self—responsible worker—not other "selves" he has suggested earlier (lonely man wanting a woman to love).

But are there other imagined audiences, "ghostly" ones?[21] Was Burt also performing for public audiences, those who might question his motivation to work? Arthur Frank remarks that "stories repair the damage that illness has done" to people's sense of where they are in their lives.[22] Burt's stories were probably told to multiple audiences, including (but not limited to) me. Language, Bakhtin reminds us, is a "field of dialogic intentions, past meanings, and future responses."[23]

Looking back on the poignant conversation, I now see gaps and omissions, and relate the text to other texts about job loss with which I am familiar. Burt's story reminds me of another performance—Willy Loman, in Arthur Miller's *Death of a Salesman*. A salesman for thirty-four years who was tired and aging, he too wanted to be known as a workingman. The employer, who extracted Willy's labor for thirty-four years and then fired him, took the work identity away. Willy confronts his boss: "You can't eat the orange and throw away the peel. . . . A man isn't a piece of fruit." Unlike Willy, Burt does not confront corporate power—it is taken for granted, rather than challenged in his dramatic presentation. Yet a pension was absent from his listing of the sources of his income, even though he had worked for twenty years for a large corporation with several factories in the Northeastern United States. The line Burt gave to his boss in the performance narrative ("Oh, it's goin' to be so good to have you back, you've been out of work for so long") masks larger corporate neglect—the job did not provide him with a pension.

In my interpretive work over time with Burt's story, I have sought additional information. I learned from a local informant (who had a relative who had been similarly employed at the factory) that the plant was downsizing during the very time I interviewed Burt. Shortly after, the plant closed. People in management and upper levels were given employment opportunities in the new corporation, and generous benefit packages. Line workers were given nothing. Factory labor had used up the able-bodied Burt. Reading the narrative now with history in mind, I see how corporate capitalism and job loss ravaged American workers like Burt. The postindustrial wasteland in manufacturing in the entire Northeastern United States, produced in the 1980s by acquisitions and mergers, capital flight, and the search for corporate profits, eclipsed the power of workingmen, bleeding the masculinity embodied in factory labor.

Attention to history also opened up another issue in that disability necessarily means confinement, which Burt (and I) took for granted in our conversation in 1983. We both assumed that access to social space is necessarily restricted for someone in a wheelchair. Looking back on the research materials with history in mind, I see his extreme social isolation in a time when the disability rights movement had not yet secured wheelchair access in communities, for disability had not yet become politicized. Burt said that "being alone" was his greatest difficulty. A personal care attendant, who helps him with "hygiene . . . exercises . . . housecleaning . . . food shopping," is his "closest relationship." With the attendant's aid, he is able to get out of the house several times a month only, to play bingo or go to a movie. Otherwise, he watched TV alone. Burt's employer did supply an electric wheelchair for the workplace, but no such provision was made for him in the community. The illness narrative (and experience of MS) would be transformed in the context of current public policies about wheelchair access. Instead, Burt was physically segregated at home. The limited possibilities he had for a public life, and the loneliness of the private sphere, are grimly apparent to me now. I am reminded of another text, the biographical account of Irv Zola (an American sociologist with polio) and his discoveries when he did ethnographic research in a Dutch village without curbs and other barriers.[24] Extreme social isolation need not accompany polio or multiple sclerosis, except as social arrangements and physical barriers make it so.

I chose to present my reanalysis of a single interview as an introduction to the dialogic/performance approach because it incorporates aspects of thematic and structural methods, while also displaying a different way of working with data that is more hidden in the two exemplars to follow (they come from published books). Determination of meaning(s) in my conversation with Burt suggests how texts play hide-and-seek with interpreters. Here, I was guided by Wolfgang Iser, who argues that meaning is not concealed within the text itself, instead we "bring the text to life [with our readings] . . . a second reading of a piece . . . often produces a different impression from the first . . . [related to the] reader's own change in circumstances."[25]

Burt's illness narrative is a "product of occasions of telling and reading"[26]—several occasions of reading, each producing different meanings. The view of the interview I take now illustrates how "the reading process always involves viewing the text through a perspective that is continually on the move."[27] More generally, the work illustrates how dialogic/performance analysis can uncover the insidious ways structures of inequality and power—class, gender, and race/ethnicity—work their way into what appears to be "simply" talk about a life affected by illness.[28] Although Burt never acknowledged objective social conditions (he "naturalized" them), his life was saturated with class and global politics—taken-for-granted inequalities inscribed in the consciousness of ordinary citizens: corporate pension plans (and their absence), the downsizing and migration of large industrial plans (benefiting executives, not workers), and restricted spaces for the disabled.

Burt was chained to a place[29] because of social arrangements that are historically and class-specific, not inevitable. Narrative investigators, even working with the limitations of single interviews, can bring these hidden dimensions of power into their readings. Obviously, other interpretive methodologies in sociology do this well, taking up C. Wright Mill's call to make public issues out of what seem on the surface to be personal troubles.[30] What close narrative study of a single case can add is displaying how larger social structures insinuate their way into individual consciousness and identity, and how these socially constructed "selves" are then performed for (and with) an audience, in this case the listener/interpreter.

Before moving on, I briefly interrogate the exemplar in relation to the core methodological issues taken up in prior chapters. The definition of narrative should be familiar to readers from Chapter 4: a bounded segment of talk that is temporally ordered and recapitulates a sequence of events. As structural analysts do, I transformed the oral narrative into a written text, parsing it into clauses, retaining key features of the oral version needed to interrogate performance features (e.g., shifts in verb tense, direct speech, creative language— "urinologist"—and expressive sounds—"shhhh"). The action unfolds in scenes, each representing a distinct time period, with a final coda that "resolves" a conflict. Once again we see how interpretation is inseparable from transcription. Unlike exemplars of structural narrative methods (see Chapter 4), context gets considerable analytic attention here. I used thematic material from earlier parts of the interview, and located the personal narrative in broader historical and economic contexts, noting how public issues are buried in a personal story about the last day at a factory job. I also include myself as an active participant in the narrative and its interpretation—a distinguishing feature of dialogic/performance analysis.

The next two exemplars go beyond the limitation of a single research interviews to look at how identities are performed in everyday settings. Both investigators worked ethnographically in schools and, in different ways, constructed situations that allowed them to see identities being developed and expressed in collaborative performances. Extending a theme from the earlier case study, the two investigations show how class and racial identities work their way into group performances. In lively classroom discussions, readers see how talk among speakers is dialogically produced and interpreted, with the investigator active throughout.

Raising Their Voices: Mad Girls in the Classroom

Psychologist Lyn Mikel Brown studied the schooling experiences of a small group of outspoken white preadolescent girls from two different cultural communities in rural Maine.[31] Brown's work is particularly interesting because detailed study of the impact of social class on white youth is rare in the United States (though common in Britain),[32] where political discourse almost always feeds on stereotypes of poor urban black youth. Research neglects whiteness as a racial identity and rural experiences of class. As a way to understand white girls' understandings of their schools and teachers, Brown "hung out" over an extended period with two groups of eleven- and twelve-year-old girls who met weekly or, in some cases, bimonthly, in their respective public schools with a teacher/facilitator. She worked collaboratively with the teacher/facilitator in each group. Group sessions were videotaped, and interviews supplemented ethnographic observation. The communities served by the contrasting schools differ significantly: "Arcadia" parents are highly educated with professional careers; "Mansfield" parents live on the edge, devastated by mill closings and industrial downsizing. In lively discussion groups in each school setting, girls spoke about their relationships with one another, their families, teachers, and schools. Raw angry emotions permeated discussions, captured in Brown's choice of a chapter title, "Mad Girls in the Classroom."

Her book draws attention to neglected subjects in educational research, namely girls' "strong feelings, particularly of anger, their critical opinions about their schools, their conceptions of what it means to be female, and their critique of (and resistance to) dominant expectations of femininity."[33] Using Bakhtin as a theoretical resource, Brown attends to the polyphonic nature of voice, or the "the non-linear, nontransparent interplay and orchestration of feelings and thoughts"[34]—what others might refer to as power and positionality in girls' talk.

A voice-centered method of data analysis (based on the Listening Guide developed earlier by Brown, Gilligan, Taylor, and colleagues[35]) required five distinct listenings (and viewings, in the case of videotapes) of each interview and group session. Note how in the first, the investigator explicitly locates her position and subjectivity in the interpretative process, before attending in the second listening to thematic elements in the talk:

> First I attended to the overall shape of the dialogue or narrative and to the research relationship—that is, I considered how my own position as a white middle-class academic with a working-class childhood affected the girls' perceptions of me, our interactions, and my interpretations of their voices and behaviors. . . . I tracked my feelings and thoughts, my questions and confusions, as I interpreted the girls voices. The second [listening] . . . attended to the girls' first-person voices, to the ways they speak for and about themselves. . . . I also listened to the girls' gossip and put-downs of their peers and siblings to established whom they considered "Other" and why.[36]

The third "listening" is particularly relevant to the thematic content of the narrative excerpts below:

> I attended to the girls' discussions of personal anger and social critique: what people, events, or experiences provoked their anger and criticism? How and to whom did they express their strong feelings? What form did their anger take? Who or what forces constrained their expression of these strong feelings?[37]

The fourth and fifth listenings "focused on the ways the girls define and speak about appropriate female behavior and, in particular, the ways in which they accommodate to and resist dominant cultural constructions of femininity":[38]

> I documented voices and gestures of strength, fluidity, irreverence, and creativity—voices that are often grounded in local understandings of white femininity in tension with the dominant ideal. . . . Here, class and culture, relevant through the various listenings, took center stage. . . ."[39]

Note how Brown draws on thematic methods in several of the listenings and details the precise procedures she devised to systematically trace themes (and the girls' voicing of them) across transcriptions. For example, she documented each listening on a worksheet:

> recording in one column the girls' voices and in another my interpretation of their words. From these worksheets I created interpretive summaries, and from these summaries generated my analysis.[40]

Watching the videotapes, she documented gestures and movement. Reading Brown's book, I noted that not all the interactions took a narrative form; there were many rapid question and answer exchanges, and lengthy arguments about a topic where everyone added a comment.

Brown adopted Bakhtin's concept of appropriation, and its cousin—ventriloquation.[41] As she examined the tapes and transcripts, she noticed instances where "one voice speaks *through* another voice or voice type."[42] Close examination of these moments led to a theoretical discovery: girls' appropriated the dominant culture's denigration of femininity, on the one hand, and struggled against it on the other. Mansfield working-class girls, for example, ventriloquized patriarchal voices, they appropriated sexist, misogynist, and homophobic language to poke fun at one another and to denigrate other girls and teachers they felt have betrayed them in some way. "She was a bitch," one girl said of a teacher after she had narrated an incident the day before when the teacher had treated her badly. Another was dismissed as "cheap ho" (meaning whore), a referent appropriated from contemporary black rap. It is a term "drenched in intensions, some parodic and some subversive . . . the girls appropriate its misogynic overtones when they use the term . . . to denigrate other girls and women they dislike." At other times girls used the word playfully with one another.

When Brown asked the girls why they use such denigrating words, the girls said they are "just fooling around." Interpretation does not stop here, for the ethnographer draws on the history contained in the words. She wonders what it means "to ventriloquate and appropriate voices that deform, devalue, or subjugate oneself."[43] Does the language serve to appropriate power? Misogynist words can command power in the world, at the same time as they carry traces of history that attenuate female power and silence women. Working-class girls, Brown posits, may find strength in "renegade voices and outlawed tongues."[44]

Discussion groups were lively and spirited, a process difficult to capture in a written transcription, but Brown does present some. One day, the girls collaboratively performed a narrative about a teacher (Miss Davis) who was unfair, abusing her power over Donna, a girl in the group. Transcript 5.2 displays the collaborative story that this group of girls develop in a lively dialogue. It recapitulates an incident in which Donna wouldn't take her coat off in the classroom, and the teacher's harsh response. The adult facilitator of the group, Diane, interrupts at three points to try to clarify what happened as the girls are rapidly performing the incident. Although a seemingly mundane moment, it had great significance for the girls and surfaced over many sessions, becoming emblematic of teacher intrusiveness. Anger filled the room as the girls collectively performed the story.

Transcript 5.2

Cheyenne:	Yesterday, Miss Davis came in from recess and was really mad and nobody knew why. And she goes to [Donna], she goes, "Take off your coat." And she wouldn't take off her coat. . . . Because she didn't feel comfortable taking it off; and she said, "Go out in the hall," and then half an hour later she went out in the hall with Donna and before she did that she was walking around and everybody would ask her for something and she'd start screaming at 'em.
Diane:	Did she say why?
Patti:	Maybe she had PMS!
Cheyenne:	Wait! No. Anyways, they were out in the hall and she asked Donna why she wouldn't take off her coat and she goes, "Because I don't feel comfortable taking it off."

(Continued)

(Continued)

Donna: No, I said, "I didn't want to."

Cheyenne: Oh, because she didn't want to. And she goes, "I want you to write me" . . . two pages on why she wouldn't take off her coat.

Donna: No, two pages why she should let me wear my jacket.

Rachel: Oh, because she always . . . wears *her* jacket. [*some of the girls start to talk*] Listen! She's like, at the end of last year, she goes, "OK, when it's wintertime I'm going to have my window open and you guys are going to have to live with it." So, okay, we're wearing our coats. *She* can wear her coat when she's cold, but we can't, we get in trouble for it.

Cheyenne: And then after that she says, "Go down to the office. I don't want your kind here."

Diane: To you?

Cheyenne: No, to Donna because she wouldn't take off her coat. And it's not fair because she can keep her coat on whenever she wants—

Rachel: She thinks she can say whatever she wants.

Donna: I wrote a two-page letter and I told her . . . that if I didn't want to take off my coat that I didn't have to and that she shouldn't make me do anything that I didn't want to do . . . and that she said that I'm going through a stage where I don't like my body.

Diane: That's what she said?

Susan [laughing, squeals in a high feminine voice]: "I don't like my body!"

Cheyenne: I don't like it when teachers say something and they don't know what's going on though, and they say something mean to you. They butt in and say, "Well, I know what's wrong with you," and think they know what is going on.

Source: Brown, L.M. (1998). *Raising their Voices: The Politics of Girls' Anger.* Harvard University Press. Copyright © Lyn Mikel Brown. Reprinted with permission.

Note how the girls take on different roles and use other devices to collaboratively reenact the incident. Although Brown doesn't treat it as a performance narrative, when I read the transcript I was struck by its likeness. For example, the text includes many of the features Wolfson identifies: direct speech ("Take off your coat" . . ."I didn't want to"); asides to the audiences ("She can wear her coat when she's cold, but we can't, we get in trouble for it"); repetition (different speakers repeat the statement about taking off the coat); expressive sounds ("squeals in a high feminine voice"); and switches in verb tense and other features of the genre. As reviewed previously, performance narrative occurs among intimates and here it is an index of the girls' commonality and shared lifeworld. Some analysts might further interrogate Patti's derogatory line, "Maybe she had PMS!" It is a good example of ventriloquation, but only if listeners and readers are familiar with the contested syndrome of PMS. A gendered discourse is being appropriated here that diminishes women.

Because Brown's thematic analysis focuses on the girls' class identities and anger, she does not "unpack" the performance narrative as a structural analyst might or look at what the narrative accomplishes for the group. Instead, she draws attention to one moment in the performance related to her thematic interest in social class, a line spoken by the teacher (Miss Davis) to Donna, "I don't want your kind here." The words speak to a recurrent perception of the working-class girls—"their kind" is not wanted in the school. Teachers do not understand "their kind." Brown further argues that teachers appropriate concepts from the clinical literature on (middle-class) girls' discomfort with body image. The ethnographer notices the explanation the teacher (Miss Davis) gives for Donna's resistance—"that I'm going through a stage where I don't like my body." As a differently situated reader, I noted in the transcript the effect of the utterance on the audience. It seems to stun the other girls and, it appears, the adult group leader (Diane). Another student (Susan) performs the jester, ventriloquating a voice from clinical texts about adolescent development, "[squeals in a high feminine voice] 'I don't like my body!'" Cheyenne, the girl who initiated the collective story, sums up its moral point: the teacher's comment was a "mean" thing to say, and presumptuous. Teachers think they know what's going on with girls, but they don't (or may not, Brown suggests, for it is unclear why Donna insists on keeping her coat on in the classroom when other girls do not).[45]

Whatever the incident signifies, Brown sees it as emblematic of the deep divide between these working-class girls and their women teachers. In an interpretive commentary, her voice is positioned alongside the girls' voices, but Brown refuses to be the "final" arbiter of meaning. Here she does share her sense of the larger significance of the coat story, and others like it that she witnessed:

[T]he intensity with which the girls express themselves speaks to the sense of both longing and loss they experience in relation to their women teachers. Their teachers, the girls say over and over, are "ignorant"—that is, they don't know anything about them—and yet many of the angry stories about their teachers are examples of possibility turned to disappointment, the possibility of being known and understood, the disappointment of lost relationships and shared knowledge.[46]

The girls cannot read their teachers and the teachers, the ethnographer posits, cannot read the girls, generating missed opportunities for communication and learning. As a result, the working-class girls become "madgirls in the classroom," resisting authority and disrupting classrooms.

Girls in Arcadia (the middle-class school) were also angry with teachers, but around different themes, and they expressed anger quietly. Girls commented over and over again about the boy-preference they perceive in classrooms. Boys, they say, get away with a lot—swearing, rudeness to teachers, fights—but when a girl steps out of line even in a small way, different standards apply. Kristin complained about a time when a teacher didn't call on her friend Theresa (see Transcript 5.3).

Transcript 5.3

Like boys get away with so much. It's just that we're good all the time. If we do something moderately bad, like Theresa got in big trouble for calling a teacher by their first name. She just was so frustrated. She must have, you know, raised her hand saying so and so, so many times, saying "Hey, listen to me," and it got [the teacher's] attention. . . . [She] was like, "Excuse me. You have no right to call me by my first name." [Theresa] was just like—she didn't say it because she was—I could tell she was [saying to herself], "You have no right to ignore me every day. Do you remember I'm in your class?"

Source: Brown, L.M. (1998). *Raising their Voices: The Politics of Girls' Anger*. Harvard University Press. Copyright © Lyn Mikel Brown. Reprinted with permission.

Theresa later expands on the theme Kristin initiated (see Transcript 5.4). She begins with "No" (answering the investigator's question about whether invisibility has to do with being a girl). Theresa suggests that it's not about being a girl, but in the next breath she begins, "See, these boys . . ." and continues to develop a narrative fragment about how boys are treated differently

Transcript 5.4

No, I think it's because these teachers, they won't listen to everyone, they just kind of. . . . See these boys—sometimes they have their hands up and everything but they never . . . They always say raise your hand but when you raise your hand they never call on you. So you end up— you have to yell out and then you get in trouble.

Source: Brown, L.M. (1998). *Raising their Voices: The Politics of Girls' Anger.* Harvard University Press. Copyright © Lyn Mikel Brown. Reprinted with permission.

in the classroom.[47] Attentive to linguistic features here, Brown draws attention to the shift in pronouns, from the first person "I" to the second person "you"—the generalized other.[48] The subtle shift in pronouns supports Brown's interpretation about gender: invisibility is not particular to one girl's experience, it is shared. "The problem for Theresa and her friends is thus not that they are girls, but that they are not boys."[49] In contrast to the working-class girls, the middle-class girls do not act on their anger in school and become disruptive. Instead, they move anger underground. Middle-class girls become skillful in an art of subtle expression—"dirty looks" and "icy stares."

In sum, the exemplar illustrates a broad interpretive approach to ethnographic data that incorporates aspects of thematic methods and some attention to language use. At the same time as it is similar, it departs in key ways from the approaches featured in earlier chapter. More like ethnographic work in general, Brown's comparative approach generates knowledge about girls' contrasting class identities and related school experiences from close observation of their collaborative performances. Girls' narratives are only a small part of a large corpus of data. I include Brown's work here because it offers insights into the kind of spontaneous narrative performances fieldworkers are likely to encounter when they enter classrooms and community settings. Stories told in group settings are less likely to be rehearsed, that is, they may not have been told similarly before. They typically emerge in fragments, with each speaker adding a thread that expands (or corrects) what another member contributed. Group stories typically lack the neat boundaries— beginnings, middles, and ends—more likely to occur in research interviews. Institutional and community settings offer opportunities for investigators to collect and examine group narratives that take the form of performance pieces— spontaneous dramatic reenactments of key moments in the group's life, performed for (and with) an audience that includes the investigator.

Looking briefly at core methodological issues, Brown's implicit definition of narrative is broad, referring (I think) to girls' accounts of their own actions, those of other girls and teachers, and the elaboration of these in group conversations. Brown does not distinguish narrative discourse sharply from other speech events that structural narrative analysts would define as arguments, question and answer exchanges, and other nonnarrative discourse.[50] The written versions of the group narratives include considerable detail (interruptions, rapid-fire exchanges, expansion by group members of a story fragment initiated by another girl, and some nonlexical features—gestures and "icy stares"), but there is little attention to narrative structure. Inquiry does isolate and interpret particular words and phrases in a sequence (e.g., "I don't want your kind here"). As is common in much ethnographic work, there is little information on transcription methods—how talk has been transformed into text. Brown's thematic focus in the excerpts presented here is anger—the emotions girls display based on events in school that make them mad.

In ethnographic work, identifying a "unit of analysis" is not really appropriate, but to be consistent in my application of the four questions, the unit for Brown appears to be the incident arousing anger. (Brown has various thematic foci in chapters of her book, and anger is only one.) There is considerable attention to local contexts such as the influence of the ethnographer, the group leader, and the other speakers on what girls say and do. Larger contexts of gender, race, and class are, of course, also central to Brown's analytic approach, reflected in the research design and shaping interpretation in major ways. Historical contexts enter her inquiry at several points when she draws on past uses of words that the girls appropriate, and the historical roots of class divisions in rural Maine (the ethnographic setting).

The exemplar provides an application of the dialogic/performative approach that can serve as a model for others. The investigator's way of coding different listenings is methodical, and well suited to analyzing complex interactions in focus groups, community meetings, and classrooms. Many voices join in these group exchanges, different speakers in a literal sense but also symbolic voices that speak through other characters (e.g., patriarchal voices denigrating women that the girls appropriated and ventriloquized). For those who want to interrogate their own data for instances of appropriation and ventriloquation (concepts from Bakhtin), Brown models the way; she questions the origins of words that narrators "naturalize." What meanings are invoked? What history do the words carry on their backs? Who have they hurt or silenced in past uses?[51] What may be accomplished when they are appropriated in the present? To address these difficult interpretive questions, dialogic investigation looks beyond superficial, literal, and consciously intended practices of language use.

The final exemplar (also from education) is in some ways the most complex in the chapter. It describes the developing identities of a young girl and her classmates over the course of a school year, reflected in their storytelling performances for (and with) each other in a classroom that includes the teacher/researcher. The investigator adopts some structural analytic methods, but adds the dimension of performativity. Even more than in the earlier studies, the investigator's presence is palpable.

Epiphanies of the Ordinary: Performances in a First Grade Classroom

Karen Gallas is a teacher/researcher who routinely interrogates her classroom practice to see how it can better aid children's learning. Knowledge of social linguistics from doctoral training in education sensitized her to the importance of narrative structure. In the section of her research presented here, she interrogates "sharing time" in her classroom, which is socioeconomically and racially diverse. The classroom event (sometimes called show-and-tell) is a familiar ritual in first and second grade classrooms in many Western countries. Although mundane and ordinary, it is often the only time in the official school day for children to speak on topics of their own choosing; they are invited to compose their own oral texts about home, community, and family.[52] As Chapter 4 reviewed, systematic study of these storytelling occasions has generated considerable knowledge about variation in children's styles of speech and how teachers' practices can create, or remove, barriers to achievement.

Gallas knew that children do not enter school with access to "discourses of power"—the authoritative ways of speaking and storytelling privileged in the dominant culture.[53] For instance, a six-year-old homeless girl said to the teacher/researcher on the fifth day in her suburban school, "My mother must not have gone to the same kind of school you went to. 'Cause she doesn't know how to speak any of those languages you speak."[54] These words from a little child reminded Gallas of the huge power language has over children's lives and their differential access to literacy. Learning from the work of Cazden and Michaels (see Chapter 4), she routinely tapes her classroom practice, trying to help children, "all children, 'speak in tongues' . . . move to broader and more powerful ways of presenting themselves to the world."[55] Her teaching is heavily influenced by Bakhtin's theory:

> Language is not a neutral medium that passes freely and easily into the private property of the speaker's intentions; it is populated—overpopulated—with the intentions of others. Expropriating it, forcing it to submit to one's own intentions and accents, is a difficult and complicated process.[56]

Interrogating "sharing time" in her classroom, Gallas finds that appropriation is multidirectional: children teach each other discourse forms, and she (the teacher) helps children expropriate—to "speak in tongues," new languages. The language development of one child, Jiana, vividly illustrates the process. The child is a tall and skinny, six-year-old African American girl who enters Gallas's racially mixed first grade class. Jiana comes to the suburban school from a shelter across the park, where she and her mother live.[57] Her father is in jail for drug related incidents. Gallas[58] relates her initial evaluation of the child, "she was functioning on a pre-kindergarten level . . . recognized only a few letters and numbers, could barely write her name, and had extreme trouble naming common objects, animals, and pictures. She appeared to have little, if any, experience with books." In the classroom Jiana was primarily interested in making friends and just "being" in school.

At first, Gallas considered referring Jiana for a speech and language evaluation; how could she deal with such severe problems properly in a class with twenty-two children? But instead, upon further thought, Gallas's commitments led her to "make room in my classroom for many different language styles"; she recognized further that she had no grasp on the reality Jiana brought with her to school—her traumatic life story. Rather than referring the child, she decided "to wait and see" and listen and watch. She wanted "to make the classroom a place that welcomed her and did not send her away."

Readers learn that even before Jiana arrived, Gallas had begun to experiment with the ritual of "sharing time" in her first grade classroom by turning the speech event over to the children to manage. Learning to take sharing time seriously in her doctoral training, Gallas experimented further. She no longer sat up front, but in the back of the audience; the sharing child was given the center chair. Each child had a designated day of the week when he or she could share a story about an event or an object brought to school. Typically, two to five children volunteered on any given day. Following the approach pioneered by Cazden and Michaels (see Chapter 4), Gallas audiotaped and made extensive field notes of the classroom process, sections of which are reproduced below. Readers can see how carefully ethnographic observation and knowledge about complexities of transcription are built into her research methods:

> Jiana wanted to share from day one, and she always tried to participate in other children's sharing by asking questions and offering comments. . . . When she got into the chair, it was as if she were sitting in a forbidden place . . . Inevitably, she would look out at me, as if asking for permission, and I'd say, "go ahead, Jiana." And then she would try to start. Her narratives were usually unintelligible, but she persevered. Here is an example of her talk in early October, when she was sharing a half-finished bookmark. (Each dot [in Transcript 5.5] indicates a pause of one second in Jiana's talk. "Karen" refers to me).

Transcript 5.5

Jiana:	I made this at LEDP [after-school program].
Teacher:	I don't think they can hear you, honey.
Jiana:	I got this in LEDP, and. . . . . . and I made it. . . . . and I didn't want it so. . . . . I'm going to give it to Karen.
Teacher:	Do you want to tell more before you take questions?
Jiana:	Questions or comments?. . . . . . . Fanny.
Fanny:	What are you going to make it out of? What are you going to make it out of?
Jiana:	I'm not gonna make it.
Fanny:	But it's not finished. . . Well, you're going to have to show Karen how to do it because she doesn't know how to do it. And also, I think you need a needle for that.
Jiana:	I know.
Fanny:	Oh, do you have a needle?
Jiana:	No.
Fanny:	A fat one.

Source: Gallas, K. (1994). *The languages of learning: How children talk, write, dance, draw, and sing their understanding of the world.* Copyright ©Teachers College Press. Reprinted with permission.

Transcript 5.5 shows how very basic Jiana's language is; there are long pauses, and other children draw her out. Another child, Fanny, teaches Jiana how to expand her brief narrative about a bookmark she made in an after-school program with a question ("What are you going to make it out of?"). Gallas writes that it was difficult in the beginning for both class and teacher to understand the child's speech plan—Jiana's intent. How were listeners to know when she had finished? Jiana brought a way of speaking to school that did not fit the mainstream. Questioning by other children continued as Jiana brought other material objects to share—rocks from the playground, and asphalt shingles she had pulled off the side of the homeless shelter. Children waited through her long pauses (carefully marked on transcripts), asking her questions about small aspects of her nascent narratives to clarify understanding, and they preserved her position in the chair. In keeping with dialogic/performance analysis, the teacher/researcher includes herself:

I found this process terribly painful to witness. Often, as she struggled, I wanted to look away and preoccupy myself elsewhere, much as one might avoid looking at a handicapped person laboring to perform a simple function. However, although I secretly despaired that Jiana would not gain fluency, I was taping and listening carefully. Apparently my attention and silence in the midst of Jiana's long pauses led the children to believe that they should take care to try and follow Jiana, and they did.

After "three interminable months," something changed. Jiana's performance began to shift. The teacher/researcher observed her get into the chair confidently with a different demeanor. She talked loudly, sat up straight, and seemed to listen to the children's questions and, in turn, followed them up and clarified. As Jiana's identity performance shifted, so, too, did the content of her speech. She introduced one narrative by saying she didn't have anything to show (e.g., a material object) just something to tell.

A great deal could be said about Transcript 5.6; note how Jiana's speech is certainly more detailed and spirited than in the previous one (5.5). The

Transcript 5.6

Jiana: Oh. Um, and we saw the rainforest, we saw um, um, there was a um, thing on a, ... like a say, tree, and there was a . . . . . a fake snake, and everybody, and, some it was a fake snake but it was long and somebody was moving it in back of the thing, and and everybody thought it was a snake and everybody screamed.

Donald: Did you scream?

Jiana: No! Because . . . . . . 'cause, a a snake couldn't be. . . . yellow.

Several: Sure it could. It can.

Jiana: . . . And we saw, . . . and we saw um, ... little kinds of shells and we went to the pickup thing, where we pick up um, um, um, this big crab . . . . . . We get to pit it, pit it, we get to pit it up, and we pitted, picked it up, with some little things and they have a lot of legs.

Several: Starfish! Starfish!

Jiana: Yeah. Starfish.

Source: Gallas, K. (1994). *The languages of learning: How children talk, write, dance, draw, and sing their understanding of the world.* Copyright © Teachers College Press. Reprinted with permission.

teacher/researcher observes subtle shifts in narrative structure, although "it is still filled with hesitancies and word-finding problems."[59] Group participation, too, has changed, for Jiana's performance engages the other children in spontaneous play. They expand her answers and she, in turn, expands theirs. A kind of group performance was beginning to happen during "sharing time."

In the weeks that followed, Gallas describes how Jiana switched back to objects and expanded other children's stories by saying she had similar objects in her life, a cat for example. The teacher/researcher was suspicious that these utterances weren't "true," but nevertheless in Jiana's stories about her cat's antics, "inflection, intonation, and personal force would change; and a different narrative style emerged, a series of linked stories, which we would sometimes have to stop because they gradually increased in length."[60] Jiana began taking longer turns at talk than was customary in show-and-tell. Gallas identifies a critical moment in her ethnography: it occurred after the holiday break, when Jiana brought a Christmas ornament to share. As she sat in the chair, she described the ornament, explaining she had gotten it "a long time ago at a Christmas party," which segued into a story about her family (see Transcript 5.7).

Transcript 5.7

Jiana: My father was on stage talking to his friends, and he did it, he was in this program. My father doing it . . . did something bad, and he's in a program, and I can't tell you why. . . . . It's something white. . . . . It starts with a C, but I don't want to tell. And it's called. . . . . . cocaine. . . . . And that's why he's in the program, and he'll never come out.

Robin: What do you mean by what you said, your father's doing it? I don't understand.

Jiana: It's like something bad, like mommy goes in a closet and I say, "what are you doing?" She says, "You don't need to know," and she's sneaking a cigarette. And I say, that's not good for you. My father sometimes . . . . Sometimes if he says he's coming to pick you up . . . and he doesn't come . . . . . . don't say he's a liar, say he's a fibber.

Source: Gallas, K. (1994). *The languages of learning: How children talk, write, dance, draw, and sing their understanding of the world.* Copyright ©Teachers College Press. Reprinted with permission.

After initial hesitancy (note the long pauses in Jiana's beginning utterances, she explained everything, "and in doing so finally established a context for her presence in our class." Writing dialogically, the teacher/researcher includes her subjectivity and reflections about Jiana's story and her father's cocaine use:

> I felt at the time that this was one of those situations that sneak up on you and create a huge dilemma. Although in my role as a member of the audience I would never stop a discussion, I was worried that this kind of talk was not appropriate for the classroom. It was similar to hearing the most secret of family secrets.

The conversation Jiana initiated about drugs continues in Transcript 5.8.

Transcript 5.8

Andy: What does "cocaine" mean?

Jiana: That means like drugs and stuff.

Andy: You mean your father used drugs?

Jiana: No. My father took drugs. . . . . and my mother kicked him out and he went in a program.

Cindy: What's a program?

Jiana: It means that when a lot of people have problems when he got kicked out he went to a program.

Robin: What's a program? I don't understand.

Jiana: A program means you don't have no place to live, and you, you just stay there for awhile and when you you're ready to go find a house, you go find a house.

Source: Gallas, K. (1994). *The languages of learning: How children talk, write, dance, draw, and sing their understanding of the world.* Copyright ©Teachers College Press. Reprinted with permission.

Gallas describes how the explanation produced extreme seriousness in the classroom. Children wanted to understand the meaning of a drug "program"—notice how they question Jiana closely about words ("What's a program? I don't understand"). Note, also, how in the dialogue, Jiana becomes the authority on the topic for classmates ("It means that when a lot of people have problems . . ."; "A program means you don't have no place to live"). Consistent with a dialogic emphasis, the teacher/researcher includes her thoughts and feelings as they intersect with children's voices:

[A]s the discussion expanded I was not uncomfortable because Jiana was very composed. She was not ashamed. She was just telling her story, and a look at her language shows how well constructed and coherent her story is, how layered her reality. . . . This is powerful talk. A question lingered, however: Was this appropriate for school? Should a child be allowed publicly to disclose to her classmates the difficult circumstances of her life? As I listened, I knew that to stop the conversation would have been akin to censoring her world. My decision to let her continue reflected, I think, my intuition that this child's wish to tell her story took precedence over my discomfort at hearing it.

Although Gallas doesn't analyze the content and form of the narrative segments in the transcripts as fully as a structural analyst might, such methods could be folded into her dialogic/performance approach. What, for example, are the linguistic markers of Jiana's increasing "authority" in the group? How is the development of her authority displayed in the sequence of stories? What makes her story about cocaine "coherent" in ways that previous stories were not, and what precisely is the "layered" reality the teacher senses in Jiana's emerging identity? We are required to fill in, thus introducing our interpretive meanings into the texts (a central feature, of course, of dialogic/performance analysis).

In late February of the school year, Gallas decided to shift the rules of sharing time to further expand the children's repertoire of languages—no more stories about objects. Several grumbled that they wouldn't have anything to say. But Jiana had no problems with the new rule because she had few objects to share. In mid-March (more than halfway through the school year in the U.S. school setting), another child talked about a trip to the zoo. Jiana then got into the chair and began a long narrative about her zoo trip, in which a zookeeper came out with gorillas on a leash for her mother to pet. Gallas courageously shares her thoughts, actions, and mistakes:

This was simply too much for me, and I blurted out "Jiana, this is a time for true stories!" But she was adamant that the event had occurred and tried to continue her story. No sooner were the words out of my mouth than all the children in the group turned around and look at me very hard and long. Time seemed to stop for me as I realized from the change in their expression what I had done. They turned slowly back, mumbling about it's not being true, how it could not be true. Jiana tried to maintain her story in the face of their questions about how a gorilla would come out. A few kind children tried to fix the story: "Maybe it was chimpanzees" and "maybe it was a petting zoo," but within those few seconds her audience had turned away from her. Afterwards I spoke with Jiana, trying to explain my actions, and really, I thought to myself, my betrayal. I was the one person who had always supported her in the chair. She admitted to me that you could not really pet a gorilla.

As readers, we have to figure out specifics again here—what exactly constitutes the "betrayal" the teacher refers to? Readers engage dialogically with the investigator's text, interpreting it in light of their positionality (teachers, for example, might read Gallas's commentary differently than those outside the profession).

Difficult as the moment apparently was for the teacher/researcher, it signaled a turning point in "sharing time" because Jiana had initiated imaginative storytelling, and it continued. Children called them "fake stories," a term Gallas says she reluctantly adopted and April would be a month for telling true or fake stories. Some children grumbled, especially the boys. In response to another child's story about a make-believe trip, Jiana raised her hand and performed a fantasy story (not reproduced here). The audience was hysterical with laughter, and "they howled and hushed each other as she talked so they could hear." Five other children followed with stories modeled on hers. A few days later, Jiana told a full-blown fantasy story, a complex collaborative narrative that turned class members (Manon, Andy, Joel, William) into characters with different roles.

The full story (only part of which is represented in Transcript 5.9) went on for five minutes, and children were beside themselves with delight, their laughter echoing through the school. Gallas observes how Jiana's performance as author/director displayed dramatic skills not used before, including a broad range of movement of her body; she sat back on the chair "as if she owned it, with her hand on her hip . . . pointing to different members of the audience. When the laughter became too hilarious, she would lean over and shake her finger, 'Shhh! Are you listening?,' and they would quiet down." She varied her inflections for different children, changing pace as she noticed whom she had forgotten, and then picking up the pace as she directed them in their roles. Again, the teacher/researcher's voice is included:

This was the first time Jiana had been fully herself in the chair. She had spent the year figuring out how to talk in sharing [time] and then had adapted the model to her own style. Once she had become fully acclimated to school, she was then able to influence our level of discourse so that she could fully participate.

As Jiana continued to take a greater role in storytelling occasions, the teacher/research notes that some of the white boys expressed discomfort with the different story styles of classmates, and several said, "this doesn't make

Transcript 5.9

Jiana:	When I went to Mars um, Karen and Karen K . um, they had little pieces of hair sticking up . (*laughter*) and um, and Karen uh, Karen (*whispers to me, pointing to the rosebud necklace I am wearing, "what are those?" I answer "roses . . . rosebuds, rosebuds"*) and when Karen had the rosebuds on she had her little kid with her . . .
Others:	She doesn't have one!
Jiana:	And it was Robin
Others:	Ahhhhhh
Jiana:	and um, . . . No! And his boy, her boy was Robin's boyfriend was um, uh, let's see. I'm not gonna pick Andy because he doesn't like it. Awww. Oh no . . . Manon. No, Bridget? No, wait, who?
Others:	You! Manon!
Jiana:	Manon. So when Manon went out with Karen, 'cause that's her mother, and, Manon's my sister. . . . Me and Manon went out and saw Andy. Manon said (*speaking in a high voice*) "Andy, um, um, will you come over to my house to have dinner?" I said (*in her own voice*) "um, ssshhh, ask him if he wants to go out to the restaurant!" And so she said, "Oh, um, um" (*high voice again*)
Others:	Eeewwww. Yuck!
Jiana:	Can we go to the restaurant? Can we go out to the restaurant? And he said (*loudly*), "NO!" And so she said, "I never can get a boyfriend." And so she asked Joel. (*loud laughter*)
Joel:	No!
Jiana:	And so Joel said, "Yesss."
Joel:	No, No!
Jiana:	Joel, Joel said, "NO!" So she asked William.
Others:	Oooohhhh!
William:	And I said, "No."
Jiana:	And he said, "No."

Source: Gallas, K. (1994). *The languages of learning: How children talk, write, dance, draw, and sing their understanding of the world.* Copyright ©Teachers College Press. Reprinted with permission.

any sense." Gallas also recorded in field notes how some boys turned their bodies away from Jiana as she spoke. In response, as she initiated storytelling performances, Jiana began to check with the boys, asking, for example, "Donald, do you want to be in it?" At first they refused, but slowly the boys relaxed as the group uproar gained momentum. After several weeks, they, too, were encouraging Jiana to tell fake stories and allowing her to use their names. Jiana was changing the rules of storytelling. She was using language "in a way that was difficult for these very articulate and privileged boys to understand." A new genre of narrative performance was being born—collaborative and inclusive—and even the boys couldn't resist participation.

Gallas relates that the genre of inclusive storytelling developed in complexity over the rest of the school year. Many children imitated the style and made it their own, some using call-and-response sequences. Children drew on aspects of the immediate context to construct their stories, for example, what other children were wearing; they created naturalistic dialogue between characters and gesture to elaborate a story and manage the audience. Several adapted Jiana's model of inclusive stories to insert themselves into friendships they wished they had. As the dialogic approach encourages, Gallas's interpretive voice is interspersed with presentation of the children's narratives:

> Duncan, for example, who had been ignored by the boys' circle for the entire year and did not appear to know how to initiate friendships, began to develop stories in which he and the boys spent time together. He was able to get their attention and support by semantically placing himself within their group and by developing the characters in his stories around each boy's particular interests.

By June, the boys had begun to include Duncan in their play and seemed to view him as a friend. Jiana's storytelling style had enabled children to find new ways of being together; a group identity was being forged. There was resistance, especially among several boys with a high level of mastery over the authoritative discourse style of mainstream parents—these boys had to be forced to narrate in a fantasy format. Gallas describes the struggles of one white, middle-class boy, and how his demeanor changed when he finally succeeded in holding the floor in front of a tittering audience with a story of aliens. An African American boy also found a style as he began sharing regularly, breaking the mold other boys had set of excluding girls. Toward the end of the school year, children pleaded with Gallas to continue storytelling during an activity time later in the day. The teacher/researcher concludes, "Something important had happened. The power of the stories, and the community of listeners that the stories had created, had become part of the fabric" of the classroom.

Gallas's work can be read in a number of ways. For my purposes in the chapter, I have read it in terms of identity performances, at both individual and group levels. We see how a child's identity changes over time in a classroom (rare in research). I have also suggested that a group identity is forged during the dialogic performances. Readers located in the field of education might interpret Gallas's work in relation to prior scholarship on differential access to literacy—how some children's modes of storytelling have been silenced in schools and how a teacher's commitment to many languages of learning can restore balance. The social justice implications of the work will resonate with many readers, recognizing that the inclusionary, sociocentric stories that Jiana introduced became a vehicle for working out divisions between boys and girls in dramatic play, enabling the group to build a more egalitarian community in first grade. Group performances enabled children to speak about belonging and exclusion, and to build a classroom culture that accommodated diversity. The practice of the investigator was also changed as children's fascination with "fake" stories stimulated Gallas to interrogate imagination in her subsequent research and teaching.[61]

To summarize key methodological points from the exemplar, the teacher/researcher worked like an ethnographer, carefully recording in field notes and tape recordings group interactions over time. As other practitioner/researchers could do, she made data collection a routine part of her practice, never hiding it from the children:

> I make it clear to my students that I am documenting *our* work. They become familiar with the tools I use and often assist me in using them. They expect the tape recorder to be on when we have discussions, and they often listen to and comment on the tapes. They expect me to have my notebook out when we are working on projects.[62]

As children ask the investigator about her note taking, "[t]heir questions enable me to be more explicit about the kinds of things I want to understand, and I share my questions with them,"[63] encouraging dialogue. Over the course of a school year, she collects vast amounts of information—artifacts that help her "reflect on the classroom and to answer my more difficult questions about teaching, learning, and the process of education."[64] As a general rule, she does not decide beforehand which categories of information are relevant, nor does she predetermine the questions she will ask of her data—a stance in narrative inquiry that should be familiar to readers from earlier chapters (and exemplars).

To return to my core questions about method, Gallas's conception of narrative is broad and collective, or "a complex of signs and texts" that render children's thinking and learning visible as they eagerly engage with one another.[65] Broader than the definitions in other exemplars, stories are viewed as evolving dialogues—brief fragments from one speaker get elaborated and expanded in group performances. These, in turn, are nested in Gallas's experiential narrative, composed from field notes. Second, looking at the investigator's representational decisions and attention to form, Gallas carefully transcribed selected segments of the children's classroom speech, adapting structural methods; the transcripts of the audiotaped conversations include "messy" features. Because pauses and other detailed features of conversation were important in marking change in Jiana's stories over time, Gallas timed pauses and indicated overlapping speech, interruptions, and break offs. Interruptions by audience members were also included in the written transcripts because they gave cues about what members—the community of listeners—needed and wanted. In dialogic/performance analysis, detail about the local conversational context is essential to interpretation. Larger politics of gender, class, and race also entered Gallas's research through their enactment in the classroom situations (e.g., boys excluding girls in their performances).

As other exemplars in the chapter suggest, readers are invited to become interpreters. When I presented Gallas's work at a seminar in the United Kingdom, several teachers and school administrators took issue with her decision to let Jiana's story about drugs continue. In the settings where they work, several imagined irate middle-class parents storming into their offices when they heard from their children that drug use had been discussed in sharing time. These seminar students added their voices to the dialogue the ethnographer had initiated. For these readers, the idea of constructing a research project that is multivoiced in their heavily regulated school environments was hard to imagine.

In a different way than the Brown exemplar did, Gallas drew on Bakhtin's concept of appropriation. Children helped Jiana appropriate forms of discourse, asking her questions that enabled her to expand her brief and fragmentary stories and, over the school year, develop "narrative competence," as it is called in education. More important, Jiana's storytelling practices changed other children, expanding their discourse repertoires beyond dominant forms. Appropriating aspects of her speech aided the language development of other children.[66] Appropriation suggests reciprocity, unlike other words that indicate unidirectional movement and passivity (e.g., the children "internalized" or "learned").[67] Identities were formed and transformed in group performance.

Conclusion

What I have named a dialogic/performance approach draws on components of thematic and structural analysis, but folds them into broad interpretive research inquiries. Attention expands from detailed attention to a narrator's speech—what is said and/or how it is said—to the dialogic environment in all its complexity. Historical and cultural context, audiences for the narrative, and shifts in the interpreter's positioning over time are brought into interpretation. Language—the particular words and styles narrators select to recount experiences—is interrogated, not taken at face value. The candidate exemplars, in very different ways, illustrate the profound importance of context in the construction and performance of narrative. They illustrate how the approach can be useful for ethnographic data, single interviews, and group conversations in settings such as classrooms.

I selected the candidate exemplars because they share a general thematic interest—the construction and performance of identities—which is central to narrative inquiry. They all treat identities as dynamically constituted in relationships and performed with/for audiences. Methodologically, too, they have some features in common. The research relationship is an unfolding dialogue that includes the voice of the investigator who speculates openly about the meaning of a participant's utterance. Readers see her subjectivity and awareness of social positioning at work. In other words, the investigator adopts an active voice (although she is never the only voice). More in the direction of first person research than is typical in thematic and structural traditions, the investigator joins a chorus of contrapuntal voices, which the reader can also join. To put it differently, intersubjectivity and reflexivity come to the fore as there is a dialogue between researcher and researched, text and reader, knower and known. The research report becomes "a story" with readers the audience, shaping meaning by their interpretations.

The three written reports (two were published as book length manuscripts) represent a departure from customary, distanced forms of social science writing. Such experimental forms challenge dominant modes of presentation (and may be difficult for graduate students to adopt in traditional social science departments) because investigators did not segregate the "methods" of an investigation from "findings" and "discussion" of them. Instead, compositional styles were purposefully self-conscious and subjective. In the Gallas exemplar, for instance, the practitioner/researcher's story about dilemmas in her teaching practice is embedded in a text that analyzes children's speech. The nested form of writing is unconventional, embodying Bakhtin's theory of the plurivocal text. Experimental writing in the human sciences can also make room for different ways of reading. We can enter a text and respond, adding perspectives. Readers actually see representations of the different voices on a page and can interrogate them, questioning (perhaps) the meaning and timing of a conversational exchange, or decisions made. Textual openness makes it especially important for investigators to be explicit about their ways of working methodologically, that is, how they came to particular interpretations (and not others) from features in the narrative text and context.

Summary Table 5.1		Dialogic Analysis of Narrative		
Author of Exemplar	*Definition of Narrative*	*How Represented; Attention to Form and Language*	*Unit of Analysis; Focus*	*Attention to Contexts*
Riessman (2004b)	Bounded, temporally ordered segment from a single research interview	Unedited segment of an interview; attention to formal features of a performance narrative	The narrator; his personal narrative as it intersects with history, the economy, and gender	Local: extensive Societal: considerable
Brown (1998)	Not explicitly defined, implicitly a sequenced exchange among girls about classroom incidents	Edited; minimal attention to form, considerable focus on language	Episodes of conflict in schools; expression of anger by girls	Local: some Societal: considerable
Gallas (1994)	Expansive: a complex system of signs and texts (Bakhtin); children's discourse during show-and-tell meetings	Unedited, language with pauses, interruptions, nonlexical utterances; investigator's observations in field notes	Child/group's narrative productions over time	Local: extensive Societal: limited

It was especially difficult to summarize the three exemplars on key methods issues in a summary table, but it may serve a heuristic purpose for students. Variability is the rule, for future investigators will not find a similar toolkit of research practices, but instead a range of perspectives adapted for different research aims. Even the meaning of "narrative" varies from exemplar to exemplar, albeit within certain bounds. Riessman adopts a narrow definition from the structural tradition (see Chapter 4), moving from that kind of analysis to inquire about her entanglement with the text. Brown, working in a school setting, employs a commonly accepted (but implicit) definition of group narrative—lively dialogic reenactments in which students take on performative roles. Regarding representations of speech, there is also considerable variation, in large part because of the different objectives of the studies. Speech was transcribed (edited in some cases) to include all participants, even the investigator.

Narrative style and language are examined by all three, but for different purposes. Gallas attends closely to the shifting narrative genres children selected over the course of a school year. Brown interrogates particular misogynist words girls used, speculating about their meanings in lives stripped of other sources of power. Riessman asks what it means when the interview participant chose at a key juncture to perform his last day on the job. What did the performance narrative accomplish for the man in a conversation with the woman interviewer? The voice of the investigator and aspects of her auto/biographical subjectivity are present in all candidate exemplars. Taken together, they illustrate a general principle of the dialogic/performance approach—investigators carry their identities with them like tortoise shells into the research setting, reflexively interrogating their influences on the production and interpretation of narrative data.

Finally and related, local (micro) contexts of the interview and/or ethnographic encounter are part and parcel of analysis in all the exemplars. Unlike the approaches described in previous chapters, meaning in the dialogic approach does not reside in a speaker's narrative, but in the dialogue between speaker and listener(s), investigator and transcript, and text and reader. Attention to broader contexts, beyond the interview or ethnographic situation, is a great strength of the dialogic approach. Exemplars vividly illustrate what attention to history and politics can add to interpretation of lives. For Burt, this was seen in the taken-for-granted segregation of the physically disabled in the early 1980s in the United States; or, for white adolescent working-class girls in rural Maine, the momentary power misogynist rap lyrics provided. In Gallas's interpretive work, the voices of history and politics were less evident (perhaps because she is writing for a practitioner audience), but readers could bring the legacy of slavery and persistent racial and class inequality to readings of the classroom exchanges. In a real sense, Brown and Gallas worked in research contexts that were small-scale versions of larger sociocultural environments. In sum, the chapter showcases a diverse set of exemplars that draw on features of thematic and structural methods, and the investigators might have made even greater use of these building blocks of narrative inquiry.

Up to now, the book has examined analytic approaches to narrative discourse, spoken and written. The next chapter examines research in the human sciences that works back and forth between images and words in a broad area I am calling visual narrative analysis.

6

Visual Analysis

N arrative research has relied on spoken and written discourse—interview transcripts, ethnographic observations in field notes, letters, documents, and other language-based materials. Words, however, are only one form of communication; other forms (gesture, body movement, sound, images) precede words in human development and continue to communicate meaning through the life course. On another level are aesthetic representations made by artists who communicate with images. How are social scientists incorporating images into narrative research? How are rapid developments in visual technology shaping narrative inquiry?

This chapter illustrates in some detail how five contemporary social scientists are integrating words and images from different visual genres (photography, painting, collage, and video diary). Interpretation in the candidate exemplars spans the continuum from "found" images to "made" ones, interrogating archival photographs and paintings in museum collections, on the one hand, and collages and video diaries that research subjects make with (and for) the researcher, on the other. Several investigators tell a story *with* images, others tell a story *about* images that themselves tell a story. Similar to previous chapters, I concentrate primarily on how the scholars did their work and do not interpret the images. But I do provide some detail on how each investigator interpreted particular images because the strategies provide models for future investigators. All the exemplars draw on thematic and dialogic/performance methods (described in previous chapters), applying them here to images that are interpreted alongside spoken and written text. The result is visual narrative inquiry that, like dialogic/performance analysis, spans a broad spectrum.

Visual representations of experience—in photographs, performance art, and other media—can enable others to see as a participant sees, and to feel. Alan Radley calls for greater use of images in research on illness, explaining how "pictures not only restore feeling but also the capacity to feel . . . [transforming] what was previously a private experience of the patient to being a shared comprehension of illness."[1] Photovoice projects (a primary method of visual inquiry in the social sciences) encourage readers "to understand the world as defined by the subject."[2] Students and their advisers are appropriately cautious, often asking how to interrogate images without background in the visual arts, media studies, or art criticism. The chapter provides guidance, and I refer readers in detailed endnotes to key resources on working with images in human science investigations.[3] As context for the exemplars, I provide some history and several caveats.

The Visual in Narrative Research

Although there has been a "visual turn" in social research, the use of images is hardly new. Visual technologies have long provided ways to collect social science data, with a history in sociology and anthropology before postmodern perspectives entered the disciplines. Gregory Bateson and Margaret Mead were some of the early pioneers in this area, documenting non-Western cultures with photography. Images of "natives" advanced anthropology as a discipline, although the activity was later criticized for exoticising the Other—part and parcel of the oppressive colonial project. Reform-oriented sociologists in the early twentieth century also used photographs, in this instance to document gross inequalities, including child labor in the cotton mills, rural and urban poverty in the United States and United Kingdom, and the demise of the family farm in the southern United States.[4] These early applications were generally based on realist epistemologies; images were not integrated into interpretation, instead they illustrated (providing evidence of something seen), a strategy that continues in documentary studies today.[5]

With the "narrative turn," investigators are moving beyond realism and illustration as images become "texts" to be read interpretively (as written transcripts are). Attention is shifting to how and why the images were produced, and are read by different audiences. In some applications (several are included as exemplars in the chapter), images are made *with* participants, not *of* them. Photo voice, in particular, goes beyond documentary photography by giving the means of production (a camera) to those "who might otherwise not have access to such a tool, so that they may record and catalyze change in their communities, rather than stand as passive subjects of other people's intentions and images."[6] New visual technologies, accompanied by the postmodern critique of documentary photography, wrests control of the camera and the images it produces from the monopoly of experts. New questions develop, requiring different methods of inquiry—a "collaboration between the subject and the photographer."[7]

Contemporary narrative scholars are now integrating photography and, more recently, video technologies into data gathering, and the power of the camera is turned over to research participants to record the images they choose, and to story their meanings collaboratively with investigators. In a particularly compelling photo voice project, Gretchen Berland (a physician/film-maker) developed a film (*Rolling*) of the lived experience of three individuals with severe physical disabilities who navigate barriers of access in the United States, and who hold cameras in their wheelchairs.[8] The film opens with a question from one participant who asks whether it is "possible for me to show you the world through my eyes, for you to see what I see?" From the perspective of these three individuals, experiences of disability become "seeable" in ways that go way beyond the "sayable."[9] Such applications disrupt the investigator's control and authority over the meanings of images.

Unlike filmmakers, social science investigators must write about images. Some say images "speak for themselves" and they "capture" something hidden from view, and therefore do not need commentary. Although a few artists continue to take this naïve realist position, it is indefensible for most of us. We have to make arguments in words about images, that is, contextualize and interpret them in light of theoretical questions in our respective fields. The camera does not simply record what is "out there" in the world (nor does a tape recorder in an interview—the message of Chapter 2). While it is certainly true that real objects reflect light rays that enter a camera's lens, eventually producing an image on film or paper, the photographer has enormous interpretive control (as the investigator working with interview material does) over selecting the image (or interview segment), its production (as in interviewing and transcription), and consequent message. Becker notes some of the interpretive decisions hidden in a photograph, made before the viewer encounters it:

> The choice of film, development and paper, of lens and camera, of exposure and framing, of moment and relation with subjects—all of these, directly under the photographer's control, shape the end product.[10]

(With the computer and digitizing, of course, the process of making photographs has become much more complicated.)

Like spoken narratives, images contain theories based upon the image-makers' understanding about what they are looking at.[11] Social scientists can ask how and why the image-maker composed a particular shot. What might have been the intended meaning at the time of production? What are other readings of the image? Is it connected to other texts? In most cases, image-makers provide some commentary (minimally, in captions that name and date a painting or photograph, sometimes in more extensive reflections). Exemplars below illustrate the ways social science investigators can interrogate "found" images (e.g., photographs in archives) and others "made" in the research situation, alongside the image-makers' (and scholars') words about them. Learning from Becker's classic essay, investigators need to get beyond ordinary ways of viewing, and help readers to do so:

> Laymen learn to read photographs the way they do headlines, skipping over them quickly to get the gist. . . . Photographers, on the other hand, study them with the care and attention to detail one might give to a difficult scientific paper or a complicated poem. Every part of the photographic image carries some information that contributes to its total statement; the viewer's responsibility is to *see*, in the most literal way, everything that is there and respond to it. To put it another way, the statement the image makes—not just what it shows you, but the mood, moral evaluation, and causal connections it suggests—is built up from those details.[12]

As in word-based methods, reading an image closely and responding to *details* is essential to visual narrative analysis.

Gillian Rose identifies three sites for visual analysis that I am adapting here in a preliminary effort to construct a set of methods for visual narrative projects: the story of the production of an image, the image itself, and how it is read by different audiences. The first interrogates how and when the image was made, social identities of image-maker and recipient, and other relevant aspects of the image-making process. The second interrogates the image, asking about the story it may suggest, what it includes, how component parts are arranged, and use of color and technologies relevant to the genre (e.g., a photograph, painting, or film). The third focus is the "audiencing" process—responses of the initial viewers, subsequent responses, stories viewers may bring to an image, written text that guides viewing (e.g., captions),[13] where the spectator is positioned, and other issues related to reception. Rose provides theoretical arguments for the importance of each site, and identifies specific questions for investigators to ask in each.[14] She treats the sites distinctly for didactic purposes but notes they are interrelated, as they certainly are in many narrative projects—researchers typically interrogate all three sites.

Turning to the exemplars of visual narrative analysis, I selected them to illustrate contemporary work with the three sites and four genres of media: photographs, paintings, video diaries, and collages. Including a range of genres opens up points of contrast, illustrating how archival photographs can "do" things in a narrative inquiry (including documenting) that paintings and collages are not suited for; versions of the same photograph can be interrogated with Becker's advice in mind—were details excluded in subsequent cropping that alters meaning? At the other end of the continuum of visual genres, video diaries "do" things that the narrative analyst can interrogate, such as a research participant's decisions about what objects to include in the moving image, subsequent edits, clips to retain in a final version, and the verbal commentary or voiceover.[15] Although the candidate exemplars differ in genre of image, they all share a thematic interest in identities and subjectivities. To understand identity, each investigator works the interface between visual and textual data, drawing connections between an image and some kind of discourse: a caption, written or spoken commentary, and/or letters of the image-maker that provide contexts for interpreting the image.

I begin with three exemplars that work with "found" images—archival photographs and paintings in museum collections—and then turn to interpretive work with "made" images—collages and video diaries produced by subjects during a research project. Readers should note narrative definitions are broader in this chapter than in previous ones, and sometimes elusive; a narrative can be the story constructed by the investigator from data (which include images), or the storyline suggested in a set of images, and/or narrative fragments from accompanying spoken or written texts. Visual analysis, then, pushes the boundaries of narrative and narrative analysis. Some might question whether several exemplars even belong in the chapter because not all the investigators identify themselves with the narrative tradition. I believe, however, that they all belong because stories can be found in moments of the research process, in some of the images, in reactions viewers bring to the images at different points in time, and sometimes in the implicit goals of a project. Because of the productivity of narrative concepts, narrative analysis keeps overflowing its container.

The first exemplar offers a case in point. The investigator does not draw on narrative concepts, but the work extends with visual data a well-established tradition in history and historiography. Scholars can present a similar sequence of events, but tell entirely different stories.[16]

1. Imaging Japanese America During World War II

Elena Tajima Creef uses archival images and historical documents to construct a story. From photographs, drawings, and historical documents, she constructs a counter-narrative to the established one about the internment of

Japanese Americans. (The internment chapter is part of a larger project on visual representations of Asian Americans, describing how racialized gendered bodies have been imaged and imagined over a half century.) To recover a collective identity and suppressed history, and tell a new story, the investigator draws on government documents, archived interviews, drawings, and the photographs of three established artists who imaged their Japanese American subjects immediately before and during internment.[17] There are missing pieces, for no images remain in archives that display the harshness of the camps, the crowded conditions there, or protests of the internees. Like all narratives, Creef's is partial and incomplete, limited in its visual history by the pictorial record preserved. She fills in some gaps in the story by drawing on textual sources that describe the agency and political resistance of Japanese Americans, both during internment and in the postwar years as a reparations movement grew. Substantively, the counter-narrative she constructs breaks the collective silence surrounding shameful events in U.S. history.

Analytically, the exemplar illustrates how working the interface of the visual and the textual—back and forth between archival photographs, drawings, interviews, and other documents—can bring into view a collective identity. In terms of sites of inquiry, the investigator examines conditions in which particular images were produced, and she interprets selected images to restory the history and collective experience of Japanese Americans. Some differences in "audiencing" are suggested (e.g., what the images mean to photographic subjects fifty years later). I limit discussion here to how she uses photographs to tell an untold story.

As background, the internment of Japanese Americans involved mass relocation of nearly 120,000, the large majority were U.S. citizens, including many second and third generation (*nisei* and *sansei*). Exile was authorized several weeks after the bombing of Pearl Harbor in 1941 when President Franklin D. Roosevelt signed Executive Order 9066; families with Japanese ancestry were uprooted from their homes and businesses along the West Coast and isolated in crowded internment camps behind concrete walls and barbed wire in eastern California, the Utah desert, Arizona, Wyoming, Arkansas, and other remote locations.[18] The events offer a reminder of the power of racist hysteria, as happened following September 11, 2001. Creef includes text from a report in 1943 to the Secretary of War by a Commanding General:

> The Japanese race is an enemy race and while many second and third generation Japanese born on United States soil, possessed of United States citizenship, have become "Americanized" the racial strains are undiluted.[19]

In the climate of "virulent wartime racism," Creef argues, "the Japanese American body and its blood became sites/sights of difference, disloyalty, danger, and degradation that must be appropriately contained, disciplined, and punished for the duration of the war."[20]

To counter this national narrative, Creef constructs a visual narrative by sequencing the images of three photographers. She interprets the archival images to make claims about historical events, drawing on the contrasting perspectives of each photographer ("implicit theory," as Becker puts it). Each artist challenged, from a different standpoint, prevailing sentiments in the United States during the war. Creef reproduces selected photographs from the corpus of each, which she interprets alongside writings by the artist and archived interviews with the subjects of portraits and relatives years later. In terms of Rose's analytic framework (cited above), focus is on context of production of the images, the images themselves, with some attention to "audiencing" over time.

Ansel Adams came to Manzanar as a civilian photographer in 1943, later writing about the eighteen months he spent at the internment camp in the California desert. He was given enormous freedom, but with three significant restrictions—he could not photograph barbed wire, the armed guards, or the guard towers. In 1944, Adams produced an exhibit of photographs and a published text, *Born Free and Equal,* that had a clear antiracist message. Creef systematically examines these images, finding that nearly one quarter are schoolgirls, who were photographed in strong outdoor light that suggests nothing to hide (see Images 6.1–6.3). Adams's captions "frame the schoolgirls as good and innocent young citizens of the nation";[21] they are educable, cooperative, and enthusiastic in an imagined postwar nation. The images disturb the national narrative about national security and substitute another: "so many visually harmless and recognizable American children in the camps."[22] The analyst attends to details in the photographs:

[T]he eye is drawn to an American style of feminine clothing and adornment, where Peter Pan collars peek out of cardigan sweaters and pinafores, hair is arranged in pig tails or Shirley Temple ringlets held together with bobby pins, barrettes, or ribbons, and faces are marked by smiles, freckles, and childhood innocence. Adams's careful selection recoups the girls from a visual Orientalist rhetoric of yellow menace, treachery, enemy, alien, and inscrutable Otherness.[23]

The girls cannot be imagined as militarized subjects but instead suggest loyalty, and the potential for motherhood (and intermarriage in multicultural America, a theme Creef develops later in her study).

Ansel Adams believed Japanese Americans were unjustly incarcerated—the implicit theory that guided his photographic choices. But he failed, Creef

Images 6.1, 6.2, & 6.3
Source: Courtesy of Library of Congress.

argues, to confront the issue of collective discrimination, explaining, "The disturbing subtext of *Born Free and Equal* is the erasure of memory of the physical, constitutional, and psychological violence of the internment experience."[24] Viewers see upbeat "good cheer"—Japanese Americans transformed into "loyal, unambiguously American citizens who, through loss of memory, offer an automatic forgiveness of the very people who sanctioned the violence of their forced removal, relocation, and internment in the first place."[25] Creef interrogates conditions of production, revealing that the images were constructed "for the wartime gaze of a suspicious white American audience that was unused to non-racist or non-stereotypical representations of the Japanese Other."[26] For wartime audiences, Adams made a strategic decision to "de-Orientalize" his subjects. (Reading the images now, they can be seen as precursors to the "model minority" discourse.)

To fill in gaps in the story she is constructing, Creef draws on images created by two other photographers. Dorothy Lange shifts the camera's gaze to the preinternment process. She went to work in 1942 for the War Relocation Authority (WRA); one assignment was to document the evacuation in northern California. Lange visited an elementary school in San Francisco and composed photographs that have become iconic—juxtaposing the American flag and several Japanese American schoolchildren. Creef interrogates one particular photograph from the series (see Image 6.4) that depicts two Japanese American schoolgirls engaged in the daily ritual around the flag; she draws attention to small details in the image, and to subsequent events. It shows two young girls, dressed in coats, holding their right hands across their hearts as the left hand holds their brown paper bag lunch sacks.[27] "The smile of the girl on the right bears no trace of anxiety on the eve of evacuation, no intimation of the tragic consequences that uprooting will bring to her life."[28]

With material from archives, Creef further contextualizes the image. Mary Ann Yahiro, the smiling seven-year-old child on the right, was interviewed fifty years later and relates she was separated from her mother (who was sent to a different camp); she never saw her mother again (she died a year after internment). Note how Creef works back and forth between the visual and the written to recover a suppressed history, and to uncover the incomplete story suggested in the image, for it fails to show the immeasurable damage done to Japanese Americans in the name of national security. Other Lange photographs depict anxious mothers with babies, and elderly *issei* (first generation) women with heavy lines on worried faces—signs missing from Ansel Adams's heroic portraits, and from the national narrative.

Image 6.4

Source: Copyright © Dorothea Lange collection, The Oakland Museum of California, city of Oakland. Gift of Paul S. Taylor.

Creef interrogates written and visual sources to map an uncharted theme in internment history—the impact on Japanese American masculine identity—using several Dorothy Lange photographs, the artist's notes about them, and archived interview data.[29] One she closely examines (see Image 6.5) represents an elder *issei* grandfather and his two young grandsons awaiting an evacuation bus. Analysis focuses on the man's position in the image, and compares audience reactions:

All three figures are tagged and ready for relocation; yet the grandfather sits tall and stiff-lipped as he leans upon his cane and returns the camera's gaze with a solid one of his own. While this photograph is usually read for its show of dignity and strength in the body of Sakutaro Aso, the elder issei grandfather, fifty years later it signifies differently to Jerry Aso, who is one of the grandsons in the photograph. In a 1992 interview, the younger Aso asserted: "When people look at grandfather's face, they see a lot of dignity. . . . I see a lot of other feelings . . . pain."[30]

Exploring the interview further, Creef discovers the silence internment left with the Aso family. They did not openly discuss the camps even after the redress checks arrived by mail some forty years later (such silence is common in Japanese American families). When asked about the lasting impact his childhood experience in the camps had on him, Jerry Aso replied, "A lot of shame, a lot of shame. . . . Even if you're innocent, you're still tainted."[31] Note how the investigator is filling in a storyline here—internment had devastating effects on families long after the war ended—by analytically working back and forth between an image and a written text.

Creef's visual story is missing the internment camp experience, a gap she fills with the photographs of an insider—Toyo Miyatake, a Japanese American who was interned at Manzanar, and became an "underground chronicler of life there."[32] A professional photographer from Los Angeles before evacuation, he

Image 6.5

Source: Courtesy of The Bancroft Library. University of California, Berkeley.

smuggled equipment into the camp when such devices were prohibited in the hands of Japanese Americans. Using scraps of lumber, he fashioned an under-cover camera that looked like a lunch box. After several months of surreptitious photography, he was caught by camp authorities but the sympathetic camp director allowed him to continue his visual history, provided a white camp worker tripped the shutter—a chilling but vital context of production. Strict military regulations were lifted eventually and Miyatake was able to send for his professional equipment from Los Angeles. Until the camp was closed in November 1945, Miyatake was able to compose a visual record that depicted daily life: sports and recreation teams, victory gardens, Christmas celebrations, and sending off young male *nisei* to serve in the U.S. military.

Like Ansel Adams, Miyatake created images of smiling schoolgirls—barelegged majorettes in short skirts and white boots, "a hyper-American and gender-specific activity in the midst of what appears to be the frigid conditions of a desert concentration camp in high winter."[33] But, unlike Adams, he provides a visual counterpoint to such images, with, for exaple, a portrait of three boys, behind barbed wire, with a guard tower behind them on the right (see Image 6.6). As with Adams's images, Creef reads Miyatake's photographs for the implicit theory of the image-maker:

> Beautiful in composition, this photograph is one of the very few unposed portraits of young adolescent boys in the camp. Their body language signals their sense of boredom, longing, and certainly confinement behind the camp's security fence. Most significantly, it remains one of the very few photographs of internment that combines the visually taboo images of barbed wire, guard towers, and internee body language that is less resilient than resigned.[34]

Image 6.6

Source: Courtesy of Toyo Miyatake Manzanar War Relocation Center. Source: Archie Miyatake.

Another taboo object is represented in "Watch Tower," which provides guards with a "panoptic gaze" (see Image 6.7). Like the analyst of a written narrative, Creef draws attention to particular features in the image, guiding the sense we make of the total composition:

> The photograph is, initially, visually reminiscent of Adams's scenic Manzanar landscapes of the snow-capped Inyo mountain range in the background, a moon just visible over the low horizon. Yet, a monstrous watch tower looms above the vista like an awkward wooden sculpture—a menacing reminder of the authority of an ever-present military gaze whose gun sights were set on the thousands of internees below its scaffolding. Indeed, this image of the watch tower signifies a pervasive view from above, where armed sentries kept a panoptic vigil on Japanese American activities below from every barbed-wire corner of Manzanar's one-square-mile perimeter.[35]

To conclude, through visual data, the exemplar extends a question often posed by contemporary historians—what events are included (and excluded) in an historical narrative?[36] Narrative here refers to the investigator's story, or the sequence of events that challenge collective silence. Creef does not treat the photographs as narrative (though certain images strongly suggest temporality— a before and after), or the archival texts, which are simply reproduced as

Image 6.7

Source: Courtesy of Toyo Miyatake Manzanar War Relocation Center. Source: Archie Miyatake.

written. Creef's strategy is instead to sequence images (in dialogue with written texts) to tell a story about the devastating effects of evacuation and internment; meaning is complicated by subjects' reflections later, and sometimes by reflections of the artist. A strength of her visual narrative approach is attention to contexts of production: the dominant wartime discourse about the threat of Japanese Americans, the severe constraints on artists permitted into the camps, and the biographical positioning of the three photographers.

The next exemplar also explores the interface of the visual and the written, but regarding an illness experience. Interpretive work with photographs brings another invisible topic into view—breast cancer.

2. Imaging an Illness Experience

Sociologist Susan Bell tells a story of stories, interpreting the auto/biographical narrative of an artist who visually represented her body in photographs that are themselves storied. Bell is a scholar of narrative and women's health, and an activist in the women's health movement. Bringing these biographical streams together, she links Jo Spence's photographs, writing, and activism—the artist's depiction of her body during breast cancer diagnosis and after, and essays about her resistance to medicalized understandings of her body. Bell's way of working with archival photographs contrasts with the previous exemplar because she tell a story about images that are narratively sequenced by a single artist.[37]

As background, Jo Spence was a widely recognized British feminist photographer, educator, and political activist who received attention during the 1970s for provocative critiques of mainstream photographic practice. From the working class, she became a portrait photographer and then moved during second wave feminism to documenting the invisible work of women in home and childcare settings. Drawing on the feminist dictum that the personal is political, she wanted to make private topics public. Her photographs serve to "unmask the everyday, normalized, institutional practices and codes of photography that represent gender, family, and the female body."[38] Also committed to making photographic technology and images accessible to women, Spence coauthored the book *What Can a Woman Do With a Camera?* urging her subjects to wield the power of the camera for themselves to "contest dominant modes of representation by picturing their heretofore unpictured selves."[39] When in 1982, at forty-eight, Spence was diagnosed with breast cancer during a routine medical exam, only pathological images of the disease were available and there was under-narrativisation of the illness experience. She turned the camera on herself and did so until she died ten years later, developing (largely in the absence of an organized breast cancer movement) a photographic politics. She intended the photographs as an ideological challenge to the medical status quo, not just as an outpouring of grief. Years later, the work serves as a resource for activists in the contemporary breast cancer movement that emerged during the decade of the 1980s and 1990s.

Bell chose three images from hundreds in the corpus about living with breast cancer (and leukemia that ultimately killed the artist). The decision to connect the images "in the course of engaging with Spence's work"[40] reflects Bell's theoretical interest. Like analysts working with oral and written narratives, Bell selects data to illuminate a neglected issue in the literature—visual representations of illness experience. The three photographs depict temporally ordered events in the progression of breast cancer and, Bell argues, temporality is also suggested in each image. (Note how the investigator holds on to temporal sequence as a defining feature of narrative here.) She examines contexts of production of each image and what's included in each, drawing on Spence's writing about her photographs, interpretations of Spence's work by art historians, and Bell's own reading of the artist's feminism. Other than captions that guide viewing, there is limited attention to audiencing.

The first photograph Bell examines is captioned "Mammogram" (see Image 6.8). The artist included a textual commentary:

> Passing through the hands of the medical orthodoxy can be terrifying when you have breast cancer. I determined to document for myself what was happening to me. Not to be merely the object of their medical discourse but to be the active subject of my own investigation. Here whilst a mammogram is being done I have persuaded the radiographer to take a picture for me. She was rather unhappy about it, but felt it was preferable to my holding the camera out at arm's length and doing a self portrait.[41]

With this information as context (the artist composed the image, perhaps cropped it after printing, but the radiographer took the picture), Bell draws attention to detail. Jo Spence stands in profile, holding the plates with her hands (standard protocol at the time). The setting is sterile, with bare walls, stripped of marks of individual identity, except in the corner where Spence's crumpled shirt appears:

> The photograph is dominated by the machine and the breast. They are at the center of the photograph and are the central characters in the photographic narrative. . . . Spence looks away from the camera and the machine, her eyes covered by her glasses.[42]

Although she asserted her right to use her camera in a medical setting, Bell questions (as the artist did) "how much control Spence has over her body once it is constructed as the body of a patient,"[43] concluding that medicine

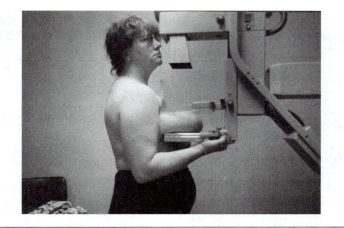

Image 6.8

Source: Courtesy of Terry Dennett. Photographer: Jo Spence.

fragments and objectifies women's bodies. Spence worked to expose the violence of orthodox medicine, using her camera to disrupt a routine medical event; her camera became "a weapon to be symbolically violent back to medicine."[44] She decided how her body would be represented, reworking the moment of the mammogram. As another woman who has experienced a mammogram (but not a lumpectomy or breast cancer), Bell also reads "Mammogram" as a story in progress—what will be the outcome of this one?

To make the second image, "I Framed My Breast for Posterity" (see Image 6.9), Jo Spence worked with her collaborator, lover and now archivist, Terry Dennett; he wrote the caption when the photograph was eventually exhibited, "I frame my breast the night before going into hospital—will the surgeon get his way and 'take it off' or will I get my wish for a 'Lumpectomy'?"[45] Although the doctor preferred to treat her with a mastectomy, she had a lumpectomy (not a common surgical treatment in 1982), winning the confrontation.

The investigator closely attends to components of the image, noting ambiguities:

> This photograph is one of Spence's many attempts to make her suffering visible and to engage audiences in the experience. Taken in her home, it places her experience of breast cancer in her life world. Spence is at the center of the photo. She is naked from the waist up, except for a string of wooden beads. On the underside of her left breast is a bandage [from a biopsy]. She holds a picture frame in front of her left breast. The top of the frame almost covers her mouth; it is not clear whether her mouth is open or shut and whether she is biting the frame or simply resting it against her mouth. Her eyes are shut, covered by glasses. Her hair is disheveled. The beads are marks of gender and the bandage a mark of medicine.[46]

Image 6.9

Source: Courtesy of Terry Dennett. Photographer: Jo Spence.

Note how the investigator reads objects and figures other interpreters might overlook; there is a poster on the left of British mineworkers engaged in collective action that includes a quotation from Karl Marx. There is the gaze of one of the workers—directly at the woman and her breasts. What can it mean? Interpretation draws the eye of the viewer to other details as well— a burning fire in a fireplace, an alarm clock on the mantelpiece, a tin mug, a greeting card, and a colored screen printed with large bright red flowers. The range of objects included, beyond the body, is puzzling. Bell relates them to the illness experience, analyzing what is inside and outside the frame:

> The frame divides Spence's identity before and after the cancer. The frame cuts through her body but it does not cut off her breast, seemingly integrating the selves before and after. . . . The frame sets her breast (and her cancer) off from Spence's previous life. It suggests that there is nothing important outside of this frame, especially on the night before she is about to have surgery for her breast cancer. Yet even inside the frame the beads she is wearing provide a connection to her previous life.[47]

The figures outside the frame are markers of Spence's working-class commitments, connecting the artist's experiences with breast cancer to her politics.

Finally, how to interpret the frame that covers Spence's mouth? It invites "reflection on silence and speech,"[48] Bell suggests, the struggle for the artist to be heard by her surgeon, and to be heard by other women. A later essay of Spence's suggests an impulse about how women could think differently about breast cancer, how they too could refuse to be passive victims of disease, and instead argue with surgeons. Anticipating organized health movements to follow, Spence wanted to create a community of "dissident cancer patients."[49] When the images were first shown, Bell discovers by reading Spence's essays, viewers were silenced, not knowing how to react. The analyst draws on Spence's later writings: "the more silence there was from audiences, the more determined she was to be heard . . . developing different languages to speak to different audiences in the world of art, photography, and health."[50] The initial reception of the images contrasts with later viewings that included women living with breast cancer, who spoke of relief at the chance to talk about the disease, including downsides of treatment from chemotherapy that only patients would know.[51]

Titles of photographs (captions) strongly shape viewers' reactions; those who work with visual materials must attend to these written texts, and learn who composed them and when. Spence captioned "I Framed My Breast for Posterity" after she knew she had not lost her breast. Bell uses the information to theorize about the illness narrative: "The title of the photograph begins a story . . . the use of the past tense positions Spence and the audience in the present, looking back at a sequence of events whose outcome was known at the time she titled the image."[52] The use of "posterity" raises other possibilities.

The third photograph in Bell's story of stories was made many years later; words do not signify the artist's intent (see "Untitled," Image 6.10). Spence had lived for ten years after the diagnosis, never agreeing to a mastectomy and defying medical orthodoxy by following traditional Chinese medicine. She worked on her art and essays, but by 1992 she could no longer work and was admitted to a hospice, where she died. Terry Dennett is credited with the photograph of Spence in her bed; a version appears on the final page of her posthumously published book, *Cultural Sniping*, with the words, "Jo Spence on a 'good day' shortly before her death, photographing visitors to her room at Marie Curie Hospice, Hampstead [UK]."[53] Working back and forth between the image and the artist's essays, Bell notes the shift in the artist's aggressive stance toward orthodox medicine. Spence wrote "that choosing to go like an Amazon into the lions' den over and over again in order to be politically useful is just too energy-consuming and too conflictual."[54]

Bell's interpretive work with "Untitled" is paradigmatic for a visual sociology of illness experience. She compares the image with those made ten years earlier:

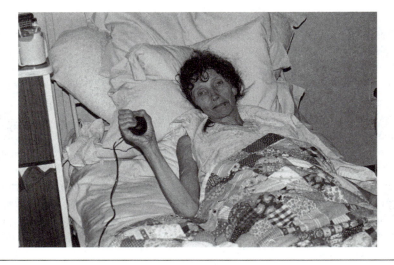

Image 6.10

Source: Courtesy of Terry Dennett. Photographer: Jo Spence.

This photograph feels more mutually nurturing than the other two ["I Framed My Breast" . . . , and "Mammogram"]. Perhaps this quality is conveyed by Spence's uncovered (unframed) eyes and her covered breasts, or by her faint smile. Perhaps it is Spence's face [and, I would add, her small frame], so gaunt in comparison to the face in the other two photographs, that makes her seem vulnerable instead of confrontational; or the implication of friends just outside of the frame instead of comrades or medical personnel. And perhaps the knowledge conveyed by the text accompanying it—that she is in a hospice and that therefore her death is imminent, and indeed that she died shortly afterwards—evokes compassion and nurturance in the audience.[55]

In "Untitled," Spence's life world has shifted:

From the quilt that covers her [and the breast] to the pillows piled on one another, to the cord attached not to the ubiquitous call button in a hospital but to the camera, this photograph decenters medicine. Still, the intravenous line and the stark background displaying the institutional character of the hospice in which she lies, make it impossible to efface medicine entirely.[56]

Note how Bell draws attention to and interprets the several cords in the image:

There are two significant cords—or lifelines—in this picture. The camera bulb, or life world lifeline, connects Spence to photography and friends. Spence is holding on to this cord, her fist clenched around it. This cord marks some of her different identities. She is a photographer about to snap a photograph of her friends. She is a collaborator on this photograph, as she has regularly been since the mid-1970s, with Terry Dennett. . . . The IV [barely visible], or medical lifeline, connects Spence to fluids, nutrients, or medicines to maintain life in her body. It marks her as a patient.[57]

The photograph vivifies a tension others have theorized in oral narratives of the illness experience, namely a conflict between the "voice of medicine" and the "voice of the lifeworld."[58]

In sum, the exemplar has aspects in common with the previous one (which also drew on archived photographs), and key differences. Bell's unit of analysis here is the individual artist and her illness experience.[59] Contexts of production of specific images (and captions) are examined; the self-portraits required collaboration, as did the photographs of Miyatake in the first exemplar, adding complexity (although neither investigator explores what collaboration might mean for a particular photograph). Bell notes ambiguities—what particular objects in the photographs may signify in the artist's feminist politics. Each photograph is treated as narrative, and the sequence forms a visual narrative of illness. The level of analytic attention to how a photograph was composed and what objects it contains mirrors exemplars in Chapter 4 that worked off spoken texts. Creef, by contrast, constructs a story from photographs composed by different artists that, taken together, bring a collective story into view. Her focus (and hence the unit of analysis) is the representation of Japanese Americans during World War II. The analyst constructs a story of the suppressed history of the group from images and texts. As in every research project, the purpose of each study shapes the ways of working with photographs and narrative concepts.

The investigator in the third exemplar also works with "found" images, but the visual genre is very different. An artist's paintings and drawings (held in public and private collections) constitute the visual data; the artist's letters and biographies about the artist are the written data.

3. Writing the Self/Painting the Self

Sociologist Maria Tamboukou tells a story of the "self" of an artist. An auto/biographical case study, it reconstructs the complex identities of a well-known Welsh painter, Gwen John (1876–1939), who like many young artists, migrated to Paris at the turn of the twentieth century to study. She created a rich collection of drawings and paintings during her life in France where she died, leaving a voluminous correspondence in archives for scholars to interpret. Connections between the letters and paintings serve as a methodological entry point for Tamboukou's inquiry into the complex subjectivity of a woman artist living in a male-dominated art environment. The investigator uses thematic narrative methods with epistolary narratives—letters—interpreted alongside visual data. Analysis concentrates on two sites: the conditions of production of images (gleaned from letters and knowledge of the historical context), and aspects of the images themselves.

Readers met the work of British sociologist Maria Tamboukou in Chapter 3, where she analyzed spatial themes in self-writings of women teachers living in Britain at the turn of the twentieth century. Theoretical interest in "a room of one's own" continues into her current research on women artists, one of whom is Gwen John. The Welsh artist painted interior scenes (modeled from her own room/studio in Paris), and many portraits, during the twenty-five years she lived in France. To support herself financially, she also worked as a model for other artists, including the sculptor Auguste Rodin. Initially serving as a model for his sculptures, Gwen John became Rodin's lover and the relationship continued for over a decade of her life. Adding more significance to her work, Gwen John wrote letters to Rodin that the investigator examined, including those contained in the archive of the Rodin museum in Paris. Many of these letters were written from her room in Paris, where she also wrote to her women artist friends, often referring to details of the room and their many meanings for her "interior life."

Working with letters is difficult (discussed further below); Tamboukou uses them as a point of departure for studying the artist's "passionate attachment to her room."[60] An exemplary letter cited by many scholars includes the statement: "my room is so delicious after a whole day outside, it seems to me that I am not myself except in my room."[61] Biographers have interpreted the statement, imagining the artist a "recluse." Tamboukou saw the entire letter in the archive and was astonished to discover that the statement contained another clause (context omitted by other scholars), "It seems to me that I am not myself except in my room and in my master's studio." The artist added, "My Master is the centre of my Paradise." (The "Master" is Rodin; the term was a common referent for a senior artist/teacher.) The full letter also reports (to "Julie") that the day had been "wasted" modeling for other artists, as it was not spent in the solitude of her room:

> I was posing for the whole day! For Mrs. Smidt in the morning and Miss O'Donnel in the afternoon. I had lunch outside, in a restaurant and it seems to me that I didn't have time to be anything else than a machine for the whole day.[62]

Further inquiry into context revealed that the letter was addressed to Rodin, though the artist used "Julie" as a fictitious female confidante in this and other letters.[63] Based on these discoveries, the investigator poses a research question: Who is the woman, Gwen John? Analysis explores the different "selves" Gwen John is grappling with—model, lover, friend, and artist—and the place of her room in these identities, and in her art. By analyzing letters and paintings together, the investigator can map the multidimensional subjectivity of the artist.

Plate 6.1 reproduces a self-portrait where the artist is contemplative, her mouth slightly open as if to speak, with a letter in her hand. As another commentator notes, "the picture unites Gwen John's speech, her correspondence and her art."[64] Thematically, the self-portrait unites Tamboukou's project, linking the artist's letters and paintings.

Tamboukou examined the artist's interior paintings (not reproduced here but available on museum Web sites[65]), noting contradictions in how she positioned herself in them. In one painting she appears as a spiritual figure, in another as an intellectual woman reading a book by an open window. In another ("The Artist in Her Room in Paris" c. 1907–9):

> [She] assertively presents herself as the artist sitting in her room, perhaps having just returned or maybe ready to go out as her hat is prominently displayed on her bed. Indeed a hat and a parasol are often depicted in her interiors probably as signs of a woman who keeps moving in and out as part of her daily routine.[66]

Note how the visual analyst compares thematic elements across several paintings to theorize about the artist. Yes, there are domestic scenes similar in some ways to ones produced by other artists of the period (Vuillard, Cassatt), but Tamboukou emphasizes that Gwen John reminds us of a woman's life outside domesticity—the hat and parasol indicate a life beyond the confines of walls of rooms. Shattering the image of the artist as "recluse," Tamboukou continues searching other paintings and letters for signs of a complex subjectivity at a time of severe constraints on women's movement (and achievement) in the public sphere.

She turns to the self-portraits; one represents the artist nude on her bed "in an expressive state of erotic anticipation."[67] Examining letters written at the time several of the portraits were made, the analyst learned the artist was boldly experimenting with technique. The nude self-portraits were also done explicitly to show to Rodin. The nude portraits "were expressing her passion for Rodin" but they were also to convince him that she was working seriously on her art—his strong admonition: "I did drawings to show my

Master that I was not lazy today. Drawings of myself in the mirror. It was difficult to draw."[68] Tamboukou argues that Gwen John's "self" includes multiple identities, consisting of "the intellectual woman, the spiritual figure, the domestic woman, the art student that still experiments with her art, the assertive artist, the new woman."[69]

The room/studio contained these many identities; it was configured as an erotic territory, "a space par excellence for her immense passion and love for Rodin to be expressed."[70] Viewing this in historical context, the investigator argues that by writing explicitly about her passion and pleasure, Gwen John "is breaking the taboo of passivity of female sexuality." Excerpts from letters to Rodin are brought to bear: "I am going to sleep. I am going to look at my naked self in the mirror. I believe that my body is more beautiful because of love."[71] The room is theorized as a "transgressive place, a corner in the world beyond the sanctioned spaces of marriage." Gwen John spent a decade of her life waiting for Rodin's occasional visit to her room/studio "and despairing when he would not turn up as expected."[72]

Analyzing spatial themes, Tamboukou found the room was also a place for solitude, a refuge from busy modeling in the studios of other artists in Paris. The investigator located many letters (some addressed to Rodin, others to friends) that included references to her pleasure in (and with) the private space, exemplified in a narrative fragment from a long letter written to a friend in London:

> I have not been posing to-day, so I washed the floor and everything is brilliant in my room, do come and see my room soon—the floor is of red bricks, and there are tiles in the fireplace and two little grates and all the furniture is brand new, light yellow. . . . I've got *an armoire a glace* which is a wardrobe with shelves and a *glace* front, and white lace curtains at the window—yes I am *Parisienne* and I feel more at home with the French than the English now, I think, at least the English over here.[73]

The tranquility of her sun-drenched room is depicted in several paintings and, given that she couldn't afford a separate studio, the Parisian room served as a space for painting. The space also functioned as a social place to receive women artists who flocked to Paris from many countries during the first decade of the twentieth century to study art and to paint. In a letter written to "Julie," Gwen John writes about a strange socialist woman who scheduled a visit to arrange modeling sessions for a Russian artist:

> She was big with grey hair dressed somehow like a socialist I believe . . . the woman . . . began talking about troubles in Russia and about her life, she was a political writer. . . . She admired my room very much and I showed her the

kitchen and the view from the window (which is very beautiful, particularly at night, my Master has not yet seen it in the dark). . . . In the end she left . . . and she also said "I would be very pleased to see you, I would also like to see your soul"! Oh Julie, I don't know what to say on this, neither do I know what she wanted, but it's a way of speaking I believe between socialists, so I promised to go and see her one evening.[74]

The investigator, as she was analyzing letters for references to the functions of the room/studio, uncovers an amusing narrative suggesting (among many things) a sense in 1906 of impending events in Russia. Again, the world outside enters into the interior space.

Turning to methodological lessons, note how the investigator analyzes letters for thematic elements, and then draws connections to thematic components in paintings. She tacks back and forth between visual images and written texts, evolving relevant concepts inductively, as she works through the data. The implicit definition of narrative (not discussed by the investigator) seems to be the auto/biography of Gwen John—the life and complex subjectivity of a woman interpreted through her art and letters. Tamboukou joins a long tradition of feminist scholars who analyze life writings to construct a story of a woman's life.[75] To be sure, there are fragments within some letters that meet narrative criteria, but there are also many letters that do not. The investigator selects relevant bits and pieces from across the corpus to craft a story about the multiple identities and complex subjectivity of the Welsh painter. The images themselves subtly imply narrative sequence (in the self-portrait on Plate 6.1, for example, the viewer is invited to imagine a "before" and "after," and the recipient of the letter—not included in the painting). The interior paintings, too, suggest movement in space over the sequence of a day—a woman has come back to her room from outside, folded up her parasol, and leaned it against a chair along with a frock, throwing her hat on the bed. But Tamboukou does not argue (as Bell does) that the images themselves are stories. Skeptics might ask, can a single image really tell a story? As noted above, visual narrative analysts push the boundaries of narrative definition.

Turning to the letters, students who want to interrogate such documents must bear context in mind at every point. To help us understand this, Liz Stanley has written a definitive paper on working with the epistolary form.[76] She notes how some social scientists are suspicious of letters because "the kind of story told shifts with the person who will read it" and they can contain a great deal of information "that strays from the researcher's concern."[77] (I would note that these are problems common to all forms of narrative data.) Stanley challenges dismissive statements about letters, drawing on the volume of work in history and literature for methodological pointers that investigators in other fields can adapt to their purposes. Letters, she argues (echoing ideas in Chapter 5), are dialogical, perspectival, and emergent in their meanings, which the exemplar vividly illustrates. Note, for example, how Tamboukou attends to forms of address, such as "Master" and "Julie," and different readings of the letters by scholars over time (the artist as recluse compared with the sociologist's passionate reading). Attention to context is a strong element in her work—the intended audience for a letter or painting, and the social milieu of *fin de siècle* Paris for unmarried women artists. (Because of space considerations, my representation of the investigator's work here does not always include the relevant context for each letter and painting; students should consult Tamboukou's papers for a fuller account.)

Finally, some issues arise about presenting language and image. As in the investigator's prior work with spatial themes in letters of women teachers (see Chapter 3), Tamboukou analyzed thematically the writings of her biographical subject, reproducing sections of texts with ellipses to indicate omission of a word or phrase. Some letters (including those to Rodin) were translated from French; Tamboukou provides no indications about translation dilemmas she may have faced[78] (readers may remember the complexity of translation illustrated in Chapter 2). As for the images, presentation of Gwen John's paintings and drawings is relatively uncomplicated. Although I reproduce only one image here, Tamboukou uses several in brilliant color in her papers, situating them strategically in the text to support her evolving discoveries in the letters. Reproductions vary substantially, of course, from "the original"—a familiar issue for all narrative analysts.

In the final two exemplars, I turn to working with "made" images, that is, visual data composed by research participants where the investigator is part of the construction process. Issues of "audiencing" come vividly to the fore. Adolescent girls are image-makers in both projects; they compose visual self-representations. Beyond these similarities many differences arise.

4. Making Art and Making Selves

How do pregnant teens see themselves, and experience the "social problem" of teenage pregnancy in their self-portraits, writings, and group conversations? Using classic ethnographic methods (visual data are only one component), Wendy Luttrell takes readers inside the stigmatizing label of "pregnant teenager," asking, what is it like to live with this label? She explores girls' subjectivities in the transition to motherhood—feelings and sense of agency—in an "activist ethnography."[79] This ethnography showcases teens' visual self-representations in collages, which are interpreted alongside girls' written and spoken texts about their art.[80] The girls (predominantly black and working class[81]) attend a school with a special program in a southern U.S. city designed to keep them in school. The investigator spent several years in the school and "curates" the girls' art, writing, and conversation—a dialogue between self ("Who am I?") and society ("Who do others think I am?").[82] Methodologically, the exemplar models for investigators a way of working collaboratively with individuals as they create visual representations of their experiences. Focus of analysis here is on production of the image, the image itself, and its audiencing.

Luttrell turned to visual and dramatic activities when traditional narrative interviewing approaches fell short. In prior research, she had elicited coherent life stories from a diverse group of working-class students about difficult schooling experiences. Because self-understandings are emergent among adolescents, attempts to interview teens produced only "bits and pieces . . . not unified or linked" stories. To fully engage the girls, the ethnographer began to view her participants as improvisational actors who gave clues about the identity-making process in a variety of ways, stating, "It seemed they enjoyed *performing,* using their bodies and the space around them as if they preferred to 'show' rather than 'tell' about their lives."[83] Luttrell designed a set of activities (for three class periods each week through an academic year—well integrated into the school day and program) that included journal writing (Who Am I?), media collages, improvisational role plays of "pregnancy stories," and (my focus here) self-portraits accompanied by text. Introduction of the activity during one class session ("You artists are going to make self-portraits") evoked gales of laughter; girls were to make a book about themselves that "will include everyone's self-portrait and written description." Students could draw themselves (none chose to) or compose collages from materials on hand.[84] Color Xerox copies of the productions would be bound together and each girl would get her own copy of the book.

What could be learned with a collaborative book project "about the girls' self- and identity-making from their self-portraits and texts . . . and from the lively, and at times intense, conversations that were sparked by a girl's self-representation?"[85] Collecting images and accompanying text from all fifty girls was difficult, since attendance at school was sporadic; "a girl might go through several iterations [of an image] before she discovered what—or settled on how—she wanted to represent herself,"[86] a complex process captured in the recordings and field notes. And, self-portraits could evoke different responses from viewers (schoolmates, teachers, boyfriends, and family members) who attended the "book signing parties" held at the end of the school year.[87]

As each girl completed her piece, the investigator asked the artist to formally present it to her classmates, explaining the meaning she intended to convey; the group then asked questions, and Luttrell asked others to elicit further reflection by the artist and her classmates. She also asked a set of questions specifically about the image:

> [S]ome were "aesthetic" questions about color choices, features of design, and perspective; others were anatomical questions about missing body parts or the varying size of body parts; others were "autobiographical," questions about the people or places depicted in a picture.[88]

All class sessions were tape-recorded and transcribed; some were videotaped.

Note the layered narrative elements in this exemplar, for there is a story in the production of each image, "each one distinct in its making and meaning,"[89] and another story contained in different viewings by audiences, including the investigator's own sense-making over time. Luttrell presents the interpretations of the girls alongside her own; she also encourages readers to interpret the images. Building on features of the dialogic/performance approach (see Chapter 5), the investigator constructs an open plurivocal text. (For students wanting to adapt Luttrell's methods, the book provides considerable detail about her way of working.[90])

Michelle's completed self-portrait is presented in Plate 6.2. In the corpus of fifty images, she was one of only two girls who represented her body in a pregnant state. Michelle was "eight months pregnant, more visibly so than any of the other girls";[91] she attended school less regularly, and typically didn't participate in the joking banter that went on in class. Other girls talked about her, complaining that she "whined" about her problems and was "spoiled" by her mother. The investigator provides some information on the life world of the artist; we learn that Michelle was living with her mother (employed as a clerk by the town) and a younger sister who had a seizure disorder. Although born "up north," her mother returned to the south to raise her daughter and be near extended kin. The student was seen by teachers as "difficult," "a handful," and someone having "lots of personal problems." Michelle was particularly engaged in the journal writing activity in classes Luttrell conducted, often writing about her emotions ("Yesterday I felt as if everyone was on my back and that I couldn't do anything right but today everything is looking up."). She wrote about her goals for independence—a job and moving out of her mother's house—and her worries, such as who would care for her ill sister. She also feared becoming dependent on her boyfriend, who said he wanted to stay involved with her and the baby, but who didn't keep his promises, provoking Michelle to write, "I don't want to get overly dependent on him or anybody."[92]

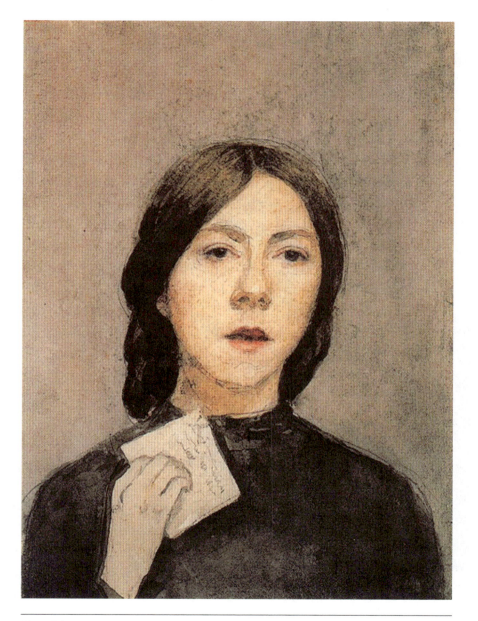

Plate 6.1

Source: Reproduced with permission of Rodin Museum, Paris.

Plate 6.2

Source: : Reproduced with permission of Wendy Luttrell.

Luttrell describes the conditions of production of Michelle's initial self-portrait in dialogue with its audiencing among the girls. To begin, Michelle selected a black piece of paper. A member of the class was critical of the choice ("Why don't you pick a nice color for the background?"). When there was no response, the classmate said, "She's in a dark mood I guess."[93] Michelle then took several days to construct the two pregnant figures facing each other; the early version did not include the hearts, explaining that one figure was her "happy" and the other her "angry" side. After the first image was made, she held it up for the rest of the group, frowned and said, "there's too much emptiness . . . I need something to fill me, I mean this space up." Luttrell writes:

> I noticed her slip and wondered if she did as well. I considered asking her about it, but decided against it. . . . Instead I asked if I could hold up her portrait for her to view from a bit of a distance.
> "What do you see?" I asked.
> "It's too dark, too empty, too much space in between the two figures," replied Michelle. "I'll fix it later."

The following day Michelle returned enthusiastically to class with a written statement to accompany her collage, which she asked Luttrell to read aloud and "correct":

> This is a picture of me. I am seventeen years old and so miserable. All I can do is think of the things I used to do and will do after I have my lovely baby. I only smile when I want to or if somebody makes me laugh. The funny feeling about being pregnant is feeling something move inside you. I'll never hold hatred toward my baby because I know it's my fault and not my baby's. I have more problems on me than usual. But now I have somebody to really love and care for—somebody who's a piece of my heart.

Luttrell speculates about possible meanings of the narrative fragment (including Michelle's conflicted feelings about the baby), and describes the artist's actions to "fix" her self-portrait:

> As I was reading her statement aloud, Michelle stopped me on the phrase "I'll never hold hatred toward my baby because I know it's my fault and not my baby's." At this point in hearing me read her statement, Michelle said, "I know what I need to do," and she picked up pieces of paper and started cutting out hearts that she placed in the empty space.

I draw students' attention to several methodological lessons in this exemplar. First, note how the investigator works back and forth among four kinds of data—visual, written, spoken, and observational. This is an unusually large and diverse data set: self-portraits (and other images not discussed here), journal entries and written commentaries on portraits, transcripts of classroom discussions (some videotaped), and field notes made over several years. Difficult transitions among the kinds of data are managed by Luttrell's skillfully constructed and accessible prose.

Second, the investigator maintains clear focus on the individual girl (the unit of analysis), at the same time as she traverses boundaries across data sets and sites of inquiry (production, image, and audiencing). She examines *how* Michelle produces the image, *what* she creates in several versions, and complex *audiencing* in classroom dialogues that include the ethnographer. Rather than seeing audiencing as a process that begins after an image is produced, Luttrell builds it into her methods, so that the ethnographer becomes one audience, Michelle's classmates another, and the artist herself is transformed into an audience for her own image. Across the different sites, however, attention remains on the teen and what insights the process of image-making generates about identity construction in the transition to motherhood.

Third, when the investigator presents spoken and written data, she cleans up the texts. Remember, Michelle asked Luttrell to "correct" her written composition. In presenting the methods for her ethnography, Luttrell writes about "editorial decisions":

> On occasion I cut repetitive, complicating, or exposing details from the conversations and stories in order to make the material readable (and in some cases to protect anonymity). I also was selective in using the girls' [black Southern] dialect; I deleted certain speech utterances (such as um or ah) and I also (reluctantly) deleted some repetition of words and phrases that were a feature of their performative style of speech because I worried about giving the wrong impression of the girls.[94]

Other ethnographers have made similar decisions, particularly when representing black English, to prevent readers from making negative racial judgments. (Social linguists preserve group-specific features of speech for their different analytic aims.) Because language was not her focus, Luttrell wanted to guard against readers misinterpreting the girls as inarticulate, contributing further to the stigma pregnant teens already encounter.

But it is important to note that Luttrell does pay attention to word choice—my fourth point. In the spoken excerpt (above), Michelle made a slip of the tongue that she quickly corrected. Given the investigator's knowledge of psychoanalytic theory, she viewed the slip as significant, using it to explore possible dynamic meanings—tentatively, because she is not working as a therapist with the girls. Building on plausible interpretations and looking to the image-making process for insight, Luttrell writes:

Michelle was coming into consciousness about her conflicted feelings, that she would "hold hatred toward her baby," and this made her want to change (in her words "fix") how she feels and sees herself. In making her self-portrait, Michelle notices or becomes more self-aware of several things about herself and her life: her feelings of "emptiness" set next to "feeling something move inside you"; her fears of holding hatred toward her baby held alongside deep feelings of love; and her conflicting sense of her own value as both "miserable" and as worth "having somebody to really love and care for."[95]

Finally, the investigator interrogates details in the image, interpreted in the context of the classroom conversation about the self-portrait. Most obviously, there are the hearts—added later to "fix" the empty space; they are symbols of love in popular culture, and here they serve to counter, perhaps, the feelings of hatred Michelle had spoken about earlier. And the missing hands: answering a question about them Michelle said, "I didn't want to mess up my picture by putting on hands; I just couldn't make hands that looked good."[96] Or about the figure representing her "happy side" (classmates said it didn't look that happy): "I tried to make a cut-out smile—you don't think it looks like a smile?" Luttrell interprets these last two features of the portrait as "technical difficulties," downplaying their significance. She adds that a therapist might disagree. (It is not always clear how an investigator decides which details represent technical difficulties, and which are significant.) More important is the color choice for the figures for Michelle had chosen white paper for her body, and she represented herself with "straight" hair (a classmate's word). These two details are significant, and Luttrell suggests that they "could be said to reflect social issues regarding race and representation as well as her own feelings regarding racial identification."[97] Throughout the ethnography, the complexities of racial identity are explored for girls in a society that privileges light skin and "good" hair; readers can bring these contexts to bear as they interpret Michelle's representation of race in her self-portrait.

The artistic representations that Luttrell facilitated are unusual for a sociologist to compile and analyze. Investigators venturing into the visual domain typically use "found" images (as in the previous exemplars), or they initiate photovoice projects.[98] The girls in Luttrell's sample didn't want pictures of themselves, and the administration forbade use of photography in school research. Constructing collaged self-portraits did not generate institutional suspicion. More than photographs do, the genre allows "those who are the subjects of research to change how they see themselves and are seen by others."[99] Given Luttrell's topic, the genre is ideal, she could see how participants "self-consciously identified with, used, assented, or resisted stereotypes about 'the pregnant teenager'" in image and text.[100] The girls' efforts to express multiple truths about their evolving identities could be represented effectively in self-portraits (and conversations about them). Analysis could focus on *what* the girls constructed, *how,* and *ways of seeing* each portrait—the image, context of production, and reception.

In current research, Luttrell is using the genre of photography with low income, ten- to twelve-year-olds, many of whom are immigrant children of color from Asia and Latin America. Since it is unusual in educational research to put cameras in the hands of kids and invite them to photograph their family, school, and community lives, and then interpret the images (individually in interviews and in group discussions), the project is designed to help teachers, and already is producing intercultural dialogue.[101]

The final exemplar also interprets images made by adolescent girls, but with several twists. The genre is the video diary, which allows girls to construct dynamic sequences of images accompanied by a running voiceover. The genre of film has possibilities for representing aspects of identities and subjectivity not possible with fixed images (photographs, paintings, or collage). At the same time, the "authenticity" and purity of the images cannot be taken at face value. The exemplar reveals the imagined audiences girls carry around in their heads, which shape what they film and say about themselves.

5. Imaging in Video Diaries

Maria Pini and Valerie Walkerdine's work (much of it yet unpublished) tells a story of stories—and it recounts a research project gone awry. When they gave camcorders to a group of working- and middle-class girls, the investigators thought their subjects would be free to compose stories of their daily lives and subjectivities. Instead, the social scientists found the gaze of the observer was ever present. I end the chapter with this exemplar because it raises cautions for human science investigators who might want to incorporate visual data made by subjects themselves. Such data require the same degree of analytic scrutiny as spoken narratives do.[102] Giving video cameras to research participants to image what they choose is a relatively new mode of data gathering in the human sciences, but well known to documentary filmmakers. I referred in the chapter introduction to the film *Rolling*—a visual narrative of three disabled individuals given camcorders to record daily life from their perspective—the wheelchair. The film provides a model (and there are others) of an investigator working collaboratively with participants and video technologies to story "invisible" lives.[103] But what does the video diary give scholars in the social sciences? Is the visual product fact or fiction, or some of both? Clearly, it is a performance, crafted with audience in mind, as the final exemplar illuminates. But first, I will provide some background on the investigators and the history of the project.

Maria Pini was based in a critical psychology department at Cardiff University in Wales. Valerie Walkerdine is a senior academic psychologist at the same university who has authored influential studies of gender and class that draw on film and other visual representations. One of her data sets—Project 4:21—studied thirty British girls (working class and middle class) to see how social class informs life trajectories over time.[104] The girls (mostly white) were four- to six years old when first studied with traditional interviews and observational methods. When they were sixteen- to twenty-one years old, they were invited to make their own video diaries. The originally white sample was augmented with a sample of black and Asian young women. At this point in the longitudinal project, British Channel 4 became involved, contributing funds and later broadcasting extracts from some of the diaries—ten, three-minute programs on prime time television broadcast throughout the UK in a series, *Girls, Girls, Girls*.[105]

The move to storytelling through video was initially seen by the social scientists as a "less invasive way of collecting research data."[106] They noted problems with many studies of youth by adults—surveillant outsiders reminiscent of the parental generation. For working-class girls who lack confidence in their literacy skills, producing visual rather than written diaries seemed a promising approach (reminiscent of the impulse behind other photovoice projects):

> Giving over the means of representation to research subjects themselves was imagined as a way of somehow "empowering" these young women; enabling them to frame their *own* lives, tell their *own* stories, represent their own situation, offer their *own* understandings.[107]

The investigators thought visual methods would generate more authentic representations of young women; they would be less mediated by the authority of psychologists and influenced instead by a feminist goal to produce more realistic representations of women, "what we might call 'counter-fictions' of femininity."[108]

Camcorders were given to the girls to make video diaries; departing from the methods used earlier in the longitudinal project. It was thought that with a camera the girl could develop her "own story." Maria Pini and Valerie Walkerdine then examined the video diaries and the girls' verbal accounts while they were filming. Superficially, it is tempting to believe they were getting something authentic. Here, for example, is their description of an extract of a video diary made by Ruth, a young British woman:

> A young black woman sits in her bedroom adjusting the video camera which she has balanced on her bed in front of her. "I'm literally whispering now

'cause the walls in my house have ears" she says to her hand-held mike. "This is quite private. It's quite personal, 'cause I don't really talk to anyone about this sort of thing in family. So most of the time, they don't know what I'm thinking or what I'm planning or anything." The woman pauses, cupping her hands beneath her chin and looking off into the distance. "So I got to keep it down" she continues, turning once more to face the camera.[109]

Ruth was introducing a familiar teenage story—a falling out with her parents—to the investigator/viewer, speaking as if to a confidante; even the "walls" were not allowed to hear her whisper a "quite personal" tale. The invitation was seductive, promising "veracity and authenticity originating in the diarist's experience."[110] In a media-driven culture, video diaries can look very innocent.

The researchers quickly began to question the innocence of the images, explaining, "We can very easily get drawn into thinking that because there is no film crew present, people act as though they were not being watched or as though the camera were not actually there."[111] These are highly problematic assumptions: "Certainly, from our own data, it very quickly became obvious that to see this exercise as somehow 'empowering' our research subjects was very naïve." So too was imagining that these young women necessarily felt less like they were being watched, studied, or scrutinized.[112] There were imagined audiences (what the authors call the "invisible observer") in deciding what to film, and what to say in voiceovers about the objects and people.

The girls' running commentaries while they were filming suggest they "often appear to be quite concerned about issues of respectability . . . very conscious of being somehow 'on show.'"[113] The researchers observe the working-class girls try to "posh up" their accents when they are filmed by a family member or friend. Some awkwardly signal an awareness of "how messy their homes are likely to look to an audience . . . [and] how uneventful or boring their lives are liable to appear"[114] (see Transcript 6.1). Young black women annotate their visual diaries with comments like "see, *this* is how people like us behave" or "see, *this* is what black people do when they're at home."[115] The extract of a diary of young black woman spoofs adults, racist stereotypes, and wildlife TV (the diarist herself is not filming this excerpt, her male friend is):

The camera pans a room full of young, black people—women and men who are talking, laughing and nibbling at snacks which they take from the coffee table which sits in the middle of the floor. The panning slows, resting momentarily on individuals, couples or smaller groups. "See the jungle" comes the voice from behind the camera. The camera person has obviously adopted a David Attenborough voice, and describes the scene as though narrating a wildlife program or an anthropological documentary. He stops and zooms in to one woman's face, "here, this one's from central Africa." He then pans further, stopping to zoom in to a couple of women sitting next to her. "Here, a couple from the depths of darkest Africa."[116]

Other girls spoke in similar ways from behind the camera to the investigator, who was imaginatively brought into performances. For many, the camera was animated, often referred to as "you." ("I'll take you with me tomorrow so you can meet my mum," said one diarist.) A triangular relationship is apparent among the camera, the girl, and the researcher/viewer—a twist on the idea of co-construction.[117]

To analyze the surprising data, Maria Pini calls on contemporary social theory as she reflexively interrogates assumptions of the study design:

> Built *into* their diaries is often the very hierarchy of cultural capital, the very judgemental structure and the same normative gaze which the researchers hoped to be side-stepping in handing the means of representation over to these women themselves.[118]

One young woman cleverly staged a comic enactment of what she imagined as a middle-class breakfast:

> Along with her friend, she has set the table with champagne and strawberries and as the women eat, drink, laugh and sway to the background music, they announce, in very obviously affected upper class accents, that for them, this is just a normal, everyday, breakfast-time.[119]

Girls enacted social class with "the imagined interpretive gaze of the academic researcher . . . very much a reference point."[120] Some of the diaries directly engaged it, others skirted around it, but whether avoided or ridiculed, the gaze of the middle-class viewer remained "a major point around which all of these diaries are structured."[121] (Other interpretations of the incident are possible, but not explored by the investigators. The breakfast table moment could be interpreted as parody—joking girls performing class distinctions—similar to the Brown exemplar featured in Chapter 5.)

Sarah, a working-class diarist, illustrates the vivid presence of an imagined audience in the enactment of her "personal" story. Transcript 6.1 displays the investigator's description of a few minutes of Sarah's diary. Reading the narrative excerpt, her discomfort is palpable, conveyed in her recurrent refrain, "That's about it really." Is she dismissing as uninteresting, for an imagined middle-class viewer, details of her working-class life world? How do different viewers "read" the objects Sarah includes from her room, and her selection and positioning of characters in the narrative she tells? What does it mean for Sarah and other teenagers to have an audience, especially one they cannot see? These and other interpretive questions could be asked of the excerpt, although the investigators focus on a broader lesson: "An autobiographical story says more about the conditions of possibility which allow certain tales to be told than it does about a subject's 'inner' reality."[122]

Transcript 6.1

Excerpt of video diary made by Sarah

A young white woman sits facing the camera from a bed in a bedroom. The room is quite dark and above the young woman, some rosettes hang on the wall. So too does a poster of a cartoon cat. Directly behind her is another single bed upon which lies a pile of clothes.

The woman has just finished adjusting the camera, clearly checking that she is in the correct position to begin filming. She appears self-conscious as she sits still, waiting to begin.

"I've been going out with Neil for four years and nearly one month at the end of this month." The woman announces, gazing directly into the camera. "So that's quite a long time. And we met at a club called X. My friend and her mum used to go there. My friend's mum used to know Neil's dad. He's called John. And that's how we met." The woman pauses.

"So I gave him a letter and he said 'yes,' and we started going out and we've been going out ever since—four years or so. So quite a long time."

Again, the woman pauses. She appears to be thinking about what to say next. "And my friends . . ." She begins but stops and begins instead on another topic. "I went to two schools. One was in Dulwich and the other one was in Catford. I left in 1990, so that's four years ago, so . . ."

She appears stuck as to what to say next. After a short gap, she continues, "I left in June 15th 1990, so that was it really."

Once more, she goes quiet.

"Neil's coming later, so I'll be able to show you him. And my friend Sally, she's coming later." Another pause. "So, that's about it really."

"My mum's just come in from work. She works down the local launderette, just down the road, which is about five minutes away." The woman pauses, "And grandma's just come out of hospital 'cause she's just had her hip done. And my sister's got a new job in Lewisham in a security company, just office stuff and that sort of thing. My dad had about five weeks off but he's got about three left now."

The woman looks around her in silence. "And that's about it really."

Source: Pini, 2001, p. 11. Reproduced with permission of Maria Pini.

Several girls spoke later with the investigators about the images they had made. Viewing the completed video diaries, some girls "hated their accents" that made them appear "common." Several of these working-class girls erased some or all the diary before handing in their videotapes, resulting in far less data for the working-class girls in the sample. Some performed their diaries with music and elaborate sets. One middle-class girl filmed herself playing the violin, then put it down to walk off screen to talk directly to the camera, developing a long account of the many activities scheduled for the next days: an essay to write, folios to prepare, babysitting, practicing the violin, a talk she has to give, dates with friends. The investigator writes that "her anxiety is . . . quite unmatched by any of the working class diarists."[123] Social class is an inescapable signifier, leaving its trace on the visual narratives:

> [it] thoroughly saturates each and every one of these diaries. It speaks through bodies, in accent, in composure, in dress, in a diarist's level of ease . . . It speaks through objects, through a room's decoration, through what hangs on a girl's wall, through what shows through her window (a large green garden or a crowded street or block of other flats for example). It speaks through the *mise en scene* of the diary. In short, it speaks itself through the whole feel, style and theme of the diary.[124]

I saw the video diaries that were broadcast on Channel 4. Each three-minute segment begins and ends with a melodic refrain, "It's great being a girl." Collectively, what is shown is certainly not "great" for girls in either social class group. As a viewer I could easily read the girls' class positions (irrespective of skin color) from the class markers Pini and Walkerdine identify, and others. Class, of course, continues to be a primary signifier of identity in Britain.

I chose the exemplar because it reinforces points made in previous chapters. Whether personal narratives are spoken, written, or visual, they do not generate unmediated and unclassed portraits of an "essential" self. Such a singular self doesn't exist (in my view). An investigator cannot elicit an autobiographical story that is separable from wider conditions in which it is situated and constructed. As the authors put it, "A diarist does not exist as an intact, unified individual whose story can be considered outside of its context."[125] Video diaries, like all self-narratives, are performances of "selves," crafted with audience in mind—a "staging of subjectivity."[126] Far from producing private and unmediated portraits of experience, the particular visual narratives were crafted by media-savvy girls living in a media-driven cultural world (British confessional day-time chat shows and "reality" TV). Funding of the project by Channel 4 (which the girls knew about) undoubtedly exaggerated performance dimensions as the girls were drawn into producing the "racey/pacey" incidents Channel 4 sought—stories of "sexy, sassy post-feminist girls"—and, reciprocally, only these kinds of diaries were selected for broadcasting; hesitant and uncomfortable girls do not appear. The investigators were very disturbed by the "docusoaps" selected for showing on Channel 4, but the girls were not.[127] The larger lesson is clear—visual narratives, like oral and written ones, are created for audiences, often blurring fact and fiction, the "natural" and the scripted, the public and the private. Visual narratives create new fictions with public performances of a "personal" self:

> Just because a young woman might hold a camcorder, this in no way means that she is now "free" to tell just any story about herself, or that she is the scriptwriter of her text. Neither does it mean that she has completely escaped the interpretive frameworks, the cultural hierarchies and the gaze of an "observer." The "observer" is as much internalized as external, and in many respects, the same interpretive dynamics are at play.[128]

The exemplar provides many lessons, and I emphasize several methodological points. First, narratives made with video cameras require the same degree of analytic scrutiny as spoken and written texts of experience do, taking into account concepts outlined in previous chapters (e.g., audience, historical context, research relationships, structures of speech, and other dimensions). Second, the work debunks simplistic notions that putting cameras in the hands of research participants produces "authentic" self-representations. As researchers we can be caught by surprise by the images participants produce. These lessons are not news to documentary filmmakers (and considerable attention is devoted in their training to interrogating representational issues), but investigators from other disciplines who have been raised in a media saturated culture don't always question the "truth" of an image; seeing is believing. Social scientists who want to understand the workings of power and culture in individual lives should, as Pini and Walkerdine do, scrutinize images for the discourses image-makers take for granted. We can ask, then, what possibilities of thought and action are closed off by dominant discourses, and how they are embodied in a piece of visual data? When we turn over the camera to research participants, how are the image-makers both more and less "free" than they first appear? The exemplar highlights a twist about audiencing—the imagined viewers participants may carry around in their heads when they have control of the camera.

Conclusion

Visual narrative analysis is a rapidly developing area of social inquiry, but must be entered cautiously, cleansed of naïve assumptions. The five exemplars offer a sampling of analytic approaches scholars are using with genres of "found" images (photographs, paintings, and drawings) and ones "made" during the research process (self-portraits in collage and video diaries). Taken together, the studies provide models of rigorous research that critically scrutinize how individual and collective identities are composed and performed visually. Spoken and written texts examined alongside visual data show how identities can be revealed, concealed, or fictionalized through images.

The summary table (Table 6.1) is an effort to outline how each investigator took up issues I believe are central to any narrative analysis. Several columns have been deleted and/or modified, and two columns have been added—genre of image and site of inquiry, which are topics specific to visual analysis. Fuller discussion of points summarized in the table can be found in my text (above).

There are many similarities between visual analysis and the word-based methods featured in earlier chapters. Interpretation remains a constant as investigators "read" images and texts for meanings related to their research questions, theories, philosophical positions, and biographies (perhaps). Just as oral and written narratives cannot speak for themselves, neither can images, although artists may have made them with a meaning in mind, indicated in a caption. As Gillian Rose puts it, "interpreting images [and textual narratives] is just that, interpretation, not the discovery of their 'truth.'"[129] Multiple readings are always possible; there is not a singular "correct" reading of an image, nor of a spoken or written text. Although visual materials make a compelling appeal to realism, they, like oral and written narratives, are produced by particular people living in particular times and places. Images may be composed to accomplish specific aims, but audiences can read the images differently than an artist intended—an entry point for narrative analysis.

The stability/fluidity of images parallels issues I raised in working with word-based data. A photograph stabilizes a moment in time, preserving a fragment of narrative experience that otherwise would be lost. Transcripts of oral narratives similarly "fix" a moment in the stream of conversation. But, as Chapter 2 shows, the same oral narrative can be transcribed in different ways, each pointing interpretation in different directions and, if the conversational context changes, the speaker would likely shape her story for the new audience. Related issues arise with images. The photographer Jo Spence, for example, produced several prints of "I Frame My Breast for Posterity," one in color that "reads" differently than the black and white version reproduced above. In the exemplars that work with "made" images, girls altered their portraits. In a word, investigators must guard against reifying a single transcript or image as the "real thing."

Working with images can thicken interpretation. Images can evoke emotions and imaginative identification, too often lacking in social science

				Summary Table 6.1 **Visual Narrative Exemplars**			

Author	Where's Narrative in the Project?	Kinds of Data	Focus of Analysis	Sites of Visual Inquiry
Creef (2004)	Story an investigator constructs about internment from photographs of artists and documents	Archived photographs; writings of the artists; archived interviews and other documents	Representation of Japanese Americans during World War II	Production; image; audiencing (limited)
Bell (2002)	Story of experience of breast cancer in photographs and writings of an artist	Archived photographs; writings of the artist	An artist's illness experience	Production; image; audiencing (limited)
Tamboukou (2006)	Auto/biography of an artist	Paintings; archived letters	Identities of an artist; spatial themes	Production (limited); image
Luttrell (2003)	Story about teenage pregnancy in production of an image and its audiencing	Self-portraits in collage; girls' written accounts; classroom conversations; ethnographic observation	Subjectivity of a pregnant teen; self-representation	Production; image; audiencing
Pini (2001) (with Walkerdine)	Stories of their lives young women choose to film	Video diary (image and speech); girls' reflections on diaries in conversations	Performance of "selves" by working-class and middle-class girls	Audiencing; image (limited)

writing. Images can generate collective critique (in contemporary times, photographs of torture at Abu Ghraib represent a case in point). But such images can also dull the senses and give a false sense of connection, as Susan Sontag argued.[130] At the same time, artworks have emancipatory potential, as Jo Spence's images have for women with breast cancer. The photographs created a discursive space to challenge the hegemony of medicine and demand doctors' respectful treatment of women patients; survivors have formed a collective identity and an organized health movement to increase public awareness and funding for research.[131] With images, forgotten moments in history can come back into view, seen in the worried faces of Japanese American subjects awaiting internment during World War II, or the posture of resistance in the body of an *issei* grandfather as he waits, tagged for internment. The averted eyes of the adolescent video diarist can also be interpreted—an expression of resistance, perhaps, to the investigator's entire project.

Finally, I mention several challenges to working with visual data. First and obviously, ethical issues arise with photographic and video data, since viewers can identify individuals and institutions. Some settings prohibit photography, or place limits on the subjects or objects that can be included. In school settings particularly, transforming research participants into image-makers requires long discussions about the "ethics of seeing,"[132] including issues of being photographed and being photographers. Even the freedom to photograph in public settings (long taken for granted by artists) is coming under closer scrutiny regarding the privacy rights of the subject of a street photograph.[133] Investigators should not be paralyzed by uncertainty and, instead, work openly and collaboratively with participants. Several excellent resources can provide guidance to the complex ethical responsibilities of investigators in the digital age.[134]

Second, publishers and academic journals are only beginning to catch up with the visual turn in social research. Reproducing color images can be especially problematic because of cost (and Kodak no longer produces black and white film). In the near future, the social sciences will have online journals with a wide readership that can embed links to color images and film clips; publishers may make provisions to include CD-ROM discs in books. In the meantime, referring journal readers to Web sites for some images may have to suffice. For archived photographs or images from museum collections, permission to reproduce can usually be secured for a nominal fee.[135]

Finally, interpreting images is no longer the practice that Becker described; digital cameras are now the norm. Digitizing introduces complications into the process of composing photographs and videos. It may be possible, for a while, to give disposable cameras to research participants to photograph aspects of their lives, collecting the cameras and developing the film in traditional ways. But I can also imagine a time when PhotoShop and other software will transform the practice of photography in photovoice projects.

Problems should not deter investigators. As Susan Bell (drawing on Becker) states, "Visual images are so thoroughly embedded in our worlds that not to take them seriously, and not to work at making them part of analysis, is to reduce our understandings of subjects' worlds."[136]

I turn, in the last chapter, to some final thoughts about the vexing question of validation.

7

Truths and Cautions

What we observe is not nature itself, but nature exposed to our method of questioning.

—Heisenberg, 1959[1]

I began the book with a story of a visit to the classroom of my granddaughter, Sage, to introduce the diverse meanings of narrative and to show how, from an early age, storytelling is encouraged. Although it may be "natural," telling and writing stories is invariably situated and strategic, taking place in institutional and cultural contexts with circulating discourses and regulatory practices, always crafted with audience in mind. The concept of narrative continues to be "elusive, contested and indeterminate . . . variously used as an epistemology, a methodological perspective, an antidote to positivist research, a communication mode, a supra-genre, a text-type."[2]

This book has focused on methodological perspectives that—as previous chapters demonstrate—have elusive, contested, and indeterminate borders. Narrative analysis (one component of the broader field of narrative inquiry) refers to a diverse set of methods, a "family" of interpretive approaches to spoken, written, and visual texts. The closing chapter provides some further guidance for students and investigators wanting to adapt one or more of the methods to their research questions. I take up two practical issues: several ways to think about the validity of narrative inquiry, and ways to develop a community for support and constructive criticism. The first is a broad and complex topic that defies easy summary. I urge students to consult the endnotes for further reading as I only touch on key concepts here.

Facets of the Validity Problem

As all storytellers do, investigators face audiences when they present their analytic stories. I end the book with some thoughts about issues that may come up as students prepare papers and dissertations using narrative methods for reception by others. Charles Bosk poses the central question: "all field work done by a single field-worker invites the question, why should we believe it?"[3] When applied to narrative projects, two levels of validity are important—the story told by a research participant and the validity of the analysis, or the story told by the researcher.

There has been a long debate in the social sciences about "truth" (although trustworthiness is a better term)—a debate with long taproots in philosophy. Recently, questions about reliability and validity have resurfaced with the growing desire among some U.S. survey researchers to give their work a human face by weaving qualitative components (including life stories) into their projects. Government funding agencies in the United States, in turn, have held conferences attempting to specify criteria for "rigor" in qualitative proposals (which neither the National Institutes of Health [NIH] nor the National Science Foundation [NSF] typically fund).[4] The documents produced from these conferences will disappoint students interested in guidance for the kinds of approaches I featured in the book. Jean Gilgun provides a trenchant analysis of a 2002 NIH document, drawing attention to the distancing language used to guide qualitative proposals:

> Where, I wondered, is recognition of the subjectivist, feminist, emancipatory, interpretivist, phenomenological, and constructivist perspectives characteristic of many types of research?[5]

Norman Denzin, reflecting on a 2003 NSF document, says, "it is as if these guidelines were written in a time warp," without awareness of decades of interdisciplinary qualitative research, now an established tradition that encompasses multiple paradigmatic formulations. Denzin continues, "Complex literatures are now attached to research methodologies, strategies of inquiry, interpretive paradigms, and criteria for reading and evaluating inquiry itself."[6] Instead, the model of a detached, disinterested, and disengaged observer is valued in the guiding documents. Fixed criteria for reliability, validity, and ethics developed for experimental research are recommended and misapplied; they are not suitable for evaluating narrative projects.

If students can't turn to documents produced by government funding agencies, where can they get help to make arguments for trustworthiness? The qualitative literature here is vast and growing.[7] In my reading of the debates, they turn on a set of questions about evidence and ethics. I prefer not to think in terms of standards or criteria, and warn students away from the "paradigm warfare"[8] that exists out there in the literature. It can paralyze and, in my view, simplify what are complex validation and ethical issues all investigators face. I hope a review of several facets of validity relevant to narrative research can help students think consciously and strategically about the trustworthiness of stories they collect, and the analytic stories they develop from them.

Situated Truths

Research projects are situated, of course, within the parameters and debates of the particular social science discipline, and by the epistemologies and theories that ground the empirical work. Consequently, ways of thinking about validity and ethics are products of the paradigms that spawn them.[9] Investigators choosing to write realist tales will have to persuade audiences with a different rhetoric than investigators adopting interpretive, feminist, constructionist, and other perspectives.[10] The validity of a project should be assessed from within the situated perspective and traditions that frame it (which, ideally, an investigator makes clear up front). I approach the issue of trustworthiness, for example, from a particular position on narrative research, which emphasizes its fluid boundaries and origins, theoretical premises, epistemologies, uses, and limitations (see Chapter 1). My position on the topics is not necessarily shared by all narrative scholars. Students will have to make arguments for the trustworthiness of their work from within their situated perspectives that, in turn, will inform the ethical parameters of the inquiry.

What follows are some sensitizing concepts about evidence and interpretation for students to consider in relation to their projects. To illustrate a concept, I draw on selected exemplars from previous chapters and refer readers to other work. I take up four facets of validity that are especially relevant to narrative research projects. They are not the only ways to look at the many-sided issue of validation and, like the facets of a cut gem, angles converge at points. Each looks at the validity question from a different perspective; some angles will be relevant to certain inquiries, epistemologies, and disciplinary imperatives, and not to others. Several interrogate the trustworthiness of data, others the investigator's analysis, and a few cross the borders of the two levels of validity.

I continue to believe, since my 1993 book, that there is no canon, that is formal rules or standardized technical procedure for validation (procedural rules are insufficient in quantitative research too, as others have shown[11]). Narrative truths are always partial—committed and incomplete.[12] Nevertheless, students in the social sciences have to make arguments to persuade audiences about the trustworthiness of their data and interpretations—they didn't simply make up the stories they claim to have collected, and they followed a methodical path, guided by ethical considerations and theory, to story their findings. This is all the more reason for students to attend closely to the methods they are using (and developing) for arriving at "valid" interpretations of the type of narrative data they are collecting.

Historical Truth and Correspondence[13]

For certain projects situated in realist epistemologies, factual truth is important. Historians, for example, may ask whether a particular story (spoken or recorded in archives) is consistent with other evidence. But stories that fail the test and diverge from established "truth" can sometimes be the most interesting, indicating silenced voices and subjugated knowledge. In the exemplar in Chapter 6, Elena Tahima Creef rewrites with images and archival documents the dominant story about Japanese Americans during World War II. The reality of what happened to families with internment and enduring effects has been edited out of the preferred narrative. Just as the Bush Administration stitched together a tale of good versus evil to justify invasion of Iraq in 2003,[14] a national narrative was cobbled together to justify the internment of Japanese Americans during World War II, which Creef challenges with evidence from archives (photographs and drawings made at the time, subsequent interviews and reflections, and government documents). Skeptics could not question, then, the validity of the stories of lives depicted in the visual evidence or the "truth" of the archival evidence, even if they wanted to challenge Creef's critical interpretative story about racialized violence. Since she meticulously documents her primary sources, and reproduces for readers the statements contained in government documents, future investigators working with archival materials can learn from the exemplar.

Students need to make their modes of inquiry explicit—how they moved from a piece of evidence, for example, to a theoretical formulation. In projects that rely on realist epistemologies, factual accuracy matters, even if contemporary historians generally eschew an ideal of absolute truth and objectivity.[15] Contemporary academic historians have standards for verification, even as they are drawing increasingly on visual and other nonwritten sources, and the interpretive perspectives of other disciplines. Students in the human sciences can learn from the debates about "truth" and evidence taking place in oral history and historiography.[16]

The idea of correspondence (the preferred term of philosophers) is one route to establishing historical truth. Does the reported sequence of events in a personal narrative match accounts from other sources, give or take an expected degree of variation? For projects that rely on realist epistemologies, establishing this first level of correspondence can be important, and some investigators go to great lengths to establish it, illustrated by the following example from epidemiology.

High rates of Post Traumatic Stress Disorder (PTSD) among Vietnam veterans have been criticized for "retrospective distortions," on the premise that veterans may exaggerate their symptoms and what they witnessed during combat. To evaluate the claim, and assess the validity of personal narratives of veterans they had in hand, Bruce Dohrenwend and colleagues quantitatively estimated the probability of exposure to war-zone trauma; a measure was constructed that took into account a veteran's military occupational specialty, the monthly killed-in-action rate during his Vietnam service, and the killed-in-action rate in his military division. To construct their measure, the team had to amass data from military personnel files, military archival sources, and historical accounts. When they related their measure of degree of exposure to the men's psychological outcomes, they found a "dose-response" relationship—the greater the exposure, the more likely a Vietnam veteran would have a PTSD diagnosis. Most relevant here, they found little evidence of falsification in men's narratives of traumatic events.[17] There was correspondence between self-reports and archival evidence, strengthening validity.

For projects relying on social constructionist perspectives, the correspondence of reported events in a personal narrative with other kinds of evidence is not as relevant as in realist tales, sometimes even beside the point. Narrative scholars would generally agree that a narrative is not simply a factual report of events, but instead one articulation told from a point of view that seeks to persuade others to see the events in a similar way. As Bruner puts it, "the distinction between narrative fiction and narrative truth is nowhere nearly as obvious as common sense and usage would have us believe." He adds further that verification has "limited applicability where human intentional states are concerned,"[18] such as in psychology.

In many exemplars featured in the book, verifying the facts was less important than understanding their meanings for individuals and groups. Carole Cain examined the relationship of the narrative of an organization—Alcoholics Anonymous—to individual members' constructed stories of drinking (see Chapter 3). The meaning-making of narrators was the focus here, not whether the drinking career of an AA alcoholic "really" unfolded in the sequence reported, or whether every detail was correct. Even those working in realist paradigms generally accept that narrators interpret the past in stories rather than reproduce it as it was; investigators, in turn, interpret the interpretations.

A second level of correspondence concerns this interpretive work by the investigator. Martyn Hammersley, writing about ethnography and qualitative work generally, says that "knowledge claims are valid if they accurately represent the relevant facts of the matter."[19] Rejecting the positions of constructivists and activist investigators who posit political use as a criterion (discussed below), Hammersley believes that "truth-as-correspondence" is the key characteristic on which research results should be assessed. Hammersley is less clear, however, about how a qualitative investigator can establish "truth-as-correspondence"; he uses concepts such as plausibility (are findings consistent with well-founded knowledge?) and credibility (is the investigator making a claim in a good position to know x is true?). In my reading, Hammersley's position on validation may come down to pragmatic use (discussed below). Hayden White notes that when historians seek to explain the past, they ask "how are the facts to be described in order to sanction one mode of explaining them rather than another,"[20] rather than "what are the facts?" The historian creates a narrative that can be evaluated along several dimensions, including coherence (developed below). Norman Denzin's words are instructive:

> Narratives do not establish the truth of . . . such events, nor does narrative reflect the truth of experience. Narratives create the very events they reflect upon. In this sense, narratives are reflections *on*–not *of*—the world as it is known.[21]

Denzin stresses the constitutive function of narrative here. Put in terms of levels of correspondence, a first person narrative (obtained, for example, from an archive of materials) reports past events that undoubtedly happened, but all we have is the reflection (what a diarist wrote, for example). Going back to verify the precise and accurate "truth" of the events he or she reports may be impossible and not necessarily important. It is the analyst's interpretive work with the document and others like it that can be interrogated.

To support theoretical claims, students must demonstrate how they developed and/or used methods appropriate to their research questions, epistemologies, and situated perspectives. Students need to document their sources, and bring the reader along with them as they uncover a trail of evidence, and critically evaluate each piece in relation to others. From the cumulative evidence, the student can then construct an interpretive account of his or her findings, storying the stories collected.[22]

Coherence, Persuasion, and Presentation

The coherence of participants' narratives, and the investigator's interpretative work with them, is a related facet of trustworthiness. Do episodes of a life story hang together? Are sections of a theoretical argument linked and consistent? Are there major gaps and inconsistencies? Is the interpreter's analytic account persuasive?

To evaluate validity at the level of the participant's story, Agar and Hobbs posit three kinds of coherence—global, local, and themal—and argue that "if an utterance is shown to be understandable in terms of the three kinds of coherence, the interpretation is strengthened."[23] The approach is conceptually neat and offers an important check on ad hoc theorizing, illustrating that interpretation of meaning by an investigator is constrained by the spoken text in important ways. But it is difficult to apply to studies in the dialogic and visual traditions, even in structural narrative research that includes talk between speakers. The model assumes a single rational speaker with a discourse plan, which does not fit many applications.

Charlotte Linde's work may be helpful to investigators who face this challenge. She argues that coherence is "both a social demand and an internal, psychological demand . . . [a] subjective sense . . . that organizes a speaker's understanding of his or her past life, current situation, and imagined future." Theorizing from her background in linguistics but with an interest in social practices, she defines coherence as a "property of texts," or a relation of parts to the whole and to other texts.[24] She rejects "factuality" (historical truth or correspondence) and instead examines three levels within a text: the structure of the participants' narrative, whether "appropriate causality and continuity" are present, and the "coherence systems" in which an individual life story is embedded—assumptions about the world the speaker invokes (scholars influenced by Foucauldian thought might refer to this level as the circulating, taken-for-granted discourses of the historical period). Application of Linde's theory requires that discontinuities in any life story be explained by the analyst, and connections forged if coherence is to be fully demonstrated in the analytic interpretation.

In my earlier writing about narrative methods, text-based coherence formed a central place, but now I am less sure about this way of demonstrating trustworthiness. The shift was influenced by reading Lawrence Langer's analytic work with Holocaust testimonies, and by scholarship questioning the idea of a coherent or unitary "self" expressed in a life story. Langer viewed videotaped interviews of survivors[25] at the Yale Video Archive and, in some cases, participated in interviews that included family members. He writes about incoherence in the testimonies, reflecting fragmented lives. Survivors spoke about events and experiences before the camps, memories from the time in

Auschwitz, and some spoke about their lives since. These are "disrupted narratives . . . that do not function in time like other[s]."[26] Speakers struggled with "the impossible task of making their recollections of the camp experience coalesce with the rest of their lives . . . [there is] temporal rupture . . . a double existence."[27] It was the "needful ears" of interviewers and the survivors' children who sought to connect the fragments, perhaps to mediate the atrocities survivors spoke about. (One interviewer interrupted a survivor to ask about whether a particular moral idea "got you through to the end?"[28] Others asked similar questions that "simplified closure.") Langer's important work suggests it may be listeners' (and investigators') need for continuity and meaning—our needful ears—that has elevated the significance of narrative coherence.

Schiff and Cohler extend this line of argument with another sample, examining how many survivors exhibited "two selves with two different streams of memory,"[29] while others wove a story of survival that brought past and present together, but in conflictual ways:

> Although some forms of putting together the past are possible in Holocaust survivors, it has a fragile character, leading, for the most part, not to a single coherent voice of purpose but to the existence of meaning and non-meaning together.[30]

Absence of coherence in the stark instance anticipates a problem investigators may confront when studying other traumatized lives. Chance events, war, natural disasters, and physical assault attack victims' identities, including beliefs about a moral order; by their very nature these events disrupt meaningful connections. In subsequent interpretive work with narratives of survivors, investigators forge links and make connections by situating the personal narratives in social and political contexts. In the final analysis, validity will rest on the coherence of data interpretation, not unlike how readers evaluate work in the historical narrative tradition (see above). But, in the spirit of postmodernism, Langer is also right when he says, "we need to search for the inner principles of incoherence that make these [survivor] testimonies accessible to us."[31]

Investigators wanting to make use of the concept of coherence to "validate" their narrative projects will travel into an epistemological jungle. As philosophers know, there is no easy correspondence between life and experience. Paul Ricoeur reminds us that life as lived does not have coherence, it is essentially prenarrative. He states, "A life is no more than a biological phenomenon as long as it has not been interpreted." With interpretation comes a story and here "fiction plays a mediating role."[32] Internal consistency of a life story may be illusory (if present at all). At another level, validity can be strengthened if the analytic story the investigator constructs links pieces of data and renders them meaningful and coherent theoretically. Instead of trying to find coherence and factuality in individuals' stories, investigators might search for coexistent realities—selves and communities that are pulling together and pulling apart at the same time. A narrative analysis of stories of trauma survivors, for example, might identify points where individuals' accounts converge thematically (creating a community of experience), and other points where they split apart. Making sense analytically of both convergence and divergence would support trustworthiness.

In the final analysis, good narrative research persuades readers. Students can present their narrative data in ways that demonstrate the data are genuine, and analytic interpretations of them are plausible, reasonable, and convincing. Every reader has had the experience of encountering a piece of research and thinking "but of course . . ." even when the author's argument was counterintuitive. Persuasiveness is strengthened when the investigator's theoretical claims are supported with evidence from informants' accounts, negative cases are included, and alternative interpretations considered. The strategy forces investigators to document their claims for readers who weren't present to witness the storytelling event, or alongside the investigator trying to make sense of it. The ethnographer's stance—"I was there"—is not sufficient for many audiences.

I insist, whenever possible, that students tape-record conversations so they can represent what was said with greater accuracy. Providing descriptive evidence of the precise words spoken or written by narrators strengthens persuasiveness, and allows the investigator (and reader) to examine language—a hallmark of narrative research. Verbatim quotations without context can be deceptive, however. Molly Andrews puts it bluntly, saying they "often assume a sense of authenticity which eludes other forms of data . . . people may appear as if they are 'speaking for themselves,' rather than as people whose words were spoken in response to specific questions [and for a specific audience], and who have little input into how their thoughts are represented in the write-up of the research."[33] Interview segments that include contexts of production (including audience) are generally more persuasive than quotations stripped of context, although the practice is rare in thematic narrative analysis, as Chapter 3 illustrates.

I also teach students to keep a diary, or log, of decisions and inferences made during the course of a research project. The practice encourages methodological awareness, as Clive Seale puts it.[34] It fosters ongoing reflexivity—critical self-awareness about how the research was done and the impact of critical decisions made along the way. A log also helps when writing up a project, jogging memory and encouraging truthfulness. Leaving an audit trail, as it is sometimes called, strengthens persuasiveness.[35]

There is an inherent problem, however, in using persuasiveness alone as an argument for trustworthiness, particularly with academic audiences. Rhetorical style alone—good writing—can convince a reader of the "truth" of findings, without offering a clue as to how an investigator got there. Journalists don't face these problems: Barbara Ehrenreich, for example, persuaded me about the situations of low-wage women workers in the United States with her skillful prose, empathic positioning, honesty about her background, and way of working. I approached her compelling descriptions with standards appropriate for journalism and creative nonfiction, but the work would not stand up to tough questioning in many academic departments.[36]

Different communities bring different expectations to a piece of writing, or "preconceptions about the kinds of truths that each is supposed to deal in."[37] Academic audiences expect to learn in some detail how a study was conducted, and moments in the interpretive process that led to particular conclusions and not others. Cronbach and Suppes's description still holds:

> The report of a disciplined inquiry has a texture that displays the raw materials entering the argument and the local processes by which they were compressed and rearranged to make the conclusions credible.[38]

Selecting the appropriate form in which to present a narrative inquiry requires careful consideration, especially by students. Established investigators have power that new investigators lack; persuasiveness alone may be enough for some audiences, but risky for young investigators. Kenneth Gergen says that the success of a work depends on "the analyst's capacity to invite, compel, stimulate or delight the audience . . . not on criteria of veracity."[39] Many social scientists would disagree. Some academics argue for emotional and aesthetic criteria for validity. For instance, does a story move us or get us to think differently about a phenomenon? Regarding autoethnography, Ellis and Bochner write:

> The narrative rises or falls on its capacity to provoke readers to broaden their horizons, reflect critically on their own experience, enter empathically into a world of experience different from their own, and actively engage in dialogue regarding the social and moral implications of the different perspectives and standpoints encountered.[40]

One could make an analogy to art: when evaluating the depiction of a landscape, viewers ask not whether it looks like the place, but whether it evokes the appearance of a place (verisimilitude). Put differently, a painting or poem does not depict a "reality" but constitutes one. For this reason, "most literary theorists seem allergic to the very idea of truth."[41] If narrative is a "blurred genre" (to adopt Clifford Geertz's felicitous phrase) with firm roots in the arts and humanities, must we give up social scientific concepts altogether? Although I welcome artistic representations and good auto-ethnographies[42] (too much academic writing is distant and formulaic), most social science audiences expect something more.

Coherence and persuasion can depend on literary practices and contingent reader response. What may be the most persuasive interpretation of an oral narrative at one historical moment may not be later, or for a differently situated interpreter. (Remember my reinterpretation of Burt's narrative in Chapter 5). The narratives we collect and interpret have shifting meanings over time.[43]

In the meantime, students can ground their claims for validity by carefully documenting the processes they used to collect and interpret data. In methods classes, I teach my general preferences for analysis and presentation of interviews (learned from Mishler[44]): reliance on detailed transcripts; attention to language, contexts of production, and (to the extent appropriate) to structural features of discourse; acknowledgment of the dialogic nature of narrative; and (if relevant) a comparative approach—interpretation of similarities and differences among participants' stories. When using visual narrative data, the procedures obviously require adaptation. I also urge students to locate themselves and the issues facing their disciplines in their research inquiries. Following a methodical path, documenting claims, and practicing reflexivity strengthens the case for validity.

Pragmatic Use

The ultimate test of validity deserves mention, even if it rarely helps individual students. Does a piece of narrative research become a basis for others' work? "Others" in this instance are members of the scholarly community, not participant communities working for social change (discussed below). Questions of validity in the academy often turn on pragmatic use, whether quantitative or qualitative, or based on realist, constructionist, or other philosophies. The "truth test" here is not abstract, instead it occurs cumulatively in the development of knowledge.

Narrative research is a form of case-centered inquiry, as Chapter 1 noted. Given that most narrative projects deal with cases of individuals and groups, not population-based samples, discussions about the trustworthiness of a narrative inquiry can descend into heated debates about generalizability (external validity). Bent Flyvbjerg refutes beliefs held by mainstream social scientists about generalizing; he illustrates with rich examples the pivotal role case studies have played in the development of the natural and the social sciences.[45] I summarize Flyvbjerg's five arguments for generalizability, and urge readers to consult the full article, which provides many specifics that could support students when they have to justify a case-centered analysis.

First, case studies produce context-dependent knowledge—essential to the development of a field or discipline. Rather than operating from rules, experts operate on the basis of detailed case knowledge. Professional schools, for example, educate students through intensive study of cases—real-life situations with all their messy detail. Rule-based knowledge and predictive theories may also be used, but they are rare in the social sciences (if existent at all). Second, carefully chosen experiments and cases, coupled with critical reflexivity, are responsible for major developments in scientific knowledge. Galileo, for example, did not randomly select a sample of different objects and watch them fall from a range of randomly selected heights under varying wind conditions; instead, the matter of gravity was settled by an individual case of gravity, carefully chosen. The theories of Newton, Darwin, Marx, and Freud were developed similarly. Formal generalizations, though important in certain instances, can be overvalued; they are but one route to accumulating knowledge.

Third, interrogating atypical, extreme, or paradigmatic cases is often necessary to extend theory about a general problem (e.g., the paradigmatic case of the Panopticon, which Foucault used to theorize aspects of contemporary surveillance). Cases can uncover social practices that are taken for granted. Fourth, case studies can "close in" on everyday situations and test how something occurs in social life. The advantage here is depth rather than breadth. Contrary to popular belief, falsification of preconceived notions is more likely to occur in case study research than is verification. Donald Campbell and Clifford Geertz, among others, report how case studies forced them to revise hypotheses.

Fifth and perhaps most relevant here, case studies focus attention on narrative detail (the "little things"). Important insights can unfold from "the many-sided, complex, and sometimes conflicting stories" of actors in the field.[46] Rather than trying to appeal to readers with an abstract rule or proposition, cases reveal facets, each attracting different readers who can decide the meaning of the case, and interrogate actors' and narrators' interpretations in relation to categorical questions (what is this a case of?). Summarizing and generalizing from case studies may not even be desirable in many instances.

Flyvbjerg's essay is a balanced and nuanced argument for the importance of case studies in creating general knowledge. His five points underscore how rigorous case-based methods have been central not only to the practice of science, but to the evolution of general knowledge about the workings of the physical and social world (external validity). In other words, trustworthiness of case-based research has been demonstrated by pragmatic use.

An individual study does not instantly enter into the collective process of knowledge accumulation in a given field, as any historian of science can document. The process happens over time as scholars working on particular questions in an area come to accept a piece of research. Elliot Mishler's words are instructive: "Knowledge is validated within a community of scientists as they come to share nonproblematic and useful ways of thinking about and solving problems."[47] Martin Hammersley makes a similar point, asserting that knowledge claims are established (or refused) "in the context of collective assessment by a whole research community."[48] A community is eventually persuaded, sometimes over several decades. "Even research specialists do not judge a conclusion as it stands alone," Cronbach observes, "they judge its compatibility with a network of prevailing beliefs."[49] In mainstream research language, it all comes down to construct validity. Research communities are segregated in the social sciences, however; paradigm and methodological warfare between communities is rife at the present time (witness, for example, the debates in psychology about method and inference[50]). Conflict and controversy have always been part of "normal science," as Kuhn demonstrated long ago. Most research reports worth their salt enter a partisan and contested terrain, and students must become accustomed to this.

On a positive note, when a group of scholars eventually comes to accept a particular way of working with narrative data as a basis for empirical investigation and theorizing, the approach can be considered trustworthy. Despite their differences, both William Labov's and James Gee's contributions to structural narrative analysis (featured in Chapter 4) have met the criterion—they have become touchstones, or points of departure for others' work. In Mishler's words:

> If our overall assessment of a study's trustworthiness is high enough for us to act on it, we are granting the findings a sufficient degree of validity to invest our own time and energy, and to put at risk our reputations as competent investigators.[51]

Pragmatic use—a functional measure of validity—may not be of immediate comfort to individual investigators wanting to make arguments for the trustworthiness of their data and interpretations. But there can be transparency (as some call it), since we can provide detailed information that will enable others to follow the path taken by: (1) making explicit how methodological decisions were made; (2) describing how interpretations were produced, including alternative interpretations considered; and (3) making primary data available to other investigators where appropriate. Ultimately, it is up to future communities of human scientists to evaluate the work as trustworthy—worthwhile to pursue as a line of inquiry and/or a springboard for future work. Such is the socially constructed nature of social science.

In the final section, I introduce a facet of the validity question rarely examined in academic explorations. It asks how a piece of research aids those individuals and communities who were part of the research.

Political and Ethical Use

Does a narrative inquiry contribute to social change? Does a researcher's work with a group to collect and interpret their stories foster social justice? These questions, posed recently by Susan Chase,[52] are important to many of us who want our scholarly work to be of use to participant communities and encourage dialogue. Going farther, Bronwyn Davies asks researchers to interrogate their own contributions "to creating and withholding the conditions of possibility of particular lives."[53]

For decades, the empowerment potential of research has appealed to scholars in oral history, critical theory, and feminism. In 1978, Paul Thompson recommended in his classic volume, *The Voice of the Past*, "giving people . . . through their own words, a central place."[54] Feminist scholars added to this, embracing Patti Lather's call for "empowering research designs" and her proposal for "catalytic validity . . . the degree to which the research process reorients, focuses, and energizes participants toward knowing reality in order to transform it, a process Freire called conscientization."[55] Lather radically reformulates the validity question, asking how a research project leads to dialogue and change—for participants, researchers, and critical social theory.

Cooperative inquiries and Participatory Action Research (PAR) projects aim for the kind of validity Lather advocates. Here, the investigator works *with* a community of informants from the outset, not taking the products *back* to them for validation as in "member checks" (discussed below). Participatory inquiry offers the best way to achieve a meaningful and sustained dialogue throughout a project.[56] The subjects of the research are ideally included in every stage of a project—design, data gathering, interpretation, and publication of results. Although variation exists in degree of inclusion, PAR projects "aimed at expanding the participation of people in research directed at their self-defined needs is booming."[57] Orlando Fals-Borda emphasizes how such projects deal with the validity question for "the results of participatory research are open to validation and judgment . . . not only by scholars and bureaucrats—who are now on a rampage to co-opt it—but also by the opinion of the subject peoples themselves."[58] There are compelling examples of PAR in the human sciences; I briefly describe one here and refer students to others (including two dissertations) that radically reformulate how we can think about validity.[59]

Brinton Lykes conducted collaborative research with rural Mayan women in Guatemala, who had survived years of violence. State sponsored terror and torture during the thirty-six-year war had silenced the population, and the adaptive silence continued. As a result, community leaders wanted to create spaces where speaking could be facilitated, and they approached Lykes (a community psychologist) who then served as a consultant to a woman's group that became an NGO. Together, they created activity projects that drew on storytelling, photography, drawing, and dramatization—ways women could give voice to what they had witnessed:

> They hoped to prevent future violence by speaking out, and, though pictures and storytelling, to build connections with other women in Guatemala and beyond who were engaged in similar processes.[60]

The outcomes of the research—participants' narratives set alongside their photographs and drawings—were published in a book, collaboratively authored. Papers designed for academic audiences narrate complex moments in the data gathering process and the difficult negotiation of ethical research relationships. [61]

Projects such as this one go a long way beyond member checks—one way investigators from a wide spectrum of qualitative traditions have made claims for the validity of an interpretation. Taking one's work back to those studied earlier strengthens trustworthiness Lincoln and Guba argue, "data, analytic categories, interpretations, and conclusions are tested with those . . . groups from whom the data were originally collected."[62] The credibility of an investigator's representation is strengthened if it is recognizable to participants. For ethical reasons alone, it is important to find out what participants think of our work. But obtaining corroboration turns out to be complicated, even illusory. Giving a transcript of an interview to a participant for commentary and correction is one thing (and even here, reactions can be unexpected[63]), while giving our interpretive conclusions back for a "check" can be quite another. Research in the social sciences is guided by theory, and our theoretical commitments may or may not be compatible (or even meaningful) to research participants.

Practically speaking, a great deal of time may have passed between an interview and full analysis of a sample of interviews; issues that were formerly salient for a given participant may no longer be several years later. Participants may not even agree with our conclusions, as we saw with Sunita (whose infertility narrative was presented in Chapter 2) when she wrote that my interpretation made sense to her, but it was not how she thought about her life. Does this render my conclusions invalid? Or do our different interpretations bring into view contrasting perspectives on the issue of infertility—a kind of triangulation?[64] Different interpretations can reveal multiple realities and "truths," as Wendy Luttrell vivifies when she sets her readings of teenage girls' oral narratives alongside their reflections (see Chapter 6).

Reformulations of the validity question can be seen in advocacy research projects that are not full PAR projects. Certainly the Latin American *testimonios*, narrated with an urgent voice, make space for previously silenced voices to speak, mapping counter-narratives to the preferred ones of repressive governments. Researcher's stories that incorporate testimonies can function politically. Other oppressed groups can better understand and change their situations—an example of "catalytic validity."

Lisa Dodson used interpretive focus groups to check out her initial readings of what a group of women living in poverty had (and had not) shared with her in interviews. She sensed there had been a fear of speaking, of saying "what's really going on" in everyday lives. She turned to community women who lived in similar circumstances to women she had interviewed, and *with them* interpreted interview themes. The strategy was not to verify with member checks, but was instead a form of coanalysis:

> [W]e sought members who had *not* been involved in the data gathering because new participants more readily assumed the role of analyst, rather than respondent. We also found that asking participants to be data interpreters right from the start interrupted the habits of sequestering knowledge; many participants were quite ready to speak on behalf of *other* women and families facing daily conditions they knew so well.[65]

Whenever possible, it is desirable to take work back to the individuals and groups who participated in the study for ethical reasons alone. Individuals can check whether their identities had been adequately disguised, and we can ask for informed consent a second time, including permission to use a particular narrative segment.[66] Such practices embody an ethical research relationship, but they are not the same as establishing "validity" with member checks. The concept has some real limits. Life stories are not static; memories and meanings of experiences change as time passes. Nor can our conclusions across a number of narratives be evaluated necessarily by individual participants. They may not even agree with our displays of their talk or what we do with it analytically, so it is important (to the extent possible) to clearly distinguish between our views of subjects' lives and their own. With the important exception of PAR and emancipatory/advocacy projects (where the investigator is aligned with the participant community), we have to take responsibility for the truths of our scholarly accounts. "Catalytic" validity cannot be demonstrated simply with member checks or the "empowering" aims of a researcher.[67]

As stressed throughout the book, practices that allow participants to speak, write, and/or make images as they chose are essential to ethical narrative research, however mediated the productions may be on closer analysis (recall the video diary exemplar in Chapter 6 and Carole Cain's work with oral narratives of members of AA in Chapter 3). I want to introduce a caution, however, to the belief that narrative research is "empowering," a claim investigators sometimes make to avoid validity questions. The claim rests on the assumption of the healing power of storytelling, especially in situations involving trauma. Molly Andrews argues that "giving voice" to participants' experiences and "empowering" marginalized groups can mask complicated questions. Who benefits from the work? Is a "speaking self" the same as a "healing self"? How are stories going to be received by differently situated audiences? Will they be heard as the author intended? How will a narrator view the investigator's representation later, particularly if her life has moved on?[68] The "empowerment narratives" investigators construct—"the story which many researchers tell ourselves about what we are doing"—do not necessarily mirror the immediate experience of participants in these settings.[69]

Investigators who want to argue for the political use of their projects need to remember that "an emancipatory intent is no guarantee of an emancipatory outcome."[70] We have to take responsibility for the validity of our interpretive conclusions, and document how we arrived at them. Alternatively, genuinely collaborative projects that serve the participant group's aims at every stage—in study design, methods of data collection and interpretation, and modes of dissemination—reposition the validity question. In these instances, the research is subject to validation and judgment by participant communities, rather than academic audiences alone.

Conclusion

I have identified several facets of the validity question and touched on several related ethical dimensions. Each facet has a potential dark side, apparent in instances where it can cloud rather than reveal "truth" and can undermine ethical relations with participant communities. Certain facets are appropriate to some research contexts, others are not. Selection depends on the situated perspectives and commitments an investigator brings to a narrative inquiry. To reiterate, there is no cannon, clear set of rules or list of established procedures and abstract criteria for validation that fit all projects. Nor are regulations currently in use by human subjects committees in the United States sensitive to the embedded ethics of many narrative inquiries.[71]

Educated disagreement exists among qualitative scholars about the process of validation, coming from differences in our situated perspectives. Research in the human sciences has several recognized epistemologies and methodologies, and in narrative research there is added diversity—the central message of this book. Let's not waste time debating others about paradigms, and instead get on with the work of building a corpus of diverse exemplars, that is, narrative research that includes the detail and specificity needed to advance the field.

I end with an invitation to students and other investigators who want to initiate narrative projects. Interrogate the four broad approaches outlined in the book and then adapt them to your research problem. Ask hard questions of your projects similar to the ones I asked of the exemplars: What definition of narrative are you working with? To what extend are you paying attention to narrative form and language, local contexts of production, and broader social discourses? What is your distinctive focus and related unit of analysis? And, at a basic level, what are the epistemological and theoretical perspectives that frame your project?

Form communities with other researchers to gain support and constructive criticism for your work. I urge those wanting to join the "narrative turn" to follow Elliot Mishler's suggestion to "look outside of your discipline" for colleagues, as "narrative pockets" exist in virtually every field.[72] Narrative research can only grow stronger as we form connections across disciplinary boundaries, identify our own exemplars, build on them, and gain support and constructive criticism for our inquiries. Where ongoing face-to-face study groups are impossible due to distance, we can form virtual communities. (A group in Australia initiated a blog that has continued after we completed work together.) There are also listservs, Web sites, international conferences, and journals that keep narrative researchers connected.[73] Use the many resources out there to find your own path. Narrative research is gaining strength in the human sciences, and the field needs voices in different registers to become a chorus.

Notes

Endnotes for Chapter One

1. Nelson, 1989.
2. White, 1981; Bruner, 1986, 1990.
3. Gubrium & Holstein, 2002; Atkinson & Silverman, 1997.
4. Smith, 1990.
5. It is beyond my scope in the book to question the term "experience," so widely used in the narrative literature. Philosophers note "the really hard problem of consciousness is the problem of experience" (Chalmers, 1995, p. 2). Its subjective and phenomenal aspects cannot be reduced to brain or cognitive processes, as Chalmers (1996) notes. For a critical analysis of the term, see Scott, 1998.
6. Polkinghorne, 1983, prefers the term "human sciences" to "behavioral science" or "social science." As he notes, the latter terms retain the specter of behaviorism, on the one hand, and the natural sciences on the other. "Human science" implies multiple systems of inquiry and is more inclusive. See Lather, 1986, p. 257, for further development of Polkinghorne's distinctions.
7. The material in this section also appears in slightly different form in Riessman & Quinney, 2005; Riessman & Speedy, 2007.
8. Hinchman & Hinchman, 1997; Riessman, 2004. Toolan, 1988, defined narrative as a perceived sequence of nonrandomly connected events—a definition that leaves out the role of audience that I emphasize in the book. For various arguments, see Herman et al., 2005.
9. For an excerpt that includes the portions of Aristotle's *Poetics* quoted here, see McQuillan, 2000, pp. 39–44
10. McQuillan, 2000; Andrews et al., in press; Bruner, 2002.
11. Barthes, as cited in Sontag, 1982, p. 251–252.
12. Mark Freeman, an unconventional psychologist, has over his research career examined St. Augustine's *Confessions*, a Tolstoy novella ("The Death of Ivan Illych"), and, in a theory-rich paper on time and memory, his last conversation with his father before a precipitous death. See Freeman, 1997, 2002.
13. Gubrium & Holstein, 2002; Atkinson & Silverman, 1997.
14. Bruner, 1991, p. 9. Others have made similar points to mine about the expanding definition of narrative, and elaborated their own definitions. See, among others, Clandinin & Connelley, 1994; Clandinin, 2007; Mishler, 1986.

15. Riessman, 1997.

16. Elliott, 2005, takes a less restrictive position, including quantitative studies in her understanding of narrative. There are other minimalist definitions of narrative, see McQuillan, 2000.

17. Salmon, in press.

18. Labov, 1982.

19. Mishler, 1999.

20. See Riessman, 1993, p. 18, and Riessman, 1990, pp. 74–119.

21. DeFina, 2003, p. 13.

22. Giddens, 1991. For a feminist critique of his theorizing of modernity, see Marshall, 1994.

23. Holstein & Gubrium, 2000.

24. Langellier & Peterson, 2004.

25. Cronon, 1992, p. 349.

26. For a thoughtful explication of the contrasting positions of White and Carr, see Brockmeier & Carbaugh, 2001, pp. 14–15. The debate is summarized in Hinchman & Hinchman, 1997.

27. Laslett, 1999, p. 392.

28. Yuval-Davis, 2006, p. 201, as quoted in Andrews, 2007, p. 9. On social and collective identities that form the basis of constructions of personal identity, see Graves, 2006.

29. Gamson, 2002. Also see Polletta, 2006.

30. Freeman, 2002, p. 9.

31. Bamberg & McCabe, 1998.

32. See Plummer, 1995.

33. Frank, 1995; White & Epston, 1990. Also see Riessman & Speedy (2007) for a review of narrative in the psychotherapy research literature.

34. See Brockmeier, 2000, p. 56, who says "every narrative about my past is always also a story told in, and about, the present as well as a story about the future." He draws on Kierkegaard who wrote long ago, "life must be understood backwards. But . . . it must be lived forwards. And if one thinks over the proposition it becomes more and more evident that life can never really be understood in time simply because at no particular moment can I find the necessary resting place from which to understand it—backwards" (cited in Brockmeier, 2000, pp. 51–52).

35. Amsterdam & Bruner, 2000; Davis, 1991.

36. See Pollotta, 2006.

37. White, 2002; White & Featherstone, 2005.

38. Amsterdam & Bruner, 2000.

39. Hall, 1997; Hall, Slembrouck, & Sarangi, 2006.

40. Charon, 2006; Charon & Montello, 2002.

41. As cited in Arendt, 1958, p. 175.

42. Didion, 1990.

43. Ochs & Capps, 2001, p. 2.

44. Bruner, 1987, p. 15.

45. Mishler, 1996.

46. Abbott, 1992, p. 428, as cited in Mishler, 1996, p. 89. On the importance of the case, see Abbott, 1992.

47. Radley & Chamberlain, 2001, p. 331.

48. When I ask students in the first class session on narrative methods to define narrative, invariably the concept of "meaning" comes up—interpretation of an event by the narrator. Issues of audience and other contexts of production are not typically raised initially by students. When we pursue questions of personal meaning— why is it important?—the connections between meaning and action are made: what individuals do in the world (behavior) is linked to the meanings events and experiences have for them.

49. Charon, 2006, p. 113.

50. Mishler, 1996, p. 80. He argues that case-based methods are no less scientific a form of inquiry than population-based, variable-centered approaches.

51. Jonsen, 1998.

52. Flyvbjerg, 2004; Radley & Chamberlain, 2001.

53. For examples from these traditions of work, see R. Atkinson, 1998, and Mishler, 1999, on life story/history; Bornat & colleagues, 2000, 2003, on oral history; Roberts, 2002; Swindells, 1985; Stanley, 1992 on autobiographical study.

54. For an example, see Riessman, 1990.

55. Bryman, 1988, as cited in Radley & Chamberlain, 2001, p. 324.

56. See Chase, 2005, pp. 653–656, for her comprehensive discussion of historical precedents for contemporary narrative inquiry.

57. Bertaux, 1981.

58. For a review of the issues, and an analysis of stories told by slaves, see Wholley, 2006.

59. Langellier, 2001a, p. 699.

60. Zussman, 2000.

61. Plummer, 2001.

62. Squire, 2005.

63. Labov & Waletzky, 1967. For a review of conversation analysis, see Silverman, 2001.

64. For overviews of narrative trends and readings in literary studies, see Smith & Watson, 1998, 2002.

65. Personal Narratives Group, 1989.

66. For examples of early feminist research in sociology that includes narrative dimensions, see Bell, 1988; Todd & Fisher, 1988; Davis, 1986. Major contributions to the narrative turn in anthropology are included in Behar & Gordon, 1995. E. M. Bruner, 1986, was an early advocate in anthropology.

67. Mishler, 1986; Sarbin, 1986; Bruner, 1986; Polkinghorne, 1988.

68. Bruner, 1991

69. Seidman, 1992.

70. Denzin, 2000, p. xiii.

71. Chris Kelly, personal communication, February 21, 2006.
72. Langellier, 2001a, pp. 699–700.
73. Chase, 2005, p. 651.
74. Van Maanen, 1988.
75. Books and edited collections emerging as I write include Andrews, 2007; Clandinin, 2007; Josselson, Lieblich, & McAdams, 2007. A partial (but outdated) listing of narrative work by field and social science discipline is included in Riessman & Speedy, 2007. For work on organizational and social movement narrative, see Boje, 1991; Davis, 2002; Feldman, 2001; Kane, 2001; Polletta, 2006. For classic work in education see Chapter 4.
76. See, among others, Cortazzi, 2001; Lieblich, Tuval-Mashiach, & Zilber, 1998; Clandinin, 2000; Mishler, 1995.
77. Kuhn, 1970, as cited in Flyvbjerg, 2004, p. 427.
78. Kuhn, 1970, as cited in Mishler, 1990, p. 420.

Endnotes for Chapter Two

1. Neander & Skott, 2006, p. 297, who draw on Mishler, 1986.
2. Mishler, 1991.
3. Mattingly, 1998, p. 8. Also see pp. 25–47.
4. Cladinin & Connelley (1994) make the distinction between three kinds of narrative data: living the experience, telling the experience, and interpreting the experience. I would stress that all three are interpretive and proxies, or imitations of life (see Riessman, 1993).
5. For examples of narrative research drawing on social work documents, see Urek, 2005; White, 2002; White & Featherstone, 2005; Hydén & Överlien, 2005.
6. Mishler, 1986, p. 67.
7. For a review of research interviewing in the social sciences that builds on Mishler, see Gubrium & Holstein, 2002.
8. Chase, 1995.
9. Devereaux, 1967.
10. DeVault, 1996, 2006; Fonow & Cook, 1991; Gluck & Patai, 1991; Reinharz, 1984/1991, 1992; Henry, 2003.
11. Riessman, 1987.
12. Elliott, 2005, p. 31. See also Holmberg et al., 2004.
13. Cortazzi et al., 2001.
14. Luttrell, 2003. For a key resource on group storytelling, see Langellier & Peterson, 2003.
15. Das, 1990, as cited in Andrews, 2007, p. 14. See Riessman, 2002, for a case study of the difficulty of listening to a report of violence.
16. For example, see Bell, 1999; Holloway & Jefferson, 2000.
17. Andrews, 2007, p. 15.
18. For more on the research, see Riessman, 2000a, 2000b, 2002, 2005. Sections of the present chapter are adapted from these publications.

19. Dube, 1986; Jeffery et al., 1989; Uberoi, 1993.

20. Mishler, 1986, p. 49.

21. Related to the epistemic issue of language, there is scholarship on transcription of oral discourse. Ochs, 1979, is the classic paper. See also Mishler, 1991; Ochs & Capps, 1995.

22. For more nuanced presentations, see Wortham, 2001; Holstein & Gubrium, 2000.

23. Salmon, in press.

24. Langellier, 2001b, p. 174.

25. For one model of transcription practices, see Ochs & Capps, 2001, pp. xi–xii. On general issues of transcription and analysis of naturally occurring talk, see Silverman, 2006.

26. Van Maanen, 1995, p. 15.

27. As cited in Jameson, 1972.

28. Merleau-Ponty, 1962/1989, p. 188.

29. Qualitative researchers often exclude the interviewer's initial question, interruptions, probing questions, back-channel utterances, and other features of everyday conversation.

30. Riessman, 2000.

31. Mishler, personal communication, May 2006.

32. Minha, 1992, as cited by Holstein & Gubrium, 2000, p. 105.

33. Emotions during fieldwork remain a neglected topic in writings about social science research, but see Kleinman & Copp, 1993.

34. Mattingly, 1998, p. 8. See also pp. 25–47.

35. Paper was eventually published in Swedish, see Riessman, 1997.

36. For a full description of the text of the letter, see Riessman, 2002.

37. See, among others, Van Vleet, 2002, 2003 for an anthropologist's perspective on translation regarding how language is used to produce emotion and kinship.

38. Temple, 1997, 2002.

39. Temple & Young, 2004, p. 164.

40. Riessman, 2005.

41. Malayalam is a member of the Dravidian family of languages spoke in South India. Pronominal reference and verb tense are often ambiguous and must be inferred from the surrounding discourse.

42. Elsewhere, I have argued that many Eurocentric assumptions are embedded in Goffman's theory of stigma; resistance strategies such as selective disclosure and "passing" privilege the individual and assume privacy and mass society, conditions that are rarely present for childless women in the South Indian context. Strangers on trains, for example, will ask a woman how many children she has and raise questions about what treatment she is getting if she has none. See Riessman, 2000.

43. Goffman, 1963.

44. On the issue of linked stories in interviews, see Bell, 1988.

45. Other human scientists have experimented in much more extreme ways with poetic representations. See Richardson, 1993; Poindexter, 2002.

46. We learned from elsewhere in the translated transcript about Celine's biography, which was typical of the life course for young women from the rural areas of

Kerala, arguably the most progressive state in India. Celine was educated for ten years in the village school, although she did not successfully complete the secondary school exams and could not go on to further education. Her family, though poor and from the *Pulaya* (formerly slave) caste, is not destitute. Both parents are employed (her mother as a day laborer and her father as a fisherman), and they own land. Celine's marriage was arranged when she was eighteen. After marriage she moved into her in-laws' house in a village some distance from her natal home. Somewhat atypically, the marriage was arranged despite religious differences between the families (hers is Christian, his is Hindu). Celine is dark-skinned in a country where "fair" skin is valued in women, and perhaps it was difficult to arrange a marriage for her. Rajiv, who was twenty-one and a fisherman, had less education than Celine and poor economic prospects. His parents pressured him into marriage, apparently because of the size of the dowry. His family's economic status was threatened because of several bad harvests, and the dowry promised to secure their situation. The marriage, however, did not make things better. His family developed further financial problems, and meanwhile the total dowry promised did not materialize. His "backward" family (Celine said) thought the new bride had brought misfortune—poverty and illness—on the family; in this context, unhappiness with Celine grew, including displeasure with her "nature" and lack of fertility. When she had failed to conceive after six months, the in-laws refused to talk to her. They pressured their son to abandon her, hoping perhaps that he would get another wife and another dowry.

47. My presence had a different meaning in the lives of this family than I experienced or intended. See Estroff, 1995; Riessman, 2005; Riessman & Mattingly, 2005.

48. There is ambiguity about timing here; in the first story Celine suggests the abuse may have continued for five years, yet the move back to her village happened six months after the marriage.

49. Temple, 1997, p. 609.

50. Paget, 1983.

51. See Riessman, 2000a, p. 146–147.

52. Rabinow & Sullivan, 1979/1987, p. 12.

53. Temple & Young, 2004, p. 171.

54. Temple, 1997, p. 614.

55. White, 1976, p. 36.

56. Mishler, 1991.

57. Ricoeur, as cited in Packer & Addison, 1989.

58. Mishler, 1986, p. 48.

59. Readers can find a full explication of the ideas found in this paragraph in Mishler, 1991.

Endnotes for Chapter Three

1. Empirical work from nursing includes Rasmussen et al., 1995; Rasmussen et al., 2000; Goodman, 2004; Salander, 2002; Phinney, 2002; Öhlen et al., 2002; Skott, 2003. See Smith & Sparkes, 2005, for an example from sports health that draws on

the work of Frank, 1995. Examples of other kinds of thematic narrative analysis include Holmberg, Orbuch, & Veroff, 2004; McAdams et al., 2001; Josselson et al., 2003; Lieblich et al., 1998; Gray, 2001; Bülow & Hydén, 2003; Baruch, 1981. Even classic work in feminist studies (Taylor et al., 1995; Gilligan et al., 2003) could be considered a form of thematic narrative analysis, since investigators do multiple readings of each transcript, with each designed to answer a particular thematic question.

2. Mishler, 1995, uses the distinction between "telling" and "told" to explore differences between reference and temporal order; they do not necessarily correspond in the various research examples he reviews.

3. Williams, 1984.

4. Bury, 1982; see also Bury, 2001; Dingwell, 1977.

5. Williams, 1984, p. 177.

6. Williams, 1984, p. 179.

7. Williams, 1984, p. 186.

8. Mills, 1959.

9. Williams, 1984, p. 197. The line of argument and theorizing about the functions of illness narrative has mushroomed in the twenty years since Williams published his research. See Hydén, 1997; Bell, 1999, 2000; Frank, 1995; Good, 1994; Mattingly, 1998; Lillrank, 2002, 2003.

10. Note, for example, the ambiguity in the final lines of the last excerpt quoted above: what does "it" refer to?

11. Williams, 1984, p. 190.

12. Williams, 1984, p. 191. In his recent research on men's everyday theorizing following the collapse of steel and mining industries in Wales, Williams, 2004, interrogates particular words participants select. Drawing the reader's attention to one man's lexical choice ("segregated") to describe his unemployment situation, Williams explores the terms' history and politics in communities of color, that is, its racial meanings. Appropriation of the word by a white working-class man in Wales is significant.

13. Ewick & Silbey, 2003, p. 1338.

14. See Abu-Lughod, 1990; Scott, 1990.

15. Ewick & Silbey, 2003, p. 1336.

16. Ewick & Silbey, 2003, p. 1337.

17. Ewick & Silbey, 2003, p. 1338. It is not clear whether "familiarity with the interviews" meant that they were ones conducted by the investigators, rather than other interviewers.

18. Ewick & Silbey, 2003, p. 1349.

19. Ewick & Silbey, 2003, p. 1349.

20. Ewick & Silbey, 2003, p. 1362.

21. Ewick & Silbey, 2003, p. 1343. Students in my graduate seminar noted that Ewick and Silbey fail to attend to power relations in the research relationship, at the same time as they focus their research on power.

22. Ewick & Silbey, 2003, p. 1344.

23. Mishler, personal communication (Minutes of Narrative Study Group's meeting with Susan Silbey, December 29, 2001).

24. Stanley (1992) argues that autobiographies and biographies are overlapping; the distinctions are not generic, consequently she introduced the slash. Her insight has been accepted by others.

25. Tamboukou, 1999, 2003, 2004.

26. Tamboukou, in press.

27. Tamboukou, 2003, p. 53. Material in sections to follow comes from personal communications (August 2004), or from Tamboukou's writings, published and in press.

28. Tamboukou draws on Foucault here; see Tamboukou, 2003, p. 11.

29. Tamboukou, 2003, p. 58.

30. Tamboukou, 2003, p. 3.

31. Tamboukou, 2003, p. 59.

32. Bamberg & Andrews, 2004.

33. Stephen, 1927, a biography of Emily Davis, cited in Tamboukou, 2003.

34. Hughes, 1946, p. 120, cited in Tamboukou, 2003.

35. Tamboukou, 2003, p. 67; source of letter, biography by Grier, 1937, p. 34.

36. Riessman, 1990, 1993.

37. On working with letters, see Stanley, 2004; Jolly & Stanley, 2005.

38. Tamboukou is currently studying several artists who are "nomadic subjects"—women who have gone beyond the boundaries of their countries and cultures to search for spaces in which to paint.

39. See Mattingly & Garro, 2000; Skultans, 2000, 2003b; Good & Good, 1994; Hurwitz, Greenhalgh, & Skultans, 2004.

40. Cain, 1991. When I have taught the paper, some students take issue with Cain's assumption about a singular identity—the AA alcoholic. What happens, they wonder, to other identity positions the speaker or writer may hold?

41. There were also written accounts by AA members (up to twenty answers to the question "Who am I?") not included in Cain's published analysis.

42. Cain, 1991, p. 210.

43. Cain, 1991, p. 234.

44. Cain, 1991, p. 235.

45. Cain, 1991, p. 228.

46. The source for the often cited term "master narrative" is Lyotard, 1984.

47. Cain, 1991, p. 237.

48. Cain, 1991, p. 215.

49. Cain, 1991, p. 216.

50. Cain, 1991, p. 229.

51. Cain, 1991, p. 239.

52. As cited in Cain, 1991, p. 227 from Alcoholics Anonymous, 1979 (*Young People and AA*. New York: Alcoholics Anonymous World Services).

53. For the full text, see Cain, 1991, pp. 225–227.

54. Cain, 1991, pp. 246–247.

55. Extract is abbreviated from Cain, 1991, pp. 247–248.

56. Cain, 1991, p. 211. Medicalization was first noted in the medical sociology literature by Zola, 1972, and Illich, 1976; the concept was further developed by Conrad & Schneider, 1980/1992; Riessman, 1983; Bell, 1987; Clarke et al., 2003.

57. Reinharz, 1984, wrote about her struggles as a graduate student with academic writing conventions in sociology. In anthropology, there was a nascent tradition of work that included the observer in cultural description, but they were senior women academics, not students; see Briggs, 1970; Myerhoff, 1978, 1992.

58. Given the representational decisions Cain made, she could not draw the reader's attention to a given narrator's lexical choice or speculate about its meanings because she chose to represent spoken narratives in synopses and reconstructed dialogues. Micro-analytic strategies are not appropriate for these reconstructed texts, although the written narrative in *The Big Book* and other AA documents might have benefited from analysis of language.

59. For a conceptual framework that could guide development of the line of inquiry, see Polletta, 2006.

60. Frank, 1995, created a compelling narrative typology of written literary narratives of severe illness and disability. He maps the contrasting ways writers interpret the rupture of illness in restitution, quest, and chaos narratives. Form and thematic content of the autobiographical accounts combine to communicate distinctive understandings of illness. Frank's typology has been adapted by others to study oral accounts of disability; see Smith & Sparkes, 2004, 2005. Although the candidate exemplars in my chapter did not explore the topic, investigators can locate personal stories in the storehouse of classical Greek and biblical storylines—genres of journey, redemption, conversion, the tragic, heroic, comic, and others genres.

61. For a review, see DeVault, 2006.

62. There is considerable diversity in grounded theory. For excellent discussion of the traditions of positivist and constructivist work within the approach, see Charmaz, 2006; Clarke, 2005. See also Coffey & Atkinson, 1996.

63. Charmaz, 2006, p. 45.

64. The idea that the analyst has to "fracture" data in the service of interpretation was Anselm Strauss's language in formulating the grounded theory coding paradigm (Strauss, 1987, p. 29). Recently, Adele Clarke wrote (citing Riessman, 1995, among others), "grounded theory and other analytic approaches have been criticized for 'fracturing' data, for 'violating the integrity of participants' narratives, for 'pulling apart' stories, and so on . . . To me, this is not a weakness or problem but the key to grounded theory's analytic, rather than (re)presentational, strength. Analysis and (re)presentation are two deeply different qualitative research approaches, both valuable and both of which I support" (Clarke, 2005, p. 8). I wholeheartedly agree. Both approaches are valuable, and they are different.

65. Charmaz, 2006, pp. 50–53.

66. See Mishler, 1979. There is also the tendency in analysis to ignore "outliers" and observations that don't fit neatly into a category or typology.

Endnotes for Chapter Four

1. Burke, 1952.

2. See Connelly & Clandinin, 1999; Clandinin, 2006. Another important tradition in education examines language acquisition. See McCabe, 1997; Allen et al., 1994.

3. For another application, see Mishler, 1999, who maps the career trajectories of a group of artist/craftpersons over time; the careers consist of mainline movements, detours, and episodes of economic work to support the artistic work.

4. See Rich & Grey, 2005.

5. Todorov, as cited in Elliott (2005), p. 46. For key theoretical texts in the structural and poststructural traditions, see McQuillan, 2000.

6. Plummer, 1995.

7. Squire, 2007.

8. Heath, 1983.

9. Heath, 1983, p. 11. Children in the black community rarely told factual straightforward stories, reserving them for serious occasions; instead they creatively fictionized details surrounding a real event, learning at home that stories were for capturing attention and winning favors, a style they brought into classrooms.

10. Health, 1983, p. 184.

11. As one teacher in Cazden's class wrote, "There's no other way to honestly get back at that moment in time and know what was going on without having a transcript. There's no other way to do it. You can take notes afterwards and that's helpful, but it's not as honest and powerful—as real—as having a transcript . . . There's nothing else that can ever come close—putting yourself back there . . . It's the only way to bring everybody else with you as well. Not only do *you* go back there, but *we* get to be there. It's always worth the price" (cited in Cazden, 2001, pp. 6–7).

12. See Michaels and Cazden, 1984; Michaels, 1981.

13. All the teachers, Michaels and Cazden stress, were "good teachers"—volunteers (mostly white, but not exclusively), who had agreed to be observed and audiotaped for the research, teachers who valued sharing time and understood and expected dialect variation among black students.

14. Michaels, 1985; Gee, 1985. When I teach these studies of children's storytelling, graduate students from communities of color in my research methods class sometimes note that the nascent forms used by the young black storytellers bear some similarity to the episodic representations in novels of African American and Latin American writers, including Gabriel Garcia Marquez.

15. Cazden, 2001, credits Delpit, 1995, with the term.

16. Charon, 2001, 2006; see also Greenhalgh & Hurwitz, 1998; Hurwitz et al., 2004.

17. Guzik & Gorlier, 2004; Herman, 1999.

18. Labov & Waletzky, 1967; A special issue/number of a narrative journal recently reprinted the paper and featured contemporary scholars' responses to it; see Bamberg, 1997.

19. Labov, 1972, p. xvi. "One major conclusion of our work . . . is that the major causes of reading failure are political and cultural conflicts in the classroom, and dialect differences are important because they are symbols of this conflict" (p. xiv).

20. Labov, 1972, p. 364.

21. Labov, 1972, p. 372. At a later point in the chapter, when discussing displacement sets (see p. 359), only lines v-y are listed as evaluation, line u remains complicating action. The ambiguity reflects how coding the function of clauses can shift with the focus of inquiry.

22. Labov, 1982, p. 235.

23. Rich & Gray, 2005.

24. Riessman, 1990, p. 77–78. I thank Dennie Wolf again for her insight; from a personal communication, May 10, 1988.

25. Elsewhere (Riessman, 1989), I discuss issues the narrative does not resolve—when and why did she finally leave the marriage? I analyze a second narrative from the interview with Gloria that addresses these and other issues.

26. See Robichaux, 2003; Robichaux & Clark, 2006.

27. Robichaux & Clark, 2006.

28. Robichaux & Clark, 2006.

29. Gee, 1985. For prior work he built on see Chafe, 1980; Hymes, 1974, 1981; Scollon & Scollon, 1981; Tannen, 1984.

30. Gee, 1991.

31. See among others Öhlen, 2003; Edvardsson et al., 2003; Poindexter, 2002a.

32. Gee, 1985, 1991.

33. Gee, 1991, p. 23.

34. Gee, 1991, p. 21.

35. Gee, 1991, p. 23.

36. Because prosodic dimensions vary across languages, Gee's method is not easily applicable to translated texts. See Chapter 2 for an adaptation and Ohlen (2003) for one an application to a text originally in Swedish.

37. Gee, 1991, p. 16, fn 1.

38. Gee, 1991, p. 36.

39. Schenkein, 1979.

40. Gee (1991, p. 25) writes about the issue of stanza length, "I don't insist on four as a privileged number here (though it is intriguing how often stanzas in English formal poetry are four lines long)."

41. See Riessman, 1990, pp. 142–149.

42. "Ninety Miles an Hour," written by H. Blair and Don Robertson (ASCAP). Lyric appears on Bob Dylan's album "Down in the Grove," Columbia Records 1988. I thank Sven Knutsen, who was a student at Linköping University, Sweden, who pointed out to me that a particular song recorded by Bob Dylan is embedded in Rick's narrative.

43. See Riessman, 1993, p. 18; Cheshire & Ziebland, 2005, p. 23–4.

44. Mishler, 1997.

45. For recent examples of structural approaches not covered here, see Quasthoff & Becker, 2005; Thornborrow & Coates, 2005. For research relevant to professional practice, health, and the human services, see Poindexter, 2002a, 2003a, 2003b; Edvardsson et al., 2003; Öhlen, 2003; Bülow & Hydén, 2003; Hydén & Överlien, 2005; Örulv & Hydén, 2006.

46. For examples that locate individual narratives about health in larger social structural contexts, see Bell, 1999.

Endnotes for Chapter Five

1. Goffman, 1963, 1969, 1981.

2. Goffman, 1974, pp. 508–509.

3. Young, 2000, p. 108.

4. See, among others, Postlewait & Davis, 2003; Butler, 1990. For a compelling and early example of performing a social scientist's text, see Paget, 1990/1994.

5. Langellier, 2001b. Another precursor to the approach I outline in the chapter can be found in Bell, 1999, who compared the illness narratives of two women, separated in time by history and the women's health movement. She historicizes illness experience, showing how a social movement changed women's conversations with doctors and a research interviewer. Arguably, some narrative studies of interaction between doctors and patients anticipate shifts that occur with dialogic/performative analysis. See, among others, Clark & Mishler, 1992.

6. "When a speaker acts out a story, as if to give his audience the opportunity to experience the event, and his evaluation of it, he may be said to be giving a performance" (Wolfson, 1982, p. 24). See also Bauman, 1977, 1986; Langellier & Peterson, 2004, Peterson & Langellier, 2006; Maclean, 1988.

7. For an introduction to Bakhtin, and excerpts of his key works, students can consult Dentith, 1995; Morris, 1994. For related sources, see Vice, 1997; Wortham, 2001.

8. Dentith, 1995, p. 13.

9. I came upon a vivid example of history in language when completing this chapter and living in Bristol, U.K., where there are streets with startling names such as "White Ladies Rd." and "Black Boy Hill." When I first arrived, it was difficult for me, a North American, even to voice these street names, since they evoked such racial meanings, but they rolled off the tongues of colleagues at Bristol University with ease, tracing back to Bristol's history as a major port in the slave trade. Black Boy Hill was one of several slave markets. The origin of White Ladies Rd. is uncertain, and it may refer to a neighborhood where the slave owner's and their wives lived, or it may refer to the visual presence of Carmelite nuns from a convent in the neighborhood. In the early 1980s, an effort was initiated to change the street names, but the black community in Bristol protested, and the idea was abandoned.

10. Iser, 1978, 1989/1993.

11. Iser 1989/1993, p. 10.

12. Broyard, 1992, p. 21.

13. Riessman, 1990, 2003, 2004b.
14. Langellier, 2001b, p. 150, who is drawing on Maclean, 1988.
15. Maclean, 1988, p. 72.
16. For excerpts and discussion of these sections, see Riessman, 2004b.
17. Wolfson, 1982, p. 109.
18. Sawin, 1992.
19. Wolfson, 1982, and others call the verb tense the conversational historical present.
20. Goffman, 1974, p. 5.
21. Minister, 1991, as cited in Langellier, 2001b, p. 151.
22. Frank, 1995, pp. 54–55.
23. Herman, 1999, p. 16.
24. Zola, 1982.
25. Iser, 1989/1993, pp. 4, 10.
26. Hall, 1997, p. 30.
27. Iser, 1978, p. 285.
28. Sarangi & Roberts, 1999.
29. Bourdieu,1993.
30. Mills, 1959.
31. Brown, 1998.
32. Social class and how it shapes youth has been a central topic of research in the United Kingdom, because class is an explicit category of personal belonging and social appraisal. For an early example, see Willis, 1977.
33. Brown, 1998, p. 21.
34. Brown, 1998, p. 32.
35. Taylor et al., 1995; Gilligan et al., 2003; Brown & Gilligan, 1991.
36. Brown, 1998, p. 33.
37. Brown, 1998, p. 34.
38. Brown, 1998, p. 34.
39. Brown, 1998, p. 34.
40. Brown, 1998, p. 35.
41. For a useful discussion of Bakhtin's concept of ventriloquation, and an application, see Wortham, 2001, pp. 62–75.
42. Wertsch, 1991, as cited in Brown, 1998, p. 232.
43. Brown, 1998, p. 123.
44. Brown, 1998, p. 128.
45. A reader from education had an alternative interpretation of Transcript 5.2, concluding that Miss Davis may be "interested and caring." Different positionings shape the reading of any text, but all readings may not be equally "valid." Brown emphasizes the recurrent pattern of anger between the working-class girls and teachers, and the excerpt in the transcript is an instance of the broad pattern.
46. Brown, 1998, p. 182.
47. Although Brown doesn't interrogate narrative form here, Theresa chooses habitual narrative to make her point, rather than story, precisely to communicate that such events happen over and over again. See Riessman,1990, pp. 98–99.

48. For more on pronoun use in narrative, see O'Connor, 1994.

49. Brown 1998, p. 166.

50. The words "narrative" and "story" do not appear in the index of Brown's book, and it is not even clear that she locates her work in narrative traditions. She does, however, use the language of narrative at places in the book. The voice-centered methods developed by Carol Gilligan and colleagues have similarities with, and differences from, narrative analysis as I develop the approaches in the book.

51. For an example, see Luttrell & Ward, 2004.

52. Cazden, 2001.

53. Delpit, 1995, as cited in Cazden, p. 6.

54. Gallas, 1994, p. xiii.

55. Gallas, 1994, p. xiii.

56. Bakhtin, 1981, p. 184. See Morris, 1994, for a lengthy excerpt from *The Dialogic Imagination* (that includes the quoted passage) and other works, along with an extensive introduction and glossary of key terms in Bakhtin's theory of language.

57. Jiana had lived with her grandmother for periods during the previous year, and attended kindergarten for only a few months.

58. The case study that follows is from Gallas, 1994, pp. 20–35.

59. Gallas, 1994, p. 22.

60. Gallas, 1994, p. 23.

61. Gallas, 2003.

62. Gallas, 1994, p. 6.

63. Gallas, 1994, p. 6.

64. Gallas, 1994, pp. 5–6.

65. Gallas, 1994, p. xiii.

66. Gallas writes that the narrative tools Jiana introduced, while unfamiliar and initially uncomfortable for white children to use, turned into skills that virtually all the children attempted to incorporate into their talk "long after Jiana had left us." The child stopped attending school toward the end of the academic year; perhaps her family had moved (hopefully securing permanent housing).

67. Cazden, 2001, p. 76.

Endnotes for Chapter Six

1. Radley, 2002, p. 21.

2. Harper, 2005, p. 757.

3. Visual studies is a vast and diverse field. For key reviews of studies in the human sciences and methodological discussion, see among others Harper, 2000, 2005; Harrison, 2002a, 2002b; Pink, 2001, 2004; Rose, 2001. For classic texts on interpreting images in relation to social worlds, see Berger, 1972; Berger & Mohr, 1982. Although not used in the five exemplars, procedures exist for coding the reading of photographs (see, for example, Lutz & Collins, 1993.

4. For examples of these images in a classic essay, see Becker, 1986.

5. Harper, 2005, calls this way of incorporating images "visual illustration" and says images can "put a face on statistical data" (p. 749).

6. Wang & Burris, 1997, pp. 370–371.

7. Harper, 2005, p. 747.

8. Available for educational use from Gretchen.berland@yale.edu. Other physicians are giving video cameras to patients to assess environmental components of illness; see Rich et al., 2000.

9. Stoller, 1997.

10. Becker, 1986, p. 241.

11. Becker, 1886, p. 242.

12. Becker, 1986, p. 231–232.

13. One could argue that a caption is part of the production process, the strategy used in several exemplars in the chapter.

14. Rose, 2001, pp. 188–190.

15. For detailed discussion of different genres of image and what they can accomplish in social research, see Knowles & Sweetman, 2004.

16. For an example that compares narratives of the environmental history of the Great Plains, see Cronon, 1992.

17. Although beyond my scope for the chapter, Creef also uses drawings, images from newspapers, and paintings to support her claims.

18. When in the camps, young Japanese American men were drafted, and they served in racially segregated units on the battlefields of Europe. In 1988, the U.S. government made a formal apology, and offered to pay reparations to the formerly interned who were still living. Estimates of the worth of lost homes and businesses (in 1999 values) was between four and five billion dollars. For more on economic and other aspects at Manzanar, see www.nps.gov.

19. General John L. Dewitt, as cited in Creef, p. 16. The report goes on to say the loyal and disloyal could not be distinguished because "undiluted" blood passed between generations.

20. Creef, 2004, p. 16.

21. Creef, 2004, p. 21.

22. Creef, 2004, p. 21.

23. Creef, 2004, p. 21.

24. Creef, 2004, p. 32.

25. Creef, 2004, p. 32.

26. Creef, 2004, p. 26.

27. Dorothy Lange's original photograph was often cropped in later prints, changing meaning.

28. Creef, 2004, p. 43.

29. A compelling image (not included here) depicts a farmer in California just after his evacuation sale; it captures "the body language of dispossession and defeat even before evacuation has begun." Other images depict patriarchal fathers "rendered impotent in their inability to protect both their property and their families" (Creef, 2004, p. 55).

30. Creef, 2004, pp. 55–56.

31. Creef, 2004, p. 56.

32. Cynthia Takano, 1987, p. 61 as cited in Creef, p. 204 (fn 105).

33. Creef, 2004, p. 61.

34. Creef, 2004, p. 62.

35. Creef, 2004, pp. 63–64.

36. Cronon, 1992.

37. Material that follows is primarily from Bell, 2002. See also Bell, 2006, Radley & Bell, 2007.

38. Grisby, 1991, as cited in Bell, 2002, p. 11.

39. Bell, 2002, p. 12.

40. Bell, 2002, p. 14.

41. Spence, 1988, p.153, as cited in Bell, 2002, p. 15.

42. Bell, 2002, p. 16.

43. Bell, 2002, p. 16.

44. Bell, 2002, p. 16.

45. Bell, 2002, p. 17.

46. Bell, 2006, pp. 37–38.

47. Bell, 2002, p. 19.

48. Bell, 2002, p. 19,

49. Spence, 1995, p. 214, as cited in Bell, 2006, p. 38.

50. Spence, 1995, p. 216, as cited in Bell, 2006, p. 38–39.

51. Radley & Bell, 2007.

52. Bell, 2006, p. 39.

53. As cited in Bell, 2002, p. 21.

54. Spence, 1995, p. 217, as cited in Bell, 2002, p. 21.

55. Bell, 2002, p. 21.

56. Bell, 2002, p. 21.

57. Bell, 2002, p. 22.

58. Bell is drawing on Mishler, 1984, about voice here. She added additional context about "Untitled" in a personal communication. She first saw the photograph in *Cultural Sniping* and wrote to Terry Dennett (Spence's archivist) to ask for permission to use it, and for a copy. He sent the photograph, a different version (with more background) than the representation in *Cultural Sniping*. Bell has since seen other versions of the photograph; one shows a camera resting next to Spence on the bed. "The different versions of it point out to me just how constructed photographic 'truth' is and how one needs to be very careful in the interpretation of photographs. To see Spence holding the shutter bulb but without a camera lying next to her is not the same as to see her with a camera resting next to her on the hospice bed." Viewers interpret the image depending on the representation, with and without cropping. Precisely the same issues arise, of course, when an investigator selects a narrative segment to analyze; the part is asked to stand in for the whole, shaping meaning (see Chapter 2).

59. In a later paper, Bell treats Spence's art, and the work of another artist representing her breast cancer, as triggers for cancer activism and an embodied health movement. See Radley & Bell, 2007.

60. Tamboukou, 2007a, p. 194.

61. Taubman, 1985, p. 18 as cited in Tamboukou, 2007a, p. 194.

62. Tamboukou, 2007a, p. 195

63. Tamboukou, 2007b, writes that Gwen John got the idea from Richardson's epistolary novel, *Clarissa,* that she was reading at the time and which had left a lasting impression on her.

64. Foster, 1997, p. 8, as cited in Tamboukou, 2005, p. 16.

65. See www.artcyclopedia.com; www.bridgeman.co.uk.

66. Tamboukou, 2007a, p. 192.

67. Tamboukou, 2007b, p. 11.

68. Tamboukou, 2007b, p. 11.

69. Tamboukou, 2007a, p. 192.

70. Tamboukou, 2007b, p. 7.

71. Tamboukou, 2007b. She notes that Rodin was irritated by John's bold articulation of passion and pleasure; he wrote, "immodesty is not charming in a woman" (Tamboukou, 2007b, quoting Chitty, 1987, p. 90).

72. Tamboukou, 2007b, p. 8.

73. Tamboukou, 2007a, p. 191.

74. Tamboukou, 2007a, p. 193.

75. Classics in feminist narrative auto/biography include Personal Narratives Group, 1989; Heilbrun, 1988; Bateson, 1989.

76. Stanley, 2004.

77. Plummer, 2001, pp. 54–55 as cited in Stanely, 2004, p. 203.

78. In a personal communication (May 2005), Tamboukou said that Gwen John's written French was basic, "easy" for her as a non-native speaker to understand and translate.

79. Luttrell, 2003, p. 147. She calls her project an "ethnography of representation and self-representations—how specific girls in a specific context confront the burden of representation regarding 'pregnant teenagers,' and as individuals" (personal communication, July 25, 2006).

80. Luttrell, 2003.

81. Luttrell, 2003, pp. xiv–xv, discusses the complexities of gender and racial identification: "Whereas I might have referred to them as 'young women,' they called themselves girls. Whereas I would have referred to the majority of the girls as 'African American,' they call themselves black. Whereas I might have referred to three of the girls as recent Mexican immigrants, the daughters of migrant workers who have settled in this Piedmont region, they called themselves 'Mexican and American.' And whereas I have chosen to refer to two of the girls as white, this was not a label I heard them use to describe themselves. Their black class mates referred to each as 'the white girl,' but not in her presence. I have also wrestled with how best to describe myself in relation to the girls: as a mother; as a middle-class, middle-aged university professor; as a self-consciously white woman in an educational setting with predominantly black students, teachers, and administrators. All these labels are problematic and incomplete. Moreover, as the girls would attest, these categories of fitting in and belonging are elusive and fluid; in fact, they can be bones of contention among people. Arguments

between the girls about racial identification occurred frequently—'If she says she is black then that's what she is, I don't care if she looks white.'"

82. Luttrell, 2003, p. 71.

83. Luttrell, 2003, p. 148.

84. The students constructed portraits with paste paper, a Japanese paper-making technique they had been taught during an art activity.

85. Luttrell, 2003, p. 48.

86. Luttrell, 2003, p. 48.

87. The investigator does not present the diverse responses to the book, focusing instead on audiencing of the self-portraits among the girls, and between herself and the girls.

88. Luttrell, 2003, p. 48.

89. Luttrell, 2003, p. 48.

90. Luttrell, 2003, see especially Chapter 6, and Appendix.

91. Luttrell, 2003, p. 68.

92. Luttrell, 2003, p. 68.

93. The material that follows is from Luttrell, 2003, pp. 68–69.

94. Luttrell, 2003, p. 42.

95. Luttrell, 2003, p. 69.

96. Luttrell, 2003, p. 70. Visual artists speak of hands as one of the most difficult anatomical features to represent.

97. Luttrell, 2003, p. 70.

98. For examples of photo voice projects, see, among others, Radley & Taylor, 2003; Lorenz, 2003, 2006; Wang & Burris, 1997; Lykes, 1991.

99. Luttrell, 2003, p. 147.

100. Luttrell, 2003, p. 151.

101. See www.gse.harvard.edu/news/features/luttre1101012005.html; Luttrell, 2006.

102. For assistance with interpreting visual diaries, see Renov, 1999.

103. For example, see "Harlem Diary" (1995) where sociologist Terry Williams worked with young African Americans who become videographers of their community.

104. Walkerdine, Lucey, & Melody, 2001.

105. The segments are archived at www.hi8us-south.co.uk. Contact info@hi8us-south.co.uk.

106. Pini, 2001, p. 2.

107. Pini, 2001, p. 3. Emphasis in original. For an example of "empowering" narrative methods for working with youth, see Martin, 1998.

108. Pini, 2001, p. 3.

109. Pini, 2001, p. 1.

110. Russell, 1999, p. 27, as cited in Pini, 2001, p. 4.

111. Pini, 2001, p. 4.

112. Pini, 2001, p. 4.

113. Pini, 2001, p. 7.

114. Pini, 2001, p. 7.

115. Pini, 2001, p. 6.

116. Pini, 2001, p. 6.

117. Walkerdine, 2003.

118. Pini, 2001, p. 7.

119. Pini, 2001, p. 7.

120. Pini, 2001, p. 7.

121. Pini, 2001, p. 7.

122. Pini, 2001, p. 11.

123. Pini, 2001, p. 11.

124. Pini, 2001, p. 8.

125. Pini, 2001, p. 11.

126. Russell, 1999, p. 276, as cited by Pini, 2001, p. 13.

127. Walkerdine, 2003.

128. Pini, 2001, p. 12.

129. Rose, 2001, p. 2.

130. Sontag, 2003.

131. Radley & Bell, 2007.

132. Sontag, 1977, p. 3 as cited in Bach, 2007.

133. Gefter, 2006.

134. Gross, Katz, & Ruby, 1998, 2003. See also Bach, 2007; Clarke, 2005, chap. 6.

135. See Pink, 2004, pp. 394–396; Clarke, 2005, pp. 259–260, fn 21.

136. Becker, 2000, as cited by Bell, 2006, p. 32.

Endnotes for Chapter Seven

1. Heisenberg, *Physics and Philosophy*, 1959.

2. Georgankopoulou, 2006, p. 1.

3. Bosk, 1979, p. 193, as cited by Maxwell, 1992.

4. A report on an NSF workshop appears in Ragin et al., 2004, as cited by Denzin, 2005.

5. Gilgun, 2002, p. 360.

6. Denzin, 2005, p. 22.

7. On the evolving issue of standards for qualitative research, see, among others Denzin & Lincoln, 1994; Lincoln, 1995; Lincoln & Guba, 1985; Hammersley, 2002; Malterud, 2001; Maxwell, 1992; Mishler, 1990; Seale, 2002, 2004b; Sparkes, 2002;   Smith, 2003. Clive Seale (2002) notes that Campbell & Stanley (1963)—a book on experimental design that many researchers were raised on—were more nuanced in the formulations of internal and external validity than usually acknowledged. Flyvbjerg (2004) shows how Donald Campbell radically changed his position about case studies later in his career. Also see Mishler (1990, p. 418) on Cronbach's views.

8. Seale, 2002, p. 98.

9. Morgan, 1983, as cited by Lather, 1986, p. 270.

10. On writing different kinds of "tales" in social research, see Van Maanen, 1988. For background in the philosophies and epistemologies suited to work in the social sciences, see Benton & Craib, 2001; Delanty & Strydom, 2003.

11. Messick, 1987.

12. Clifford, 1986, p. 7.

13. The term "historical truth" comes from Spence, 1982, pp. 30–33. A psycho-analyst, he makes the distinction between historical/factual and narrative truth in therapeutic work.

14. On falsity in the case for war made by the Bush and Blair administrations, see Falk, Gendzier, & Lifton, 2006; Rich, 2006; Ricks, 2006.

15. Realism underpins some auto/biographical research (whether focused on a single case or the life history of a group). For an example, see Bertaux, 1981. For a debate about "truth" among Fischer-Rosenthal, Kochuyt, and Bertaux, see *Biography and Society Newsletter*, 1995 and 1996 (ISA Research Committee 38). In this debate, Bertaux (1995, p. 2) takes the position that self-reported factual data in personal narratives should be verified for sociological purposes, and analyzed for "recurrent patterns concerning collective phenomena or shared collective experience in a particular milieu." For an excellent exposition of the debates in biographical research about reflexivity and "truth," see Davis, 2003.

16. For a summary and key readings in historiography, see Ankersmit, 2005. On oral history, see Bornat, 2003. Bain Attwood, 2005, compares the procedures contemporary academics use to demonstrate veracity in their narrative histories of Australia with the "public" or vernacular histories that have sprung from the democratization of history in Indigenous social movements. Vernacular histories developed by documentary film makers and Aboriginal leaders about the violence of white settlement draw on different principles of veracity.

17. Dohrenwend et al., 2006.

18. Bruner, 1991, pp. 13, 18.

19. Hammersley, 2002, p. 9.

20. White, 1976, p. 44.

21. Denzin, 2000, pp. xii–xiii. For an elegant essay on the "truths" of experience, see Personal Narratives Group, 1989, pp. 261–264.

22. McCormack, 2004.

23. Agar & Hobbs, 1982, p. 29.

24. Linde, 1993, p. 220.

25. Langer rejects the term "survivors," preferring "former victims" or "witnesses."

26. Langer, 1991, p. xi.

27. Langer, 1991, p. 3 & 5.

28. Langer, 1991, p. 15.

29. Schiff & Cohler, 2001, p. 115.

30. Schiff & Cohler, 2001, p. 135.

31. Langer, 1991, pp. 16–17.

32. Ricoeur, 1991, pp. 27–28.

33. Andrews, 2007, p. 41.

34. Seale, 2002, p. 98. His position echoes Gadamer's advocacy of critical self-awareness—a way to move closer toward (greater) objectivity in perception. Self-reflexivity is the way methodological awareness is practiced in feminist research.

35. Lincoln & Guba, 1985.

36. Ehrenreich, 2001. Robert Coles's (1967) study of children living in poverty and more recent work are less persuasive in part because he is an academic psychiatrist, not a journalist, and avoids methodological issues.

37. White, 1976, p. 22.

38. Cronbach & Suppes, 1969, p. 16 as cited in Lincoln, 2005, p. 171.

39. Gergen, 1985, p. 272.

40. Ellis & Bochner, 2000, p. 748.

41. Gorman, 2005, p. 621.

42. On the issue of evaluating autoethnography, see Sparkes, 2002; Atkinson, 1997; Atkinson & Delamont, 2006; Clough, 2002; Josselson & Lieblich, 2005.

43. Gadamer, 2004, the German philosopher in his classic text on hermeneutics, argues that we bring our personal experience, cultural traditions, and prior understandings to any perception, which renders them unstable. Perceptions shift in the interplay between an author's intentions and readers' responses.

44. Mishler, 1986, 1999.

45. Flyvbjerg, 2004. Also see Radley & Chamberlain, 2001.

46. Flyvbjerg, 2004, p. 430.

47. Mishler, 1990, p. 422.

48. Hammersley, 2002, p. 17.

49. Cronbach, 1988, p. 6, as cited in Misher, 1990, p. 415.

50. Camic, Rhodes, & Yardley, 2003.

51. Mishler, 1990, p. 419.

52. Chase, 2005.

53. Davies, 2006, p. 182.

54. Thompson, 1978, p. 2, as cited in Andrews, 2007, p. 41.

55. Lather, 1986, p. 272. Empowering research designs include three interwoven elements: reciprocity (through member checks, collaborative interpretation, and a vigorous self-reflexivity); dialectical theory-building rather than theoretical imposition; and interrogating the validity of interpretation.

56. Reason observes that cooperative inquiry is one articulation of action research. See Reason, 2002, 2003. On PAR, see Reason & Bradbury, 2001.

57. Feagin & Vera, 2001, p. 166.

58. Fals-Borda, as cited in Feagin & Vera, 2001, p. 173.

59. Wang & Burris, 1997, describe a participatory needs assessment that used photovoice methods with a rural community in China. Two strong dissertation projects can aid students. First, Janet Kapetas conducted a cooperative action project with a group of marginalized Indigenous people in Western Australia. She worked intensively with a group over a six-year period in creative writing workshops and they produced a book. Participants crafted written narratives, visual images, and performance texts to recount their parents' histories of being taken away from families by

authorities to be raised as white (the "stolen generation") and forced from Aboriginal lands to Christian missions. Some participants who could barely read and write when the groups began, crafted many stories and tales of the bush, and all developed literary skills over time; several went on to become teachers, nurses, and artists (see Kapatas et al., 2000; Kapatas, 2006). When I talked in 2006 to several Aboriginal women who had been part of the book project, one said that when she began "the course" she was reluctant to read her work to the group, so she "asked Jan to do it." Now she "speaks up everywhere"—at community meetings and to government authorities. I asked whether writing about the "stolen generation" had opened up the topic in conversations with parents. One woman said "no" emphatically, because the pain of remembering was too strong; she then educated me about what had happened in the missions. In terms of contemporary Australian politics, the "truth" of the dissertation lies in its political use for Aboriginal communities, including current efforts to acquire native title to land in Western Australia. The second dissertation project is from Fay Martin (Martin, 1998), a Canadian social worker. She turned the agency of authorship over to a sample of youth coming out of foster care in Britain, a group whose difficult lives had been constructed into "cases" over the years by various child welfare workers. She gave power back to the young speakers, who became authors. They then produced a monograph (in dialogue with the radical social work investigator) that challenged how they had been represented in case records. The dissertation amplified muted voices of youth in child protection, initiated dialogue, and the book that was collaboratively produced (Fay, 1989) forged alliances among radical social workers critical of child welfare practices.

   60. Women of PhotoVoice/ADMI & Lykes, 2000, p. 17.

   61. See Women of PhotoVoice/ADMI & Lykes, 2000. For academic discussions, see Lykes, 1989, 1996.

   62. Lincoln & Guba, 1985, p. 314.

   63. On the reactions of narrators to our constructions of their stories, see Andrews, 2007; McCormack, 2004; Mishler, 1999. Also see the conversations of Jean Clandinin with three senior narrative scholars, where Mishler related his experience, "I mean you go back to your subjects and they kind of shrug . . . they find what we're doing dull . . . not that interesting to them" (as cited in Clandinin & Murphy, 2007, p. 649). Also see Page, Samson, & Crockett, 2000, who report taking their work back to participants and the conversations that ensued. When I sent *Divorce Talk* back to nearly one hundred participants (it appeared years after the interviews), I had no responses—lives had moved on, I assume. See Riessman, 1990.

   64. Seale, 2002, p. 102. For a variety of perspectives that bear on triangulation (of data sources and perspectives about the data), see Carspecken, 1996.

   65. Dodson & Schmalzbauer, 2005, pp. 954–955.

   66. For examples, see Bell, 1999, 2002. Also see conversation with Amia Lieblich, in Clandinin & Murphy, 2007, p. 647, who relates how she went back four times to the women she interviewed about the "new families" they were creating without husbands or male partners in residence, taking book chapters as they evolved to ensure that identities had been sufficiently concealed. Women could also pick their pseudonyms. Lieblich then went back to the women again for permission when a playwright

asked to depict their stories, even though it may not have been technically necessary. The ongoing process of ethics negotiation was driven by her beliefs about narrative interviewing: "It is a relationship" (p. 647). At the institutional level, obtaining informed consent in qualitative research inquiries is complex and parameters have shifted over time. See Christians, 2005; Lincoln, 2005. For issues in narrative research in particular, see Lykes, 1991; special issue of *health: An Interdisciplinary Journal for the Social Study of Health, Illness and Medicine* (Riessman & Mattingly, 2005).

67.   Researchers in the early days of second wave feminism wrote about "giving voice" to women and other marginalized groups in interviews and interpretations of them. The language is troubling. I prefer "amplifying" the voices of others, in dialogue with one's own. Even more preferable is the formulation of Maori scholar Russell Bishop who suggests that in creating knowledge we are "repositioned in such a way as to no longer need to seek to give voice to others, to empower others, to emancipate others, to refer to others as subjugated voices, but rather to listen and participate . . . in a process that facilitates the development in people of a sense of themselves as agentic and having an authorative voice . . ." (1998, pp. 207–208, as cited in Kapetas, 2006, p. 55).

68.   Andrews, 2007, chap. 6. Sue Estroff provides an example of what happens when a participant sees herself represented and doesn't like the portrait. Years after the ethnography of a mental hospital was published (Estroff, 1981), the anthropologist received a phone call in the middle of the night from an irate informant who recognized herself in the book. The informant felt "wounded by the images of herself in the past . . . exploited . . . misunderstood . . . unmasked." Estroff (1995) uses the disturbing event to explore complex ethical issues of ethnographic authority, voice, and responsibility in field research.

69.   On the "empowerment narratives" of researchers, see Walkerdine, 2003.

70.   Acker, Barry, & Essevelt, 1983, p. 431 as cited in Lather, 1986, p. 267.

71.   For a passionate challenge to research regulation that is creeping into U.S. universities in the guise of ethical scrutiny, see Lincoln, 2005. She takes on the "evidence-based" discourse dominating the professions, which "obscures the larger discourse of what evidence, which evidence, whose evidence, evidence gathered under what circumstances, evidence gathered for what uses, and for whom . . ." (p. 175). Testimonies lack the protections required by ethics committees for interview research with vulnerable populations, necessitating a high degree of personal scrutiny about possible effects on human subjects and their families. Scholars who work with archival testimonies and oral histories are exempt from official ethical scrutiny, requiring individual investigators to monitor their ethical practice as they elicit and write about narrative data.

72.   Mishler, as quoted in Clandinin & Murphy, 2007, p. 645.

73.   Important Web sites include www.uel.ac.uk/cnr/ and www.narrativenetwork australia.org.au.

References

Abbott, A. (1992). "What do cases do?" Some notes on activity in sociological analysis. In C. C. Ragin & H. S. Becker (Eds.), *What is a case? Exploring the foundations of social inquiry* (pp. 53–82). Cambridge: Cambridge University Press.

Abu-Lughod, L. (1990). The romance of resistance: Tracing transformations of power through Bedoin women. *American Ethnologist, 17*, 41–55.

Agar, M., & Hobbs, J. R. (1982). Interpreting discourse: Coherence and the analysis of ethnographic interviews. *Discourse Processes, 5*, 1–32.

Allen, M. S., Kertoy, M. K., Sherblom, J. C., & Pettit, J. M. (1994). Children's narrative productions: A comparison of personal event and fictional stories. *Applied Psycholinguistics, 15,* 149–176.

Amsterdam, A. G., & Bruner, J. (2000). *Minding the law.* Cambridge, MA: Harvard University Press.

Andrews, M. (2007). *Shaping history: Narratives of political change.* Cambridge, UK: Cambridge University Press.

Andrews, M., Squire, C., & Tamboukou, M. (Eds.). (forthcoming). *Doing narrative research in the social sciences.* London: Sage.

Ankersmit, F. (2005). Historiography. In D. Herman, M. Jahn, & M. Ryan (Eds.), *Routledge encyclopedia of narrative theory* (pp. 217–221). London & New York: Routledge.

Arendt, H. (1958). *The human condition.* Chicago: University of Chicago Press.

Atkinson, P. (1997). Narrative turn or blind alley? *Qualitative Health Research, 7*(3), 325–344.

Atkinson, P., & Delamont, S. (2006). Rescuing narrative from qualitative research. *Narrative Inquiry, 16*(1), 164–72.

Atkinson, P., & Silverman, D. (1997). Kundera's *Immortality:* The interview society and the invention of self. *Qualitative Inquiry,* 304–325.

Atkinson, R. (1998). *The life story interview.* Thousand Oaks, CA: Sage.

Attwood, B. (2005). *Telling the truth about Aboriginal history.* London: Allen & Unwin.

Bach, H. (2007). Composing a visual narrative inquiry. In D. J. Clandinin (Ed.), *Handbook of narrative inquiry: Mapping a methodology* (pp. 280–307). Thousand Oaks, CA: Sage.

Bakhtin, M. M. (1981). *The dialogic imagination: Four essays* (C. Emerson, M. Holquist Trans.). Austin: University of Texas Press.

Bamberg, M. G. W. (Guest Ed.). (1997). *Oral versions of personal experience: Three decades of narrative analysis.* Mahwah, NJ: Journal of Narrative and Life History/Lawrence Erlbaum.

Bamberg, M. G., & Andrews, M. (Eds.). (2004). *Considering counter-narratives: Narrating, resisting, making sense.* Amsterdam & Philadelphia: John Benjamins.

Bamberg, M. G. W., & McCabe, A. (1998). Editorial. *Narrative Inquiry, 8,* iii–v.

Baruch, G. (1981). Moral tales: Parents' stories of encounters with the health professions. *Sociology of Health and Illness, 3,* 275–295.

Bateson, M. C. (1989). *Composing a life.* New York: Atlantic Monthly Press/Grove.

Bauman, R. (1977). *Verbal art as performance.* Prospect Heights, IL: Waveland.

Bauman, R. (1986). *Story, performance, and event: Contextual studies of oral narrative.* Cambridge, UK: Cambridge University Press.

Becker, H. S. (1986). Photography and sociology. In *Doing things together: Selected papers* (pp. 223–271). Evanston, IL: Northwestern University Press.

Behar, R., & Gordon, D. A. (1995). *Women writing culture.* Berkeley: University of California Press.

Bell, S. E. (1987). Changing ideas: The medicalization of medopause. *Social Science and Medicine, 24*(6), 535–542.

Bell, S. E. (1988). Becoming a political woman: The reconstruction and interpretation of experience through stories. In A. D. Todd & S. Fisher (Eds.), *Gender and discourse: The power of talk* (pp. 97–123). Norwood, NJ: Ablex.

Bell, S. E. (1999). Narratives and lives: Women's health politics and the diagnosis of cancer for DES daughters. *Narrative Inquiry, 9,* 1–43.

Bell, S. E. (2000). Experiencing illness in/and narrative. In C. E. Bird, P. Conrad, & A. M. Fremont (Eds.), *Handbook of medical sociology.* Upper Saddle River, NJ: Prentice Hall.

Bell, S. E. (2002). Photo images: Jo Spence's narratives of living with illness. *Health, 6,* 5–30.

Bell, S. E. (2006). Living with breast cancer in text and image: Making art to make sense. *Qualitative Research in Psychology, 3,* 31–44.

Benton, T., & Craib, I. (2001). *Philosophy of social science: The philosophical foundations of social thought.* Basingstoke, UK: Palgrave.

Berger, J. (1972). *Ways of seeing.* London: Penguin Books.

Berger, J., & Mohr, J. (1982). *Another way of telling.* Cambridge, UK: Granta Books.

Bertaux, D. (1981). *Biography and society: The life-history approach in the social sciences.* London & Beverly Hills, CA: Sage.

Bertaux, D. (1995). A response to Thierry Kochuyt's 'Biographical and empiricist illusions: A reply to recent criticism'. *Newsletter* of Biography and Society Research Committee 38, International Sociological Association.

Boje, D. M. (2001). *Narrative methods for organizational and communication research.* London: Sage.

Bornat, J. (2003). A second take: Revisiting interviews with a different purpose. *Oral History, 31,* 47–53.

Bornat, J., Perks, R., Thompson, P., & Walmsley, J. (Eds.). (2000). *Oral history, health and welfare.* London: Routledge.

Bourdieu, P. (1993). Site effects. In P. Bourdieu et al. (Eds.), *The weight of the world: Social suffering in contemporary society* (pp. 123–129). Stanford, CA: Stanford University Press.

Briggs, J. (1970). *Never in anger.* Cambridge, MA: Harvard University Press.

Brockmeier, J. (2000). Autobiographical time. *Narrative Inquiry, 10,* 51–73.

Brockmeier, J., & Carbaugh, D. (Eds.). (2001). *Narrative and identity: Studies in autobiography, self, and culture.* Amsterdam & Philadelphia: John Benjamins.

Brown, L. M., & Gilligan, C. (1991). Listening for voice in narratives of relationship. In M. J. Packer & M. B. Tappan (Eds.), *Narrative and storytelling: Implications for understanding moral development* (Vol. 54). San Francisco: Jossey-Bass.

Brown, L. M. (1998). *Raising their voices: The politics of girls' anger.* Cambridge, MA: Harvard University Press.

Bruner, E. M. (1986). Ethnography as narrative. In V. Turner, & E. Bruner (Eds.), *The anthropology of experience* (pp. 139–155). Chicago: University of Chicago Press.

Bruner, J. (1987). Life as narrative. *Social Research, 54*(1), 11–32.

Bruner, J. (1990). *Acts of meaning.* Cambridge, MA: Harvard University Press.

Bruner, J. (1991). The narrative construction of reality. *Critical Inquiry, 18,* 1–21.

Bruner, J. (1986). *Actual minds, possible worlds.* Cambridge, MA: Harvard University Press.

Bruner, J. (2002). *Making stories : Law, literature, life.* New York: Farrar, Straus and Giroux.

Bülow, P., & Hydén, L. C. (2003). In dialogue with time: Identity and illness in narratives about chronic fatigue. *Narrative Inquiry, 13,* 71–97.

Burke, K. (1952). *A rhetoric of motives.* New York: Prentice Hall.

Bury, M. (1982). Chronic illness as biographical disruption. *Sociology of Health and Illness, 4,* 167–182.

Bury, M. (2001). Illness narratives: Fact or fiction? *Sociology of Health and Illness, 23,* 263–85.

Butler, J. (1990). *Gender trouble: Feminism and the subversion of identity.* New York: Routledge.

Cain, C. (1991). Personal stories: Identity acquisition and self-understanding in Alcoholics Anonymous. *Ethos, 19,* 210–253.

Camic, P. M., Rhodes, J. E., & Yardley, L. C. (Eds.). (2003). *Qualitative research in psychology: Expanding perspectives in methodology and design.* Washington, DC: American Psychological Association.

Campbell, D. T., & Stanley, J. C. (1963). *Experimental and quasi-experimental designs for research.* Chicago: Rand McNally & Co.

Capps, L., & Ochs, E. (1995). *Constructing panic: The discourse of agoraphobia.* Cambridge, MA: Harvard University Press.

Carspecken, P. F. (1996). *Critical ethnography in educational research: A theoretical and practical guide.* New York: Routledge.

Cazden, C. B. (2001). *Classroom discourse: The language of teachng and learning.* Portsmouth, NH: Heinemann.

Chafe, W. L. (Ed.). (1980). *The pear stories: Cognitive, cultural, and linguistic aspects of narrative production.* Norwood, NJ: Ablex.

Chalmers, D. (1995). Facing up to the problem of consciousness. *Journal of Consciousness Studies, 2*(3), 200–219.

Chalmers, D. (1996). *The conscious mind: In search of a fundamental theory.* NY: Oxford University Press.

Charmaz, K. (2006). *Constructing grounded theory.* Thousand Oaks, CA: Sage.

Charon, R. (2001). Narrative medicine: Form, function, and ethics. *Annals of Internal Medicine, 134,* 83–87.

Charon, R. (2006). *Narrative medicine: Honoring the stories of illness.* New York: Oxford University Press.

Charon, R., & Montello, M. (Eds.). (2002). *Stories matter: The role of narrative in medical ethics.* New York: Routledge.

Chase, S. E. (1995). *Ambiguous empowerment.* Amherst: University of Massachusetts Press.

Chase, S. E. (2005). Narrative inquiry: Multiple lenses, approaches, voices. In N. K. Denzin & Y. S. Lincoln (Eds.), *Handbook of qualitative research* (3rd ed., pp. 651–679). Thousand Oaks, CA: Sage.

Cheshire, J., & Ziebland, S. (2005). Narrative as a resource in accounts of the experience of illness. In J. Thornborrow & J. Coates (Eds.), *The sociolinguistics of narrative* (pp. 17–40). Amsterdam & Philadelphia: John Benjamins.

Christians, C. G. (2005). Ethics and politics in qualitative research. In N. K. Denzin, & Y. S. Lincoln (Eds.), *Handbook of qualitative research* (3rd ed., pp. 139–164). Thousand Oaks, CA: Sage.

Clandinin, D. J. (Ed.). (2007). *Handbook of narrative inquiry.* Thousand Oaks, CA: Sage.

Clandinin, D. J., & Connelly, F. M. (1994). Personal experience methods. In N. Denzin & Y. S. Lincoln (Eds.), *Handbook of qualitative research.* Thousand Oaks, CA: Sage.

Clandinin, D. J., & Murphy, M. S. (2007). Looking ahead: Conversations with Elliot Mishler, Don Polkinghorne, and Amia Lieblich. In *Handbook of narrative inquiry* (pp. 632–650). Thousand Oaks, CA: Sage.

Clandinin, D. J., (2000). *Narrative inquiry: Experience and story in qualitative research.* San Francisco: Jossey-Bass.

Clark, J. A., & Mishler, E. G. (1992). Attending to patients' stories: Reframing the clinical task. *Sociology of Health and Illness, 14,* 344–370.

Clarke, A. E. (2005). *Situational analysis: Grounded theory after the postmodern turn.* Thousand Oaks, CA: Sage.

Clarke, A. E., Shim, J. K., Mamo, L., et al. (2003). Biomedicalization: Theorizing technoscientific transformations of health, illness, and U.S. biomedicine. *American Sociological Review, 68*(2), 161–194.

Clifford, J. (1986). Partial truths. In J. Clifford, & G. E. Marcus (Eds.), *Writing culture: The poetics and politics of ethnography* (pp. 1–26). Berkeley: University of California Press.

Clough, P. (2002). *Narratives and fictions in educational research.* Buckingham: Open University Press.

Coffey, A., & Atkinson, P. (1996). *Making sense of qualitative data: Complementary research strategies.* Thousand Oaks, CA: Sage.

Coles, R. (1967). *Children of crisis.* Boston: Little, Brown.

Connelly, F. M., & Clandinin, D. J. (1999). *Shaping a professional identity: Stories of educational practice.* New York: Teachers College Press.

Conrad, P., & Schneider, J. W. (1980/1992). *Deviance and medicalization: From badness to sickness.* Philadelphia: Temple University Press.

Cortazzi, M. (2001). Narrative analysis in ethnography. In P. Atkinson, A. Coffey, S. Delamont, J. Lofland, & L. Lofland, (Eds.), *Handbook of ethnography.* Thousand Oaks, CA: Sage.

Cortazzi, M., Jin, L., Wall, D., & Cavendish, S. (2001). Sharing learning through narrative communication. *International Journal of Language and Communication Disorders, 36,* 252–257.

Creef, E. T. (2004). *Imaging Japanese America: The visual construction of citizenship, nation, and the body.* New York: New York University Press.

Cronon, W. (1992). A place for stories: Nature, history, and narrative. *Journal of American History, 78,* 1347–1376.

Davies, B. (2006). Collective biography as ethically reflexive practice. In B. Davies, & S. Gannon (Eds.), *Doing collective biography* (pp. 182–189). Berkshire, UK: Open University Press.

Davis, K. (1986). The process of problem (re)formulation in psychotherapy. *Sociology of Health & Illness, 8,* 44–74.

Davis, K. (2003, February). Biography as critical methodology. *Biography and Society RC 38 Newsletter,* pp. 5–11.

Davis, P. C. (1991). Contextual legal criticism: A demonstration exploring hierarchy and "feminine" style. *New York University Law Review, 66,* 1635–1681.

Davis, J. E. (Ed.). (2002). *Stories of change: Narrative and social movements.* Albany: State University of New York Press.

De Fina, A. (2003). *Identity in narrative: A study of immigrant discourse.* Amsterdam: John Benjamins.

Delanty, G., & Strydom, P. (2003). *Philosophies of social science: The classic and contemporary readings.* Maidenhead, UK: Open University Press.

Dentith, S. (1995). *Bakhtinian thought: An introductory reader.* New York: Routledge.

Denzin, N. (2000). Preface. In M. Andrews et al. (Eds.), *Lines of narrative: Psychosocial perspectives* (pp. xi–xiii). New York: Routledge.

Denzin, N. (2005). Whose science is behind the science in qualitative methodology? American Sociological Association, *Footnotes, 22.*

Denzin, N. K., & Lincoln, Y. S. (Eds). (1994). *Handbook of qualitative research.* Thousand Oaks, CA: Sage.

DeVault, M. (1996). Talking back to sociology: Distinctive contributions of feminist methodology. *Annual Review of Sociology, 22,* 29–50.

DeVault, M. (2006). Knowledge from the field. In C. Calhoun (Ed.), *Sociology in America: A history* (pp. 155–182). Chicago: University of Chicago Press.

Devereux, G. (1967). *From anxiety to method in behavioral sciences.* The Hague, The Netherlands: Mouton.

Didion, J. (1990). *The white album.* New York: Noonday.

Dingwall, R. (1977). "Atrocity stories" and professional relationships. *Sociology of Work and Occupations, 4*, 371–396.

Dodson, L., & Schmalzbauer, L. (2005). Poor mothers and habits of hiding: Participatory methods in poverty research. *Journal of Marriage and Family, 67*, 949–959.

Dohrenwend, B. P., Turner, J. B., Turse, N. A., Adams, B. G., Koenen , K. C., & Marshall, R. (2006). The psychological risks of Vietnam for U.S. veterans: A revisit with new data and methods. *Science, 313*, 979–982.

Dube, L. (1986). Seed and earth: The symbolism of biological reproduction and sexual relations of production. In L. Dube et al. (Eds.), *Visibility and power: Essays on women in society and development.* New Delhi: Oxford University Press.

Edvardsson, D., Rasmussen, B. H., & Riessman, C. K. (2003). Ward atmospheres of horror and healing: A comparative analysis of narrative. *health: An Interdisciplinary Journal for the Social Study of Health, Illness and Medicine, 7*, 377–398.

Ehrenreich, B. (2001). *Nickel and dimed: On (not) getting by in America.* New York: Metropolitan Books.

Elliott, J. (2005). *Using narrative in social research.* London: Sage.

Ellis, C., & Bochner, A. P. (2000). Autoethnography, personal narrative, and reflexivity: Researcher as subject. In N. Denzin, & Y. S. Lincoln (Eds.), *Handbook of qualitative research* (2nd ed., pp. 733–767). Newbury Park, CA: Sage.

Estroff, S. E. (1995). Whose story is it anyway? In K. S. Toombs, D. Bernard, & R. A. Carson (Eds.), *Chronic illness: From experience to policy* (pp. 77–102). Bloomington: Indiana, University Press.

Estroff, S. E. (1981). *Making it crazy: An ethnography of psychiatric clients in an American community.* Berkeley: University of California Press.

Ewick, P., & Silbey, S. (2003). Narrating social structure: Stories of resistance to legal authority. *American Journal of Sociology, 108*, 1328–1372.

Falk, R., Gendzier, I., & Lifton, R. J. (Eds.). (2006). *Crimes of war: Iraq.* New York: Nation Books.

Fay, M. (Ed.). (1989). *Speak out: An anthology of stories by youth in care.* Toronto: Page Adolescent Resource Centre.

Feagin, J. R., & Vera, H. (2001). *Liberation sociology.* Boulder, CO: Westview.

Feldman, C. F. (2001). Narratives of national identity and group narratives. In J. Brockmeier & D. D. Carbaugh (Eds.), *Narrative and identity: Studies in autobiography, self, and culture* (pp. 129–144). Amsterdam & Philadelphia: John Benjamins.

Flyvbjerg, B. (2004). Five misunderstandings about case-study research. In C. Seale, G. Gobo, J. F. Gubrium, & D. Silverman (Eds.), *Qualitative research practice* (pp. 420–434). London: Sage.

Fonow, M. M., & Cook, J. A. (Eds.). (1991). *Beyond methodology: Feminist scholarship as lived experience.* Bloomington: Indiana University Press.

Frank, A. (1995). *The wounded storyteller: Body, illness, and ethics.* Chicago: University of Chicago Press.

Freeman, M. (1997). Death, narrative integrity, and the radical challenge of self-understanding: A reading of Tolstoy's *Death of Ivan Illych. Aging and Society, 17*, 373–398.

Freeman, M. (2002). The presence of what is missing: Memory, poetry and the ride home. In R. J. Pellegrini & T. R. Sarbin (Eds.), *Critical incident narratives in the development of men's lives* (pp. 165–176) New York: Haworth Clinical Practice Press.

Gadamer, H. G. (2004). *Truth and method.* London & New York: Continuum.

Gallas, K. (1994). *The languages of learning : How children talk, write, dance, draw, and sing their understanding of the world.* New York: Teachers College Press.

Gallas, K. (2003). *Imagination and literacy: A teacher's search for the heart of literacy.* New York: Teachers College Press.

Gamson, W. A. (2002). How storytelling can be empowering. In K. A. Cerulo (Ed.), *Culture in mind: Toward a sociology of culture and cognition* (pp. 187–198). New York: Routledge.

Gee, J. P. (1985). The narrativization of experience in the oral style. *Journal of Education, 167,* 9–35.

Gee, J. P. (1991). A linguistic approach to narrative. *Journal of Narrative and Life History/Narrative Inquiry, 1,* 15–39.

Gefter, P. (2006, March 19). The theater of the street, the subject of the photograph. *New York Times.*

Georgankopoulou, A. (2006). Thinking big with small stories in narrative and identity analysis. *Narrative Inquiry, 16*(1), 122–130.

Gergen, K. J. (1985). The social constructionist movement in modern psychology. *American Psychologist, 40,* 266–275.

Giddens, A. (1991). *Modernity and self-identity: Self and society in the late modern age.* Stanford, CA: Stanford University Press.

Gilgun, J. F. (2002). Conjectures and refutations: Governmental funding and qualitative research. *Qualitative Social Work, 1,* 359–375.

Gilligan, C., Spencer, R., Weinberg, M. K., & Bertsch, T. (2003). On the listening guide: A voice-centered relational method. In P. M. Camic, J. E. Rhodes, & L. Yardley (Eds.), *Qualitative research in psychology: Expanding perspectives in methodology and design* (pp. 157–172). Washington, DC: American Psychological Association.

Gluck, W. B., & Patai, D. (Eds.). (1991). *Women's words: The feminist practice of oral history.* New York: Routledge.

Goffman, E. (1963). *Stigma: Notes on the management of spoiled identity.* Englewood Cliffs, NJ: Prentice Hall.

Goffman, E. (1969). *The presentation of self in everyday life.* New York: Penguin.

Goffman, E. (1981). *Forms of talk.* Oxford, UK: Blackwell.

Goffman, E. (1974). *Frame analysis: An essay on the organization of experience.* Cambridge, MA: Harvard University Press.

Good, B. J. (1994). *Medicine, rationality, and experience: An anthropological perspective.* Cambridge, UK: Cambridge University Press.

Good, B. J., & DelVecchio, M. J. (1994). In the subjunctive mode: Epilepsy narratives in Turkey. *Social Science & Medicine, 38,* 835–842.

Goodman, J. H. (2004). Coping with trauma and hardship among unaccompanied refugee youths from Sudan. *Qualitative Health Research, 14,* 1177–1196.

Gorman, D. (2005). Truth. In D. Herman, M. Jahn & M. Ryan (Eds.), *Routledge encyclopedia of narrative theory* (pp. 621–622). London and New York: Routledge.

Graves, E. T. (2006). Theorizing collective identity: Structural and moral narratives. Paper presented at the American Sociological Association annual meeting, Montreal, Quebec.

Gray, D. E. (2001). Accommodation, resistance and transcendence: Three narratives of autism. *Social Science & Medicine, 53*, 1247–1257.

Greenhalgh, T., & Hurwitz, B. (Eds.). (1998). *Narrative based medicine: Dialogue and discourse in clinical practice.* London: BMJ Books.

Gross, L., Katz, J. S., & Ruby, J. (Eds.). (1998). *Image ethics: The moral rights of subjects in photographs, film and television.* New York: Oxford University Press.

Gross, L., Katz, J. S., & Ruby, J. (Eds.). (2003). *Image ethics in the digital age.* Minneapolis: University of Minnesota Press.

Gubrium, J. F., & Holstein, J. A. (2002). From the interview to the interview society. In J. F. Gubrium & J. A. Holstein (Eds.), *Handbook of interview research: Context and method* (pp. 3–32). Thousand Oaks, CA: Sage.

Guzik, K., & Gorlier, J. C. (2004). History in the making: Narrative as feminist text and practice in a Mexican feminist journal. *Social Movement Studies, 3*, 89.

Hall, C., Slembrouck, S., & Sarangi, S. (2006). *Language practices in social work: Categorisation and accountability in child welfare.* London & New York: Routledge.

Hall, C. J. (1997). *Social work as narrative: Storytelling and persuasion in professional texts.* Oxford, UK: Ashgate.

Hammersley, M. (2002). Ethnography and the disputes over validity. In G. Walford (Ed.), *Debates and developments in ethnographic methodology* (Vol. 6, pp. 7–22). Boston & London: JAI Press.

Harper, D. (2000). Reimagining visual methods: Galileo to neuromancer. In N. K. Denzin & Y. S. Lincoln (Eds.), *Handbook of qualitative research* (pp. 717–732). Thousand Oaks, CA: Sage.

Harper, D. (2005). What's new visually? In N. Denzin & Y. S. Lincoln (Eds.), *Handbook of qualitative research* (3rd ed., pp. 747–761). Thousand Oaks, CA: Sage.

Harrison, B. (2002a). Photographic visions and narrative inquiry. *Narrative Inquiry, 12*, 87–111.

Harrison, B. (2002b). Seeing health and illness worlds—Using visual methodologies in a sociology of health and illness: A methodological review. *Sociology of Health & Illness, 24*, 856–872.

Heath, S. B. (1983). *Ways with words: Language, life and work in communities and classrooms.* New York: Cambridge University Press.

Heilbrun, C. (1988). *Writing a woman's life.* New York: Ballantine.

Heisenberg, W. (1959). *Physics and philosophy: The revolution in modern science.* London: George Allen & Unwin.

Henry, M. S. (2003). "Where are you really from?": Representation, identity and power in the fieldwork experiences of a South Asian diasporic. *Qualitative Research, 3*, 229–242.

Herman, D. (1999). *Narratologies: New perspectives on narrative analysis.* Columbus: Ohio State University Press.

Herman, D., Jahn, M., & Ryan, M. (Eds.). (2005). *Routledge encyclopedia of narrative theory.* London & New York: Routledge.

Hinchman, L. P., & Hinchman, S. K. (Eds.). (1997). *Memory, identity, community: The idea of narrative in the human sciences.* Albany: State University of New York Press.

Holmberg, D., Orbuch, T. L., & Veroff, J. (2004). *Thrice told tales: Married couples tell their stories.* Mahwah, NJ: Lawrence Erlbaum.

Holstein, J. A., & Gubrium, J. F. (2000). *The self we live by: Narrative identity in a postmodern world.* New York: Oxford University Press.

Hurwitz, B., Greenhalgh, T., & Skultans, V. (Eds.). (2004). *Narrative research in health and illness.* Malden, MA: BMJ Books/Blackwell.

Hydén, L. C. (1997). Illness and narrative. *Sociology of Health & Illness, 19,* 48–69.

Hydén, M., & Överlien, C. (2005). Applying narrative analysis to the process of confirming or disregarding cases of suspected child abuse. *Child and Family Social Work, 10*(1), 57–65.

Hymes, D. (1974). *Foundations in sociolinguistics: An ethnographic approach.* Philadelphia: University of Pennsylvania Press.

Hymes, D. (1981). *"In vain I tried to tell you": Essays in Native American ethnopoetics.* Philadelphia: University of Pennsylvania Press.

Illich, I. (1976). *Medical nemesis.* New York: Pantheon.

Iser, W. (1978). *The act of reading: A theoretical aesthetic response.* Baltimore: Johns Hopkins University Press.

Iser, W. (1989/1993). *Prospecting: From reader response to literary anthropology.* Baltimore: Johns Hopkins University Press.

Jameson, F. (1972). *The prison-house of language.* Princeton NJ: Princeton University Press.

Jeffery, P., Jeffery, R., & Lyon, A. (1989). *Labour pains and labour power: Women and childbearing in India.* London: Zed.

Jolly, M., & Stanley, L. (2005). Letters as/not as genre. *Life Writing, 2*(2), 74–101.

Jonsen, A. R. (1988). *The abuse of casuistry: A history of moral reasoning.* Berkeley: University of California Press.

Josselson, R., & Lieblich, A. (2005). Book review of Carolyn Ellis, The ethnographic I: A methodological novel about autoethnography. *Life Writing, 2*(2), 187–194.

Josselson, R., Lieblich, A., & McAdams, D. P. (Eds.). (2003). *Up close and personal: The teaching and learning of narrative research.* Washington, DC: American Psychological Association.

Josselson, R., Lieblich, A., & McAdams, D. P. (Eds.). (2007). *The meaning of others: Narrative studies of relationships.* Washington, DC: American Psychological Association.

Kane, A. (2001). Finding emotions in social movement processes: Irish land movement metaphors and narratives. In J. Goodwin, J. M. Jasper, & F. Polletta (Eds.), *Passionate politics: Emotions and social movements* (pp. 251–266). Chicago: University of Chicago Press.

Kapetas, J. G. (2006). *Telling our stories: Making a difference.* Unpublished PhD dissertation. Perth, Western Australia: Curtin University of Technology, Centre for Aboriginal Studies.

Kapetas, J. G., Dodd, I., Walley, V. D., Stafford, F., & Walley, K. (Eds.). (2000). *From our hearts: An anthology of new Aboriginal writing from Southwest Western Australia.* South Fremantle, Western Australia: Kadadjiny Mia Walyalup Writers.

Kleinman, S., & Copp, M. A. (1993). *Emotions and fieldwork.* Newbury Park, CA: Sage.

Knowles, C., & Sweetman, P. (Eds.). (2004). *Picturing the social landscape: Visual methods and the sociological imagination* London & New York: Routledge.

Labov, W. (1972). *Language in the inner city: Studies in the black English venacular.* Philadelphia: University of Pennsylvania Press.

Labov, W. (1982). Speech actions and reactions in personal narrative. In D. Tannen (Ed.), *Analyzing discourse: Text and talk* (pp. 219–247). Washington, DC: Georgetown University Press.

Labov, W., &Waletzky, J. (1967). Narrative analysis: Oral versions of personal experience. In J. Helm (Ed.), *Essays on the verbal and visual arts* (pp. 12–44). Seattle: American Ethnological Society/University of Washington Press.

Langellier, K. M. (2001a). Personal narrative. In M. Jolly (Ed.), *Encyclopedia of life writing: Autobiographical and biographical forms* (Vol. 2, pp. 699–701). London: Fitzroy Dearborn.

Langellier, K. M. (2001b). "You're marked": Breast cancer, tattoo and the narrative performance of identity. In J. Brockmeier & D. Carbaugh (Eds.), *Narrative identity: Studies in autobiography, self, and culture* (pp. 145–184). Amsterdam & Philadelphia: John Benjamins.

Langellier, K. M., & Peterson, E. E. (2004). *Storytelling in daily life: Performing narrative.* Philadelphia: Temple University Press.

Langer, L. L. (1991). *Holocaust testimonies: The ruins of memory.* New Haven & London: Yale University Press.

Laslett, B. (1999). Personal narrative as sociology. *Contemporary Sociology, 28,* 391–401.

Lather, P. (1986). Research as praxis. *Harvard Educational Review, 56,* 257–277.

Lieblich, A., Tuval-Mashiach, R., & Zilber, T. (1998). *Narrative research: Reading, analysis, and interpretation.* Thousand Oaks, CA: Sage.

Lillrank, A. (2002). The tension between overt talk and covert emotions in illness narratives: Transition from clinician to researcher. *Culture, Medicine and Psychiatry, 26,* 111–127.

Lillrank, A. (2003). Back pain and the resolution of diagnostic uncertainty in illness narratives. *Social Science and Medicine, 57,* 1045–1054.

Lincoln, Y. S. (1995). Emerging criteria for quality in qualitative and interpretive inquiry. *Qualitative Inquiry, 1,* pp. 275–289.

Lincoln, Y. S. (2005). Institutional review boards and methodological conservatism: The challenge to and from phenomenological paradigms. In N. K. Denzin & Y. S. Lincoln (Eds.), *Handbook of qualitative research* (3rd ed, pp. 165–181). Thousand Oaks, CA: Sage.

Lincoln, Y. S., & Guba, E. G. (1985). *Naturalistic inquiry.* Beverly Hills, CA: Sage.

Linde, C. (1993). *Life stories: The creation of coherence.* New York: Oxford University Press.

Lorenz, L. (2003). *Photovoice: Girls' vision, girls' voices: A community activism project*. New York: Girls Incorporated.

Lorenz, L. (2006). Living without connections: Using narrative analysis of photographs and interview text to understand living with traumatic brain injury. Paper presented at European Sociological Association, Qualitative Methods Research Network, Conference on Advances in Qualitative Research Practice, Cardiff, Wales.

Luttrell, W. (2003). *Pregnant bodies, fertile minds: Gender, race and the schooling of pregnant teens*. New York: Routledge.

Luttrell, W. (2006). Making culture visible: Children's photography, identity and agency. Paper given at annual meeting of American Sociological Association, Montreal, Canada.

Luttrell, W., & Ward, J. (2004). The "N-word" and the racial dynamics of teaching. *Harvard Education Letter, 20*, 4–6.

Lutz, C. A., & Collins, J. L. (1993). *Reading National Geographic*. Chicago: University of Chicago Press.

Lykes, M. B. (1989). Dialogue with Guatemalan Indian women: Critical perspectives on constructing collaborative research. In R. Unger (Ed.), *Representations: Social constructions of gender* (pp. 167–185). Amityville, NY: Baywood.

Lykes, M. B. (1991). Creative arts and photography in participatory action research in Guatemala. In P. Reason & H. Bradbury (Eds.), *Handbook of action research* (pp. 363–371). Newbury Park, CA: Sage.

Lyotard, J. F. (1984). *The postmodern condition: A report on knowledge*. Minneapolis: University of Minnesota Press.

Maclean, M. (1988). *Narrative as performance: The Baudelairean experiment*. London & New York: Routledge.

Malterud, K. (2001). Qualitative research: Standards, challenges, and guidelines. *Lancet, 358*, 483–488.

Marshall, B. L. (1994). *Engendering modernity: Feminism, social theory, and social change*. Boston: Northeastern University Press.

Martin, F. E. (1998). Tales of transition: Self-narrative and direct scribing in exploring care-leaving. *Child and Family Social Work, 3*, 1–12.

Mattingly, C. (1998). *Healing dramas and clinical plots: The narrative structure of experience*. New York: Cambridge University Press.

Mattingly, C., & Garro, L. C. (Eds.). (2000). *Narrative and the cultural construction of illness and healing*. Berkeley: University of California Press.

Maxwell, J. A. (1992). Understanding and validity in qualitative research. *Harvard Educational Review, 62*, 279–300.

McAdams, D. P., Josselson R., & Lieblich, A. (Eds.). (2001). *Turns in the road: Narrative studies of lives in transition*. Washington, DC: American Psychological Association.

McCabe, A. (1997). Developental and cross-cultural aspects of children's narration. In M. Bamberg (Ed.), *Narrative development: Six approaches* (pp. 137–174). Mahwah, NJ: Lawrence Erlbaum.

McCormack, C. (2004). Storying stories: A narrative approach to in-depth interview conversations. *International Journal of Social Research Methodology, 7*, 219–236.

McQuillan, M. (Ed.). (2000). *The narrative reader.* London & New York: Routledge.

Merleau-Ponty, M. (1989). *Phenomenology of perception.* (C. Smith, Trans.). London: Routledge. (Original work published 1962)

Messick, S. (1987). *Validity.* Princeton, NJ: Educational Testing Service.

Michaels, S. (1981). 'Saring time': Childrens' narrative styles and differential access to literacy. *Language and Society, 10,* 423–442.

Michaels, S. (1985). Hearing the connections in children's oral and written discourse. *Journal of Education, 167,* 36–56.

Michaels, S., & Cazden, C. B. (1984). Teacher-child collaboration as oral preparation for literacy. In B. B. Schieffelin (Ed.), *Acquisition of literacy: Ethnographic perspectives.* Norwood, NJ: Ablex.

Mills, C. W. (1959). *The sociological imagination.* New York: Oxford University Press.

Mishler, E. G. (1979). Meaning in context: Is there any other kind? *Harvard Educational Review, 49,* 1–19.

Mishler, E. G. (1984). *The discourse of medicine: Dialectics of medical interviews.* Norwood, NJ: Ablex.

Mishler, E. G. (1986). *Research interviewing: Context and narrative.* Cambridge, MA: Harvard University Press.

Mishler, E. G. (1990). Validation in inquiry-guided research: The role of exemplars in narrative studies. *Harvard Educational Review, 60,* 415–442.

Mishler, E. G. (1991). Representing discourse: The rhetoric of transcription. *Journal of Narrative and Life History/Narrative Inquiry, 1,* 255–280.

Mishler, E. G. (1995). Models of narrative analysis: A typology. *Journal of Narrative and Life History, 5,* 87–123.

Mishler, E. G. (1996). Missing persons: Recovering developmental stories/histories. In R. Jessor, A. Colby, & R. A. Shweder (Eds.), *Ethnography and human development: Context and meaning in social inquiry* (pp. 74–99). Chicago: University of Chicago Press.

Mishler, E. G. (1997). The interactional construction of narratives in medical and life-history interviews. In B. L. Gunnarsson, P. Linell, & B. Norbert (Eds.), *The construction of professional discourse* (pp. 223–244). London & New York: Longman.

Mishler, E. G. (1999). *Storylines: Craftartists' narratives of identity.* Cambridge, MA: Harvard University Press.

Morris, P. (Ed.). (1994). *The Bakhtin reader: Selected writings of Bakhtin, Medvedev and Voloshinov.* London: Edward Arnold.

Myerhoff, B. (1978). *Number our days.* New York: Simon & Schuster.

Myerhoff, B., with Metzger, D., Ruby, J., & Tufte, V. (Eds.). (1992). *Remembered lives.* Ann Arbor: University of Michigan Press.

Neander, K., & Skott, C. (2006). Important meetings with important persons: Narratives from families facing adversity and their key figures. *Qualitative Social Work: Research and Practice, 5,* 295–311.

Nelson, K. (1989). *Tales from the crib.* Cambridge, MA: Harvard University Press.

Ochs, E. (1979). Transcription as theory. In E. Ochs & B. B. Schieffelin (Eds.), *Developmental pragmatics* (pp. 43–72). New York: Academic Press.

Ochs, E., & Capps, L. (2001). *Living narrative: Creating lives in everyday storytelling.* Cambridge, MA: Harvard University Press.

O'Connor, P. E. (1994). "You could feel it through the skin": Agency and positioning in prisoners' stabbing stories. *Text, 14,* 45–75.

Öhlen, J. (2003). Evocation of meaning through poetic condensation of narratives in empirical phenomenological inquiry into human suffering. *Qualitative Health Research, 13,* 557–566.

Öhlen, J., Bengtsson, J., Skott, C., & Segesten, K. (2002). Being in a lived retreat: Embodied meaning of alleviated suffering. *Cancer Nursing, 25,* 318–325.

Örulv, L., & Hydén, L. C. (2006). Confabulation: Sense-making, self-marking and world-making in dementia. *Discourse Studies, 8*(5), 647–673.

Packer, M. J., & Addison, R. B. (Eds.). (1989). *Entering the circle: Hermeneutic investigation in psychology.* Albany: State University of New York Press.

Page, R. N., Samson, Y. J., & Crockett, M. D. (2000). Reporting ethnography to informants. In B. M. Brizuela, J. P. Stewart, R. G. Carillo, & J. G. Berger (Eds.), *Acts of inquiry in qualitative research,* vol. 34 (pp. 321–352). Cambridge, MA: Harvard Educational Review.

Paget, M. A. (1983). Experience and knowledge. *Human Studies, 6,* 67–90.

Paget, M. A. (1994). Performing the text. In M. L. DeVault (Ed.), *A complex sorrow: Reflections on cancer and an abbreviated life* (pp. 23–42). Philadelphia PA: Temple Univeristy Press.

Personal Narratives Group. (Ed.). (1989). *Interpreting women's lives: Feminist theory and personal narratives.* Bloomington: Indiana University Press.

Peterson, E. E., Langellier, K. M. (2006). The performance turn in narrative studies. *Narrative Inquiry, 16,* 173–180.

Phinney, A. (2002). Fluctuating awareness and the breakdown of the illness narrative in dementia. *Dementia, 1,* 329–344.

Pini, M. (2001). Video diaries: Questions of authenticity and fabrication. *Screening the Past.* Retrieved from http://www.latrobe.edu.au/screeningthepast/firstrelease/fr1201/mpfr13a.htm

Pink, S. (2001). *Doing visual ethnography: Images, media and representation in research.* London: Sage.

Pink, S. (2004). Visual methods. In C. Seale, G. Gobo, J. F. Gubrium, & D. Silverman (Eds.), *Qualitative research practice* (pp. 391–406). London: Sage.

Plummer, K. (1995). *Telling sexual stories: Power, change, and social worlds.* London & New York: Routledge.

Plummer, K. (2001). *Documents of life 2: An invitation to critical humanism.* London: Sage.

Poindexter, C. (2002a). Meaning from methods: Re-presenting stories of an HIV-affected caregiver. *Qualitative Social Work, 1,* 59–78.

Poindexter, C. (2002b). Research as poetry: A couple experiences HIV. *Qualitative Inquiry, 8,* 707–714.

Poindexter, C. (2003a). Sex, drugs, and love in middle age: A case study of a sero-discordant heterosexual couple coping with HIV. *Journal of Social Work Practice in the Addictions, 3,* 57–83.

Poindexter, C. (2003b). The ubiquity of ambiguity in research interviewing: A case study. *Qualitative Social Work, 2*, 383–409.

Polkinghorne, D. (1983). *Methodology for the human sciences: Systems of inquiry.* Albany: State University of New York Press.

Polkinghorne, D. (1988). *Narrative knowing and the human sciences.* Albany: State University of New York Press.

Polletta, F. (2006). *It was like a fever: Storytelling in protest and politics.* Chicago: University of Chicago Press.

Postlewait, T., & Davis, T. C. (2003). *Theatricality.* Cambridge & New York: Cambridge University Press.

Quasthoff, U. M., & Becker, T. (Eds.). (2005). *Narrative interaction.* Amsterdam & Philadelphia: John Benjamins.

Rabinow, P., & Sullivan, W. M. (1987). *Interpretive social science: A second look.* Berkeley: University of California Press. (Original work published 1979)

Radley, A. (2002). Portrayals of suffering: On looking away, looking at, and the comprehension of illness experience. *Body & Society, 8*, 1–23.

Radley, A., & Bell, S. E. (2007). Artworks, collective experience and claims for social justice: The case of women living with breast cancer. *Sociology of Health & Illness, 29*(3), 366–390.

Radley, A., & Chamberlain, K. (2001). Health psychology and the study of the case: From method to analytic concern. *Social Science & Medicine, 53*, 321–332.

Radley, A., & Taylor, D. (2003). Images of recovery: A photo-elicitation study on the hospital ward. *Qualitative Health Research, 13*, 77–99.

Rasmussen, B. H., Jansson, L., & Norberg, A. (2000). Striving for becoming at-home in the midst of dying. *American Journal of Hospice & Palliative Care, 17*, 31–43.

Rasmussen, B. H., Norberg, A., & Sandman, P. O. (1995). Stories about becoming a hospice nurse: Reasons, expectations, hopes, and concerns. *Cancer Nursing, 18*, 344–354.

Razack, S. (1993). Story-telling for social change. *Gender and Education, 5*, 55–70.

Reason, P. (2003). Doing co-operative inquiry. In J. A. Smith (Ed.), *Qualitative psychology: A practical guide to research methods* (pp. 205–231). London: Sage.

Reason, P. (2002). The practice of co-operative inquiry [Special issue]. *Systemic Practice and Action Research, 15.*

Reason, P., & Bradbury, H. (2001). *Handbook of action research: Participative inquiry and practice.* London & Thousand Oaks, CA: Sage.

Reinharz, S. (1991). *On becoming a social scientist.* New Brunswick, NJ: Tansaction Publishers.

Reinharz, S., with Davidman, L. (1992). *Feminist methods in social research.* New York: Oxford University Press.

Renov, M. (1999). Domestic ethnography and the construction of the "other" self. In J. M. Gaines & M. Renov (Eds.), *Collecting visible evidence* (pp. 140–155). Minneapolis & London: University of Minnesota Press.

Rich, F. (2006). *The greatest story ever sold: The decline and fall of truth from 9/11 to Katrina.* New York: Penguin.

Rich, J. A., & Grey, C. M. (2005). Pathways to recurrent trauma among young black men: Traumatic stress, substance use, and the "code of the street." *American Journal of Public Health*, 95, 816–824.

Rich, M., Lamola, S., Amery, C., & Chalfen, R. (2000). Video intervention/prevention assessment: A patient-centered methodology for understanding the adolescent illness experience. *Journal of Adolescent Health*, 27, 155–165.

Richardson, L. (1993). Poetics, dramatics, and transgressive validity: The case of the skipped line. *The Sociological Quarterly*, 34(4), 695–710.

Ricks, T. E. (2006). *Fiasco: The American military adventure in Iraq.* New York & London: Penguin.

Ricoeur, P. (1991). Life in quest of narrative. In D. Wood (Ed.), *On Paul Ricoeur: Narrative and interpretation* (pp. 20–33). London: Routledge.

Riessman, C. K. (1987). When gender is not enough: Women interviewing women. *Gender & Society*, 1, 172–207.

Riessman, C. K. (1989). Life events, meaning and narrative: The case of infidelity and divorce. *Social Science and Medicine*, 29, 743–751.

Riessman, C. K. (1990). *Divorce talk: Women and men make sense of personal relationships.* New Brunswick, NJ: Rutgers University Press.

Riessman, C. K. (1993). *Narrative analysis.* Newbury Park, CA: Sage.

Riessman, C. K. (1997). A short story about long stories. *Journal of Narrative and Life History*, 7, 155–159.

Riessman, C. K. (1997). Berätta, transkribera, analysera: En metodologisk diskussion om personliga berättelser i samhällsvetenskaper. In L. Hydén & M. Hydén (Eds.), *Att studera berättelser: Samhällsvetenskapliga och medicinska perspektiv* (pp. 30-62). Stockholm: Lieber.

Riessman, C. K. (2000a). "Even if we don't have children [we] can live": Stigma and infertility in South India. In C. C. Mattingly & L. C. Garro (Eds.), *Narrative and cultural construction of illness and healing* (pp. 128–152). Berkeley: University of California Press.

Riessman, C. K. (2000b). Stigma and everyday resistance practices: Childless women in South India. *Gender & Society*, 14, 111–135.

Riessman, C. K. (2002). Positioning gender identity in narratives of infertility: South Indian women's lives in context. In M. C. Inhorn & F. van Balen (Eds.), *Infertility around the globe: New thinking on childlessness, gender, and reproductive technologies* (pp. 152–170). Berkeley: University of California Press.

Riessman, C. K. (2003). Preforming identities in illness narrative: Masculinity and multiple sclerosis. *Qualitative Research*, 3, 5–33.

Riessman, C. K. (2004a). Narrative analysis. In M. S. Lewis-Beck, A. Bryman, & T. Futing Liao (Eds.), *Encyclopedia of social science research methods* (pp. 705–709). Thousand Oaks, CA: Sage.

Riessman, C. K. (2004b). A thrice told tale: New readings of an old story. In B. B. Hurwitz, T. Greenhalgh, & V. Skultans (Eds.), *Narrative research in health and illness* (pp. 309–324). London: British Medical Journal Books/Blackwell.

Riessman, C. K. (2005). Exporting ethics: A narrative about narrative research in South India. *health: An Interdisciplinary Journal for the Social Study of Health, Illness and Medicine, 9*, 473–490.

Riessman, C. K., & Mattingly, C. (Eds.). (2005). Informed consent, ethics, and narrative [Special issue]. *health: An Interdisciplinary Journal for the Social Study of Health, Illness and Medicine, 9.*

Riessman, C. K., & Quinney, L. (2005). Narrative in social work: A critical review. *Qualitative Social Work, 4*, 383–404.

Riessman, C. K., & Speedy, J. (2007). Narrative inquiry in social work, counseling and psychotherapy: A critical review. In J. Clandinin (Ed.), *Handbook of narrative research methodologies* (pp. 426–456). Thousand Oaks, CA: Sage.

Roberts, B. (2002). *Biographical research.* Buckingham, UK, & Philadelphia: Open University Press.

Robichaux, C. (2003). *The practice of expert critical care nurses in situations of prognostic conflict at the end of life.* Unpublished doctoral dissertation, University of Texas, Austin.

Robichaux, C., & Clark, A. (2006). The practice of expert critical care nurses in situations of prognostic conflict at the end of life. *American Journal of Critical Care, 15*, 480–491.

Rose, G. (2001). *Visual methodologies: An introduction to the interpretation of visual materials.* Thousand Oaks, CA: Sage.

Salander, P. (2002). Bad news from the patient's perspective: An analysis of the written narratives of newly diagnosed cancer patients. *Social Science & Medicine, 55*, 721–732.

Salmon, P. (forthcoming). Some thoughts on narrative research. In M. Andrews, S. Squire, & M. Tamboukou (Eds.), *Doing narrative research in the social sciences.* London: Sage.

Sarangi, S., & Roberts, C. (1999). The dynamics of interactional and institutional orders in work-related settings. In S. S. Sarangi, & C. Roberts (Eds.), *Talk, work, and institutional order: Discourse in medical, mediation, and management settings* (pp. 1–57). New York: Mouton de Gruyter.

Sarbin, T. R. (1986). *Narrative psychology: The storied nature of human conduct.* New York: Praeger.

Sawin, P. E. (1992). "Right here is a good Christian lady": Reported speech in personal narratives. *Text and Performance Quarterly, 12*, 193–211.

Schenkein, J. (Ed.). (1979). *Studies in the organization of conversational interaction.* New York: Academic Press.

Schiff, B., & Cohler, B. J. (2001). Telling survival backward: Holocaust survivors narrate the past. In G. Kenyon, P. Clark, & B. de Vries (Eds.), *Narrative gerontology: Theory, research, and practice* (pp. 113–135). New York: Springer.

Scollon, R., & Scollon, S. B. K. (1981). *Narrative, literacy, and face in interethnic communication.* Norwood, NJ: Alblex.

Scott, J. C. (1990). *Domination and the arts of resistance: Hidden transcripts.* New Haven, CT: Yale University Press.

Scott, J. W. (1998). Experience. In S. Smith & J. Watson (Eds.), *Women, autobiography, theory: A reader* (pp. 57–71). Madison: University of Wisconsin Press.

Seale, C. (2002). Quality issues in qualitative inquiry. *Qualitative Social Work, 1*, 97–110.

Seale, Clive. (2004a). *Qualitative research practice.* London & Thousand Oaks, CA: Sage.

Seale, C. (2004b). Quality in qualitative research. In C. Seale, G. Gobo, J. F. Gubrium, & D. Silverman (Eds.), *Qualitative research practice* (pp. 409–419). London: Sage.

Seidman, S. (1992). Postmodern social theory as narrative with moral intent. In S. Seidman & D. Wagner (Eds.), *Postmodernism and social theory* (pp. 47–81). Blackwell.

Silverman, D. (2006). *Interpreting qualitative data: Methods for analyzing talk, text, and interaction,* 3rd ed. London: Sage.

Skott, C. (2003). Storied ethics: Conversations in nursing care. *Nursing Ethics, 10*, 368–376.

Skultans, V. (1998). *The testimony of lives: Narrative and memory in post-Soviet Latvia.* New York & London: Routledge.

Skultans, V. (2000). Editorial: Narrative, illness and the body. *Anthropology and Medicine, 7*, 5–13.

Skultans, V. (2003a). Editorial: Culture and dialogue in medical psychiatric narratives. *Anthropology & Medicine, 10*, 155–165.

Skultans, V. (2003b). From damaged nerves to masked depression: Inevitability and hope in Latvian psychiatric narratives. *Social Science & Medicine, 56*, 2421–2431.

Smith, B., & Sparkes, A. C. (2004). Men, sport, and spinal cord injury: An analysis of metaphors and narrative types. *Disability & Society, 19*, 613–626.

Smith, B., & Sparkes, A. C. (2005). Men, sport, spinal cord injury, and narratives of hope. *Social Science & Medicine, 61*, 1095–1105.

Smith, G. (1990). Political activist as ethnographer. *Social Problems, 37* (4), 629–648.

Smith, J. A. (2003). *Qualitative psychology: A practical guide to research methods.* London & Thousand Oaks, CA; Sage.

Smith, S., & Watson, J. (1998). *Women, autobiography, theory: A reader.* Madison: University of Wisconsin Press.

Smith, S., & Watson, J. (2002). *Interfaces: Women, autobiography, image, performance.* Ann Arbor: University of Michigan Press.

Sontag, S. (Ed.). (1982). *A Barthes reader.* London: Jonathan Cape.

Sontag, S. (2003). *Regarding the pain of others.* New York: Farrar, Straus and Giroux.

Sparkes, A. C. (2002). Autoethnography: Self-Indulgence or something more? In A. P. Bochner & C. Ellis (Eds.), *Ethnographically speaking* (pp. 209–232). Walnut Creek, CA: Altamira.

Spence, D. P. (1982). *Narrative truth and historical truth: Meaning and interpretation in psychoanalysis.* New York & London: Norton.

Squire, C. (2005). Reading narratives. *Group Analysis, 38*, 91–107.

Squire, C. (2007). *HIV in South Africa: Talking about the big thing*. London: Routledge.

Stanley, L. (1992). *The auto/biographical I*. Manchester, UK: Manchester University Press.

Stanley, L. (2004). The Epistolarium: On theorizing letters and correspondences. *Auto/Biography, 12*, 201–235.

Stoller, P. (1997). *Sensuous scholarship*. Philadelphia: University of Pennsylvania Press.

Strauss, A. L. (1987). *Qualitative analysis for social scientists*. Cambridge, UK: Cambridge University Press.

Swindells, J. (1985). *Victorian writing and working women*. Cambridge, UK: Polity Press.

Tamboukou, M. (1999). Spacing herself: Women in education. *Gender and Education, 11*(2), 125–139.

Tamboukou, M. (2003). *Women, education and the self: A Foucauldian perspective*. London and New York: Palgrave/Macmillan.

Tamboukou, M. (2005). *Spatial stories/narratable selves: Rethinking the private-privacy contour*. Paper presented at the British Sociological Association Annual Conference, York, UK.

Tamboukou, M. (in press). A Foucauldian approach to narratives. In M. Andrews, S. Squire, & M. Tamboukou (Eds.), *Doing narrative research in the social sciences*. London: Sage.

Tamboukou, M. (2007a). Interior styles/extravagant lives: Gendered narratives of sensi/able spaces. In E. H. Huijbens & Ó. P. Jónsson (Eds.), *Sensi/able spaces* (pp. 186–204). Reykjavik, Iceland: Cambridge Scholars Press.

Tamboukou, M. (2007b). The force of narrative: Making connections between the visual and the textual. Paper Presented at Centre for Narrative and Transformative Learning, Graduate School of Education, University of Bristol, UK.

Tannen, D. (1984). *Conversational style: Analyzing talk among friends*. Norwood, NJ: Ablex.

Taylor, J. M., Gilligan, C., & Sullivan, A. M. (1995). *Between voice and silence: Women and girls, race and relationship*. Cambridge, MA: Harvard University Press.

Temple, B. (1997). Watch your tongue: Issues in translation and cross-cultural research. *Sociology, 31*, 607–618.

Temple, B. (2002). Crossed wires: Interpreters, translators, and bilingual workers in cross-language research. *Qualitative Health Research, 12*, 844–854.

Temple, B., & Young, A. (2004). Qualitative research and translation dilemmas. *Qualitative Research, 4*, 161–178.

Thompson, P. (1978). *The voice of the past: Oral history*. Oxford, UK: Oxford University Press.

Thornborrow, J., & Coates, J. (Eds.). (2005). *The sociolinguistics of narrative*. Amsterdam & Philadelphia: John Benjamins.

Todd, A. D., & Fisher, S. (1988). *Gender and discourse: The power of talk*. Norwood, NJ: Ablex.

Toolan, M. (1988). *Narrative: A critical linguistic introduction*. New York: Routledge.

Uberoi, P. (1993). *Family, kinship and marriage in India*. New Delhi: Oxford University Press.

Urek, M. (2005). Making a case in social work: The construction of an unsuitable mother. *Qualitative Social Work, 4*(4), 451–467.

Van Maanen, J. (1988). *Tales of the field: On writing ethnography*. Chicago: University of Chicago Press.

Van Maanen, J. (1995). *Representation in ethnography*. Thousands Oaks, CA: Sage.

Van Vleet, K. (2002). The intimacies of power: Rethinking violence and affinity in the Bolivian Andes. *American Ethnologist, 29*(3), 567–601.

Van Vleet, K. (2003). Adolescent ambiguities and the negotiation of belonging in the Andes. *Ethnology, 42,* 349–363.

Vice, S. (1997). *Introducing Bakhtin*. Manchester UK: Manchester University Press.

Walkerdine, V. (2003). Video diaries as data and as television. Paper presented at Visual Narrative Conference, Centre for Narrative Research, University of Cambridge.

Walkerdine, V., Lucey, H., & Melody, J. (2001). *Growing up girl: Psychosocial explorations of gender and class*. Basingstoke, UK: Macmillan.

White, M., & Epston, D. (1990). *Narrative means to therapeutic ends*. New York: Norton.

Wang, C., & Burris, M. A. (1997). Photovoice: Concept, methodology, and use for participatory needs assessment. *Health Education & Behavior, 24,* 369–387.

White, H. (1976). The fictions of factual representation. In A. Fletcher (Ed.), *The literature of fact* (pp. 21–44). New York: Columbia University Press.

White, H. (1981). The value of narrativity in the representation of reality. In W. J. T. Mitchell (Ed.), *On narrative* (pp. 1–23). Chicago: University of Chicago Press.

White, S. (2002). Accomplishing the case in pediatrics and child health: Medicine and morality in inter-professional talk. *Sociology of Health and Illness, 24,* 409–435.

White, S., & Featherstone, B. (2005). Communicating misunderstandings: Multi-agency work as social practice. *Child and Family Social Work, 10,* 207–216.

Whooley, O. (2006). The political work of narratives: A dialogic analysis of two slave narratives. *Narrative Inquiry, 16*(2), 295–318.

Williams, G. (1984). The genesis of chronic illness: Narrative re-construction. *Sociology of Health & Illness, 6,* 175–200.

Williams, G. (2004). Narratives of health inequality: Interpreting the determinants of health. Paper presented at annual meeting, American Sociological Association, San Francisco.

Willis, P. E. (1977). *Learning to labour: How working class kids get working class jobs*. Farnborough, UK: Saxon House.

Wolfson, N. (1982). *The conversational historical present in American English narrative*. Dordrecht, the Netherlands: Foris Publications.

Women of PhotoVoice/ADMI & Lykes, M. B. (2000). *Voices e Imagenes: Mujeres Mayas Ixiles De Chajul/Voices and Images: Mayan Ixil Women of Chajul*. Guatemala: Magna Terra.

Wortham, S. (2001). *Narratives in action: A strategy for research and analysis.* New York: Teachers College Press.

Young, K. (2000). Gesture and the phenomenology of emotion in narrative. *Semiotica, 131,* 79–112.

Zola, I. K. (1972). Medicine as an institution of social control. *American Sociological Review, 20,* 487–504.

Zola, I. K. (1982). *Missing pieces: A chronicle of living with a disability.* Philadelphia: Temple University Press.

Zussman, R. (2000). Autobiographical occasions: Introduction to the special issue. *Qualitative Sociology, 23,* 5–8.

Index

About the Author

Catherine Kohler Riessman is Research Professor in the Department of Sociology at Boston College, and an *Emerita* Professor at Boston University. She serves as a Visiting Senior Fellow at the Centre for Narrative Research in the Social Sciences, University of East London. Beginning her career in social work, she earned a Ph.D. in Sociomedical Sciences/Sociology from Columbia University. Riessman has authored four books and numerous articles and book chapters in medical sociology and narrative inquiry.